Repeal
of the
Blues

Repeal of the Blues

by Alan Pomerance

A Citadel Press Book
Published by Carol Publishing Group

First Carol Publishing Group Edition 1991

Copyright © 1988 by Alan Pomerance

A Citadel Press Book
Published by Carol Publishing Group
Citadel Press is a registered trademark of
Carol Communications, Inc.

Editorial Offices   Sales & Distribution Offices
600 Madison Avenue   120 Enterprise Avenue
New York, NY 10022   Secaucus, NJ 07094

In Canada: Musson Book Company
A division of General Publishing Co. Limited
Don Mills, Ontario

Manufactured in the United States of America

10 9 8 7 6 5 4 3 2 1

Carol Publishing Group books are available at special discounts
for bulk purchases, for sales promotions, fund raising, or
educational purposes. Special editions can also be created to
specifications. For details contact: Special Sales Department,
Carol Publishing Group, 120 Enterprise Ave., Secaucus, NJ 07094

Library of Congress Cataloging-in-Publication Data

Pomerance, Alan.
    Repeal of the blues.

    Bibliography: p.
    Includes index.
    1. Afro-Americans in the performing arts.
2. Afro-American entertainers. 3. Afro-Americans--
History--1877-1964. 4. United States--Race relations. I. Title.
PN1590.B53P6   1988   792'.08996073   88-25706
ISBN 0-8065-1244-X

I have long wanted to write this book not only as an expression of thanks to black performers who have so affected and enriched my life, but because no one else had thought to weave their talents completely into the social, political and racial struggles that make up the fabric of my generation's time.

This book is dedicated to the memory of John Hammond, who taught us all about color blindness and the nurturing of talent.

And to my friends Ivory Stuckey, Paul Zuber, Emily Winkfield and Janice Lamb who, at various stages of my life, showed me just how beautiful black can be.

Acknowledgments

I want to thank the many people who helped me during the writing of this book, and if there is anyone I've unintentionally omitted, I hope they'll be kind enough to forgive me.

I'm indebted to Charlie McWhorter, Amy Greene, Mikey Harris, Chuck Jones, Lorraine Gordon, Josephine Mangiaracina, Rigmor Newman, Sara Frank and Randy Paul.

Special salutes go to the efficiency and dedicated assistance of Vicki Simons, Audrey Windhorst, Pat Banks, Nancy Merolle, the New York Public Library staffs handling the special collections at both Lincoln Center and the Schomburg Center for Research in Black Culture, and Barbara and Diane of Flashback.

And I'm ever grateful for the encouragement and loyalty of my wife, Molly, Ruth Pomerance, the Cataldos—Carol, Jim and Simon—Lorie and Harold Alexander, Teddy Koryn, Harvey Granat, Raphael Bernstein, and my agent Ivy Fischer Stone, of the Fifi Oscard Agency.

Contents

Preface		vii
I.	1932 (It Was a Very Bad Year)	1
II.	John Henry Hammond, Jr.	19
III.	Barney and Max (Or Is It Max and Barney?)	47
IV.	The NAACP (The National Association for the Advancement of Colored People)	68
V.	Blacks in Hollywood	86
VI.	Blacks in Las Vegas	114
VII.	Blacks in Radio and TV	136
VIII.	Blacks in World War II	165
	(Discrimination in Training)	
	(Civilian Riots)	
	(Effect of Roosevelt, Hitler, Eisenhower)	
	(Integration in Battle)	
	(Final Positive Residue of War)	
IX.	The Aftermath (Blacks in the Cold War and the McCarthy Era)	184
X.	Paul Robeson (All the Complexities of the Times in One Life)	213
Epilogue	(Where It All Is Today)	247
Bibliography		252

Preface

This is a chronicle of social change—the desegregation of blacks in the entertainment world between 1933 and 1952. Call this a civil rights movement if you'd like, although it predated this label by twenty years.

Nearly seven decades after the Civil War and Reconstruction, this particular phase of the movement started struggling the instant the ink dried on President Roosevelt's signature repealing Prohibition in 1933. It was energized by the social and political ferment that accompanied the Great Depression, the New Deal, the rise of Adolf Hitler and World War II. And it flourished until the House Un-American Activities Committee was convened, resulting in a temporary inhibition of the creative community.

It seemed to confine its scope to the entertainment world—to "show biz"—but without its strides, the pure, political civil rights movement of 1955 to 1969 could never have evolved.

Performers are often maligned as one-dimensional exhibitionists and narcissistic children. But they have an enormous impact on the public in a manner that seeps into all facets of life.

Of all the antidotes to the pain people feel as they struggle with everyday problems of illness, death, the difficulty of scratching out a living, and just plain loneliness, entertainers—singers, dancers, actors, clowns, musicians—are the most effective means of helping someone forget his or her troubles for however brief a time, at least long enough for the depression and anguish to pass their peak.

And as we are exposed to any entertainer repeatedly over the years, he or she becomes familiar—like a neighbor or a relative. We begin to identify with them, and suddenly this person who is providing a pleasurable experience for us is not objectionable, threatening or foreign any more.

This evolving familiarity with black performers of the 1930's and 1940's, like Ethel Waters, Paul Robeson, the Nicholas Brothers, Bessie Smith, Bill Robinson, Eddie (Rochester) Anderson, Billie Holiday, Lena Horne, Duke Ellington, Cab Calloway—and later, Sammy Davis, Jr., Harry Belafonte and Sidney Poitier—changed the public's image of blacks, and slowly induced in the white audience an understanding of what it meant to be colored in a white society.

And so without this "early" civil rights movement it might have taken longer than the 13 years of intense struggle between 1956 and 1969—the marches, the fervor, the danger, the loss of life—to galvanize the country into the kind of action that would not only guarantee the enforcement of the existing law of the land in the area of individual rights and liberties, but would insist on abrogating "separate but equal" statutes that undercut the concept of democracy.

And, of course, without it we couldn't have arrived at the present startling period of dominance of black performers in films, TV, recordings and concerts. It is a fact that in 1988 black stars in the main bring in the highest grosses, command the biggest salaries, are offered the choicest properties and basically control their own career destinies. And this only 50 years after the segregated indignities of the mob-controlled Prohibition era.

Anyone who has memories of the wounds of the Bessie Smiths, the Billie Holidays, the Stepin Fetchits and the Butterfly McQueens can only find it staggering to realize the power and position of black superstars in the 80's.

Pick up any issue of *Variety*, the "show biz" bible, and you find that Bill Cosby is in a class by himself in the TV sitcom arena, both as a performer and producer; his overall combined earnings for 1986 and 1987 are estimated by *Forbes Magazine* to be 84 million dollars. Oprah Winfrey, as talk show hostess and actress, was to earn $31 million in 1987, according to the December 31, 1986, issue of the New York *Post*, making her the highest paid female star in history for a single year. Eddie Murphy and Richard Pryor command the highest salaries in comedy, either in films or HBO cable specials. Whoopie Goldberg takes Broadway by storm in a Mike Nichols directed one-woman show, and then gets an Oscar nomination for her very first movie, Steven Spielberg's *The Color Purple*. Diana Ross gives a concert in Central Park and pulls in the largest audience to ever listen to live music in Manhattan. Stevie Wonder turns out wondrous film scores and wins Grammy after Grammy only to be topped by Wynton Marsalis, who in his early twenties arrives from New Orleans with such exquisite trumpet technique that he has to be given both a Jazz Grammy and a Classical Music Grammy—the first artist ever to achieve that plateau.

Today no one blinks at these feats. No one raises an eyebrow. It is a fact of our daily life that we can enjoy the virtuosity of black talent any time, any place, anywhere, and this has had a healing effect on interracial relations.

It would be ridiculous to infer that hatred and bigotry along color lines are things of the past. The headlines in any newspaper in any city across the country indicate how much of a problem still exists. But the situation is better than ten years ago and certainly far better than twenty years ago, and if we think back to racism 55 years ago, we might as well be considering life on a different planet.

To avoid offending any modern reader, only the term black will be used in these pages, except in quotes, but it should be understood that before 1956 even the most militant Afro-American writer would have referred to himself as Negro or colored. Cab Calloway says that in those days, "To call somebody black was an insult, and of course, to call me black, light-skinned as I was, was a triple insult." Everyone backs this up. Marion Montero Johnson, a childhood playmate of Lena Horne, said in 1982, "Why, if I ever called a colored person black when I was a girl, they would have been deeply offended."

The New York of Prohibition and mob control would have been unrecognizeable to any young person of today. In fact since science-fiction is so much a part of movies and MTV, it might be amusing to borrow the plot devices used so effectively in *Back to the Future* and *Peggy Sue Got Married* and travel back in time to the Harlem of 1932—a very different Harlem than we know today.

Let the camera pan to the Cotton Club, and, after entering, focus specifically on a beautiful girl, as young as the protagonists of those two popular movies, but flesh and blood and alive in history. She'll never move on from the chorus to stardom like Ada Ward or Lena Horne. She's just passing through for a while. And if we look really closely, the Club and the girl aren't actually what they seem to be—one, a throbbing palace of "rag" and "hooch" and "Minnie the Moocher," the other, a nearly naked odalisque; both were much more in 1932.

Repeal
of the
Blues

CHAPTER I

1932

(It Was a Very Bad Year)

She was sixteen, beautifully "high yella" and trembling with fear as she waited in the wings to make her debut as the newest girl in the famous Cotton Club line. The Nicholas Brothers were on stage and she started to feel the elegant energy generated by this satin-smooth pair of kids as they turned their taps into mated metronomes. The rhythm built and built, and she couldn't keep her butt from twitching and her shoulders from rocking, and the worry began to sweat out of her gut.

She ran her palms over the rough texture of her sequinned costume and marveled at how the wardrobe lady had taken her still immature figure and flattened it here, billowed it out there, with a few flashy moves of her needle and thread, until that body looked the way the men at ringside wanted it to look—paid to see it look—those tuxedoed men with their elegant women in that sea of pink and white ofay skin that she could just glimpse from her backstage perch.

There'd be no black or tan or "yella" brothers or sisters in the audience of this or any other elegant club in Harlem. "Nigger" patrons could only mix with whites at the lowdown joints, joints where dancers her age wore no pants under their skirts—"yeah, no panties"—and not because it was a strip joint—"it was worse!" Because at curtain time, instead of a bow, they had to snatch money from the ringsiders by first exposing themselves with a wide stance, and then, as a crisp bill was held against their crotch, clapping their thighs together and slowly slinking off with the money held between their lips.

She smiled at her confusion the first time she heard street boys call that part of a woman a "snatch," and at her own unanswered question to her Mama, "What did he mean?"

She leaned to the left, went up on her toes to see if she could recognize any big shots at ringside—a Jimmy Walker or an Al Capone or a Jolson. The best she could come up with in her small field of vision was a peroxide movie doll whose name she could never remember. All those blondies looked the same. It'd be nice to meet someone big and famous and have them invite her for a drink. But from what the other girls told her, you could never "plunk your black ass" down at the table next to them. Not unless you wanted the bouncers to break your toes. It was as if the leather seats would have to be scrubbed clean with ammonia. Oh, any admirer could send a drink or a bottle backstage and you could drink it together back there—but what fun was that?

A sharp shove from the girl behind snapped her back to the business at hand and she heard "The Duke" playing their intro.

"Wake up girl! We're on!"

Many things were "on" in 1932, most of them negative and downbeat and not working out for a people drowning in an ever-rising financial depression.

One of them was Prohibition, a Congressional experiment that was a conceptual disaster. The well-meaning but naïve and unworldly forces that insisted on alcohol abstinence and persisted until the bill was passed, unleashed far greater immorality than they were attempting to curb.

The U.S. has always been a puritanical society, religiously, socially and politically, and Congressional candidates of the post-Victorian era of 1911, when the legislation was passed, would never have had the courage to face up to the religious zealots who felt that "demon rum" was the source of all of America's problems.

What the puritans failed to recognize was that the moment

they made alcohol consumption illegal was the moment they bestowed unlimited power on the underworld, giving them astronomical incomes from the sale of illegal booze and beer in speakeasies, and providing a moral climate that stimulated major revenues from drugs and prostitution.

With this wealth, the "mob" became the power brokers for the entire country. To maintain the success of their operation, they required "bought" politicians, "bribed" law enforcement officials, "cooperative" labor unions and a docile public.

Such a docile public meant no tampering with the status quo, especially no unrest in the ethnic, immigrant community and no rumblings from the segregated black population. Prejudice, white supremacy, knowing one's place, all suited the mob's security and control. And since the world of night life and entertainment was closest at hand to their own operations, that is where they imposed their style first and foremost.

Various "beer mobs" owned nightclubs in the major cities. The Cotton Club, for instance, was controlled by an English-born hood named Owney Madden, who, with his silent partner Al Capone as back-up, bought the club from black ex-heavyweight champ Jack Johnson. But whichever the controlling gang, the pattern was the same. Great booze, adequate food, pseudo-classy art deco furnishings, an all "sepia" cast of the greatest entertainers (always smiling, giving 100 percent of their talent and knowing their place) and a "whites only" audience of swells and celebrities who didn't care how much they spent for a good time.

Whatever the city, these clubs were always located in black neighborhoods, but the local residents could never partake of the fun or the profits.

As long as the operation was going smoothly, the mob wanted no trouble, no violence, no publicity—why mess with a system that was a perpetual money machine?

But if anything threatened to interfere with that smoothness, it was removed rapidly, dramatically and permanently—both to solve the immediate problem and to prevent its reoccurrence.

When Madden wanted Duke Ellington as his house band and the owner of the Philadelphia Theater where Duke had a long-running contract refused to release him, Owney sent around

one of his most persuasive goons, a tough-as-nails Jew named
Yonkel Schwartz, who advised the theater owner, "Be big or be
dead." During these negotiations, someone had suggested the
great Louis Armstrong as an alternative to the light-skinned
Duke. Madden shook his head, "Too Negro"—and he never,
ever employed the genius trumpeter.

Cab Calloway didn't admit publicly to being a victim of mob
muscle, until he wrote in 1976:

"I want to set the record straight. Take my first manager, Moe
Gale. Moe was the one who booked me into the New Plantation
Club in 1930. Later I went over to the Cotton Club, about the
biggest place to be in Harlem and all New York in those days—
and the mob muscled Moe out. You read it right. I was managed
by the mob for a number of years. In those days, that was about
the only way a black entertainer could make it."

Most of the risk of violence came from overambitious competition and the documented blood baths were against their own
kind. Otherwise the well-greased city officials were always cooperative and there was no need for muscle.

Harold Nicholas and his brother Fayard were eight and fourteen respectively when they began starring in the Cotton Club
shows. This was totally counter to all the existing child labor
laws. After all, what was a little kid doing working all night long,
show after show, in that kind of atmosphere? But Harold remembers being told not to worry, it was all taken care of, and no
investigating social worker ever came around to question him.
Management treated him like a darling mascot. The Nicholas
Brothers played at the club off and on for so many years that it
was really his growing-up place, and because of his size and age
and the mob's paternal attitude, he was given special dispensa-
tions.

As previously mentioned, no entertainer was ever allowed to
sit with the patrons, but for this charming talented child an ex-
ception was made and he was often spoiled and fawned over by
ringsiders between shows. After closing time, he and Fayard
would run over to the Savoy Ballroom to hear the great bands of
Jimmy Lunceford and Erskine Hawkins and watch the latest
Harlem dance steps develop. The doorman knew that no kids
were allowed in under city licensing codes. But he also knew

that these boys were special to the gangsters and so the doors were open to them whenever they wanted to come in gratis.

If, however, a Nicholas relative or black friend wanted to watch Fayard and Harold dance at the Cotton Club, they were ushered to a couple of booths next to the kitchen which were used for this purpose because they were out of the sight lines of the rest of the audience and no one would know.

Jimmy Durante, "the Schnozz," such a lovable pixie to his fans, in truth had a darker side that needed to rub elbows with hoods. He touted the club to his buddies. "It isn't necessary to mix with colored people if you don't like it. You have your own party and keep to yourself, but it's worth seeing them step."

Lena Horne at age sixteen auditioned for Herman Stark, Madden's stout, cigar-chewing manager. At that early age she could hardly have been called a singer and only danced in a rudimentary way. But she was tall, thin, very light-skinned, with an exquisite face that had very little trace of negroid features, and there was an aura of innocence overlaying the beauty and sexuality. This is what the mob wanted because it was what turned on the white patrons, and she was hired immediately.

Later, in her writing, she explained some of the antipathy middle-class blacks felt then toward the Harlem jazz world.

"My going to work in the club caused quite a stir in the Negro press to which my grandmother and her good works were well known. It caused more than a little stir in bourgeois Brooklyn where respectable girls were not supposed to go to work in Harlem night clubs known to be owned by white hoodlums or any other hoodlums for that matter.

"Actually there was nothing to worry about. My very youth protected me. I was 'jail bait' and no one ever made a pass at me or suggested I go out with the customers, which happened all the time to the older girls. The owners probably figured that any kind of fooling around with underage girls was the quickest way to lose their license.

"I was also protected in another way. On my way into the club I was always being stopped by Negro men who were friends of my father's—gamblers, people who were in numbers, or who had the binocular concessions at the track or were partners in some syndicate. They were people who knew their way around the world I was now inhabiting. They would say things like 'we're friends of your father's and we've known you since you were a baby.' They formed a sort of underground protection association for me."

The feeling of middle-class blacks in 1932 that this nightclub scene in their own neighborhoods was foreign to their lifestyles and aspirations, and something to be ashamed of, was fairly common. James Lincoln Collier made the point that jazz was not a black music performed for black audiences, but a black music performed to a large extent for white audiences. And Art Farmer, the fine flugelhorn player from Kansas City, recollects that many black parents in his home town despised jazz and forbade their children to listen to the likes of Fats Waller and Billie Holiday.

Even Negro intellectual establishments, in their anxiety to emulate and enable their students to rise in a white world, often ignored black cultural history, particularly jazz. Benny Golson majored in classical clarinet at Howard University, and because of the official contempt for jazz at this black college, he practiced his jazz saxophone licks in the laundry room so no one would hear him.

Afro-Americans were hurting financially more than whites during those Depression times, and were more insecure than ever in their always precarious social status. To properly understand any of these attitudes in the black community, it is important to get an overview of all the complicated events happening simultaneously in America in 1932.

Economically the picture was bleaker than at any time since Revolutionary War days. Unemployment had reached 13 million. National wages were 60 percent less than in 1929. Dividends were 56.6 percent less than in 1929. Business losses across the nation were six billion dollars. U.S. industry was operating at less than one-half of maximum 1929 volume. Wages were 60 percent less than the 1929 level.

Oscar Ameringer, the editor of the newspaper *American Guardian* in Oklahoma City, made a tour of workers and found the country to be suffering from overproduction and underconsumption at the same time. In Oregon, ewes were being killed by sheep ranchers because they did not bring enough in the market to make it worth paying the cost of freight to ship them to New York or Chicago. At the same time, World War I veterans in those cities were unemployed and picking in garbage dumps for scraps of food. In Montana, wheat fields were left uncut because the low price didn't cover the labor costs of harvesting, while nearby emaciated mothers, unable to nurse, fed their starving babies on formulas of 90 percent water and 10 percent flour.

The populace couldn't buy what they themselves produced, and unless ways and means were found to make able customers out of the millions of unemployed wage earners and bankrupt farmers, no recovery would be possible.

World War I veterans trying to obtain cash for the full value of their Bonus Certificates marched to Washington, D.C., and camped out by the hundreds of thousands. After the Senate rejected payment, they were fired upon and removed forcibly by the U.S. Army units under the command of General Douglas MacArthur.

Banks were failing everywhere, causing the total loss of savings for not only individuals but also the unions. So a destitute worker couldn't even look to the union fund he'd been contributing to for assistance.

It was a presidential election year, and the economic panic of the voters was reflected in the results. The Democrats, with Franklin Delano Roosevelt promising a "New Deal" in his nomination acceptance speech, won 472 electoral votes to 59 for the Hoover Republicans. The Socialist Party ran Norman Thomas and he pulled in 800,000 votes, while the Communist Party chose a team of William Z. Foster and a black, James M. Ford from Alabama, as his vice-presidential running mate. Despite heavy campaigning among the unemployed, the Communists tallied only 102,785 votes.

All the candidates spoke out in favor of John D. Rockefeller's crusade to repeal the Volstead Act—the prohibition experiment—and, in fact, this led to its actual repeal a few months later on February 2, 1933.

The lack of funds in sponsors' and producers' bank accounts and the shrinking audience solvent enough to pay an admission fee were paralyzing the arts. Opera houses in Chicago and Philadelphia gave no performances. Few orchestral works of any serious stature came forth. Broadway had one sole hit in 1932, the Theater Guild's production of Philip Barry's the *Animal Kingdom*.

Pulitzer Prizes went to works that dealt with current problems, like Pearl Buck's *The Good Earth* and *Of Thee I Sing*, the political musical created by George Kaufman, Morrie Ryskind and George Gershwin. "Brother Can You Spare A Dime?" was understandably the most popular song, and the semi-classical "Grand Canyon Suite" by Ferdé Grofé became a favorite.

Academy Awards in film went to *Grand Hotel*, to Helen Hayes for *The Sins of Madelon Claudette*, to Fredric March for *Dr. Jekyll and Mr. Hyde*, to Wallace Beery for *The Champ*, and a special award to Walt Disney for his new creation, Mickey Mouse.

Books that made a critical stir but didn't sell were Erskine Caldwell's *Tobacco Road* and John Dos Passos's *1919*.

Amelia Earhart became the first woman to cross the Atlantic alone, while America's previous aerial hero Charles Lindbergh suffered the loss of his baby son in a kidnap-murder plot.

Only three creative spheres seemed to be flourishing with energy and excellence: motion pictures, jazz, and science. In that single year of 1932 hundreds of astounding scientific landmarks were established: the discovery of the neutron, the first production of gamma rays, the isolation of Vitamin C, the first computer machine, Edwin Land's first Polaroid glass, the building of the Empire State Building, and on the other coast the San Francisco Bay Bridge, and the construction of a musical oddity "The Rhythmicom," Henry Cowell and Leon Theremin's instrument to reproduce all rhythmical combinations.

Not so incongruously, the bad times were also stimulating an outpouring of great jazz; singers were wailing the truest blues and young instrumentalists were squeezing more soul than ever before from their solos. The names emerging in 1932 remained bona fide stars far into future decades—Duke Ellington, Louis Armstrong, Benny Carter, Fats Waller, Fletcher Henderson, Jimmy Lunceford, Bessie Smith and Billie Holiday. A renaissance of Afro-American artistry was beginning at a moment when few black people had the cash to enjoy sharing in it.

The roles of the black filmmaker and screen actor are so complex that they warrant detailed inspection in a later chapter, but suffice it to say that at that moment they were on the scene in Hollywood and New York, but making very few waves.

But it was the unknown, unheralded minority citizen who was having the toughest time fitting into the fabric of a country going through its most turbulent year. Certainly the black labor force was abused and advantage taken. With everyone of every color scratching, crawling and even begging for work at any salary level, blacks took home less than whites for the same job. Listen to Louis Banks, a cook, talking about that era.

"I had 15 or so jobs. Each job I would have, it would be so hard. From six o'clock in the morning 'til seven o'clock at night, I was fixing the meat, cooking, washing dishes and cleaning up. Just like you threw the ball at one end and run down and catch it on the other. You're Jack of all trades. You're doin' it all. White chefs were gettin' 40 dollars a week, but I was gettin' 21 dollars for doin' what they were doin' and everything else. The poor people had it rough. The rich people was livin' off the poor."

Something good is somehow distilled from the residue of any human misery, and the Depression, by tormenting all classes and colors was breaking down barriers between these groups, bringing them into direct daily contact in ways that would have been impossible in better times. All strata of society were being exposed to the common enemies of displacement and hunger, and down there on their knees together they were beginning to understand and tolerate at least a little more.

The same Louis Banks tells of riding the rails in search of work.

"I'd ride atop a boxcar and went to Los Angeles four days and four nights. The Santa Fe, we'd go all the way with the Santa Fe. I was going over the hump and I was so hungry and weak, cause I was goin' into the d.t.'s and I could see snakes draggin' through the smoke. I was sayin', Lord help me. Oh, Lord help me until a white hobo named Callahan, he was a great big guy looked like Jack Dempsey, and he got a scissor on me, took his legs and wrapped 'em round me. Otherwise I was about to fall off the flyer into a cornfield there. I was sick as a dog until I got into Long Beach, California.

"Black and white, it didn't make any difference who you were 'cause everybody was poor. All friendly, sleep in jungle. We used to make a big pot and cook food, cabbage, meat, and beans all together. We all set together. We made a tent—25, 30 would be out on the side of the hill, white and colored. They didn't have no mothers or sisters, they didn't have no home. They were dirty, they had overalls on. They didn't have no food, they didn't have anything."

And then the other side of the coin from Kentucky born Peggy Terry, living now in uptown Chicago and talking there:

"I didn't like black people. In fact I hated 'em. If they just shipped 'em all out, I don't think it woulda bothered me."

She recalls her feelings of white superiority, then discovers, "If I really knew what changed me. . . I don't know. I've thought about it and thought about it. You don't go anywhere because you always see yourself as something you're not. As long as you can say I'm better than they are then there's somebody below you can kick, but once you get over that, you see that you're not any better off than they are. In fact, you're worse off 'cause you're believin' a lie. And it was right there in front of us. In the cotton field, chopping cotton, and right over in the next field, there's these black people—Alabama, Texas, Kentucky—never once did it occur to me that we had anything in common.

"After I was up here for a while and I saw how poor white people were treated, poor white southerners, they were treated just as badly as black people are, I think maybe that just crystallized the whole thing."

But the contact of black and white on those freight trains that symbolized the odyssey of search for jobs from region to region wasn't always so ideal, and one explosive incident late in 1931 led to a series of trials that lasted two years and scandalized the United States in the eyes of its own citizens and people all over the world.

Nine black males from the age of twelve to twenty were riding a freight from Chattanooga to Memphis, Tennessee, living a hobo existence looking for work. They jumped from a boxcar into a gondola in which nine whites were huddled, fought with them over some racial slight and then threw six of them off the slow moving train. These six made their way ahead to a stationmaster who called the sheriff at Scottsboro, Alabama, where the train was stopped.

A search of the 42 cars turned up the nine blacks and three whites, two of them girls wearing men's caps and clothing. Twenty minutes later, one of the girls, Ruby Bates, claimed that she and her friend, Victoria Price, had been raped by the blacks.

A local judge appointed an elderly, nearly senile lawyer to defend the boys and the southern press tried the case in wild, inflammatory print, long before it reached a courtroom. Headlines screamed of the violation of southern womanhood by black brutes. And one by one the nine youths were declared guilty by the regional juries.

The national press, smelling a frame-up, aroused the rest of the country. The NAACP—The National Association for the Advancement of Colored People—reacted very slowly and cautiously, not wanting to appeal unless there was evidence that the boys were innocent or had been denied constitutional rights.

Into the void stepped the American Communist Party, quickly seizing on an American dilemma in which it could score points vociferously and get across-the-board press coverage. Its allied legal arm, the I.L.D., convinced the boys to designate them as counsel, and an appeal to the Alabama Supreme Court was honored, resulting in a new trial.

The tentativeness of the NAACP's reaction earned the organization contempt in this instance from many blacks.

Walter White, its president, tried desperately to gain control of the case, and for a time there was a day-by-day switching of allegiance by the boys or their parents from I.L.D. to NAACP and back again. But the Afro-American press was in no mood for caution, and it backed what it felt was the humanity of the communist approach, and finally the NAACP withdrew from the case.

In the emotion of the moment, those supporting the communists didn't suspect their opportunism, or analyze the irony and futility in the party's campaign of self-determination for blacks. This plan would result in formation of a 49th state to be gerrymandered out of the territory in the deep South where blacks

were in the majority. Those with cool heads who truly were interested in the future of the Afro-American citizens of the
United States called the concept self-destruction rather than
self-determination.

In an attempt to woo black members, the communists appointed a black lawyer, William L. Patterson, as national secretary of the I.L.D. Patterson was a Democrat and Tammany Hall
figure, not a Communist Party member. First on his agenda was
to raise much-needed cash to defend the boys in their new trial,
and he realized that a major benefit show featuring great-name
entertainers was the best means. He approached the one white
person he knew who would have the interracial, financial and
musical contacts to produce it. That man was John Henry Hammond, Jr., then just emerging in his career as social journalist
and jazz critic. In fact, Hammond, an anti-communist with liberal leanings, only took on the production because he was cov-
ering the Scottsboro Trial for *The Nation* magazine and realized
that the boys were not receiving proper American justice.

The benefit was held at the Rockland Palace in the Bronx,
very near the Polo Grounds, and it raised a great deal of money.
Hammond put together a show that included Benny Carter's
orchestra and Duke Ellington, minus his own band but playing
piano for Carter.

Duke's agent, Irving Mills, threw in a new client of his, who at
the tender age of fifteen was a jazz singer. Her name was Martha
Raye. And so Martha, later on a clown, comedienne and spokeswoman for denture commercials, made her singing debut with
no less than Duke Ellington as her accompanist.

Hammond returned to the trial and in his first article stressed
the hermetically sealed minds of the local Alabama citizenry.

"The prevailing feeling was one of annoyance at the expense
of the trial. The townsfolk were fully aware of the fact that the
schools of Scottsboro and Jackson County had been shut down
by the cost of the original trial and appeal. The defendants of
course were guilty. The average southern family believes that
blacks desire above everything to have intercourse with white
women. But there was little animosity shown the prisoners.
They would be found guilty and executed!"

The prosecutor, Thomas Knight, Jr., the attorney general of

Alabama, was 34, clever, but not too sure of himself and somewhat out of control. For the defense, the choice had been curious—a flamboyant, Jewish New York criminal lawyer named Samuel S. Leibowitz, looking for a case that would earn him a reputation as a champion of lost causes.

This strange trial was covered by every well-known reporter from all the powerful newspaper and magazine chains. Leibowitz, a master showman, made his point. The arbitrary exclusion of blacks from the jury rolls meant that the original grand jury was illegally constituted. He established that for at least two of the boys rape was physically unlikely if not impossible. One was so crippled by syphilis that he couldn't have sexual intercourse, and the youngest was only twelve years old.

When he cross-examined Victoria Price, he made his points too aggressively, trying to crack her sullen composure and instead alienating the jury. Leibowitz proffered testimony that both girls had had sex with two white men 36 hours before the alleged rape and this explained why only non-motile, inert sperm had been found in their bodies during the medical exam. This same exam turned up no signs of emotional distress or marks of physical or sexual assault. But Victoria was a tough witness and played her role of southern womanhood to the end.

Desperately, Leibowitz played his strong card. Ruby Bates appeared as a defense witness to retract her earlier testimony, and to absolve the boys of any criminal act. But Tom Knight made her a laughing stock under cross-examination when he got her to admit that she had been up north, and that the defense had bought the clothes she was wearing. The jury brought in a sentence of death and Leibowitz again appealed for a new trial.

Judge Horton, at the hearing of this motion, developed a long analysis of the testimony, concluding that the verdict was not justified by the evidence. Later on he was decisively defeated for re-election, his house was stoned and when his wife contracted polio, someone painted on his front gate:

"This is God's Will"

A third and fourth trial followed, each being appealed to the U.S. Supreme Court where the lower court was reversed. The years passed, the boys languished in jail, legal tactics continued and, from constant retelling, the prosecution's case fell apart. Finally, in 1937, four of the boys were released. One by one the others died in prison or on the outside. In 1976 the only defendant left alive received an official pardon, and a degrading chapter in American history was finally closed. No one had won. Everyone had lost.

Another incident that underlined both the economic desperation of 1932 and the anti-liberal attitudes of the South in that year, took place in the Kentucky coal mines, where miners were striking to improve their non-union conditions.

Again, a communist-front group called the National Miner's Union (not John L. Lewis's United Mine Workers) had convinced the workers to strike and had invited a group of very famous authors, sympathetic to radical causes, to go to Harlan County to observe the situation first-hand.

The communist inroads into the miners' unions had been made easier by the fact that the only national labor group then in existence, the AFL, was strictly segregationist, and the largest independent union, Lewis's United Mine Workers, still had not made much effort to organize blacks in the deep South.

The communists were having difficulty organizing non-union white workers in this area, so they decided to accomplish this with blacks first. This promptly enraged the whites and may have set back the labor movement twenty years since it shifted the central issue from workers' rights to racial animosities, which ultimately increased segregation.

To discover the truth of the situation and to bring food and medical supplies to the families of the striking miners, a caravan of writers headed for Harlan County. They included John Dos Passos, Edmund Wilson, Malcolm Cowley, Quincy Howe, Waldo Frank, Allan Taub, and, again, John Hammond. They bought 1500 dollars' worth of milk and canned food, but when they reached the edge of town, sheriff's deputies broke into their trucks, dumped the milk and confiscated the food. The writers were arrested and allowed out on bail, but not before Malcolm Cowley was slugged unconscious for protesting. However, a Paramount Newsreel cameraman had managed, without discovery, to capture all these violent scenes on film, and he urged Hammond, who had his own car, to drive him away from the area before Kentucky law enforcement got wise. They reached Knoxville, Tennessee, and the film was processed and shown in movie houses all over the country.

When the others in the group staggered into Knoxville 24 hours later, they told of being kidnapped by masked men and brought to the state line where the two Jewish writers, Waldo Frank and Allan Taub, had been severely beaten.

All these conditions and incidents clearly show why 1932 was often considered the low point in U.S. history economically, socially and racially.

Under these circumstances, it isn't surprising that a small percentage of Americans of all races, disillusioned with the status quo, started to investigate the alternatives that communism seemed to offer. The black population, having more to be dissatisfied with than whites, were courted vigorously by the Party.

The involvement of Paul Robeson—the black American with the most talent and potential in the history of the U.S. to that date—will be analyzed in a separate chapter that his career deserves. But hundreds of thousands of his race at least investigated what the Leninists had to offer.

In 1932 the Soviet Union's expanding film industry wanted to make a film that would tell the "true" story of race relations in the U.S. No motion picture with that subject matter would be produced in Hollywood, so it was simple for them to convince 23 Afro-American artists to come to Russia for the venture. Only a couple of those who accepted were actual communists. Langston Hughes, Henry Moon, Ted Poston, Lauren Miller and Wayland Rudd, all considerable talents, waited over there month after month while authorities assured them the project was about to begin. Finally, after the sixth month, it was canceled, obviously because the Soviet Government had just been recognized by the U.S., and it was more important to the Russians to have amicable relations than to honestly portray black viewpoints. It wasn't to be the last time that black Americans were to discover Russia as their fair weather friend. The group was sent home with the realization that you could only tell the truth in the Soviet Union when it bolstered Communist Party goals.

Another unfortunate example of left-of-center ideology failing to come through for black interests took place in New York at the same moment as the abortive Russian project. WEVD, a radio station whose call letters were the initials of the brilliant socialist Eugene V. Debs, had studios located in the Broadway Central Hotel and featured programs in Yiddish, Polish, Rumanian and German to get the interest of New York's first and second generation immigrant listeners.

For one-half hour on Saturday nights it broadcast live jazz jam sessions paid for personally by John Hammond, and featuring instrumentalists of the caliber of Art Tatum, Chick Webb, Chu Berry, Dickie Wells, and Frankie Newton, among others.

Suddenly, the station was given an opportunity to upgrade itself when the Claridge Hotel offered it the use of its air-conditioned penthouse as a studio, in return for air plugs for the hotel. During the second week of these sessions, the hotel flatly stated that guests had complained about blacks in the regular elevators, and that from now on all musicians had to get to the studio via the freight elevator.

This was a standard insult that all black musicians had faced in their constant exposure to discrimination. But to have it happen at a station named for America's ranking socialist made it even harder to stomach. Everyone realized that it was the hotel policy that was at fault not the station's, but the station also didn't stand up to defend their rights, so the musicians quit and the jam session program ended.

The cynicism that constant abuse aroused was not exclusive to New York black sidemen. A piano player, named Little Brother Montgomery, and Red Saunders, a band leader, sounded like this rappin'.

Montgomery: "I left around the early thirties and organized a band around Jackson, Mississippi. Sometimes we'd play a dance and make fifteen cents apiece. You'd travel maybe two, three hundred miles in a second-hand Cadillac and a beat-up Lincoln, the whole band. We'd go to a place and couldn't make gas money. Places like Meridian, Hattiesberg, Vicksburg, all up the Delta—the main time is when they're pickin' cotton. They got a dollar a hundred pickin'. Some people could pick two or three hundred pounds in a day. We played in tobacco barns down through the South. I remember one band was burned up in one of those warehouses. We played a white dance tonight and a colored tomorrow. But we didn't mix."

Saunders: "In those days the black artist was at the mercy of the promoters. In later years M.C.A. and others took 'em on, but at first they weren't booking black bands. The hotels and ballrooms were for white bands. This was a time when radio was great. White musicians were having a field day, making all kinds of money in studios, in concerts and legitimate theaters. Big money. The poor black musicians just had the beat-up Lincoln. They were what you called Starvation Bands. Did you know black musicians created the one-nighters?

"They didn't have any homes. Out of five years they'd maybe sit down ten weeks . . . the only time they would sit down would be like the Apollo in New York, the Regal in Chicago, the Howard in Washington."

Montgomery: "Even their music was taken from them. Clarence Williams wrote 'Sugar Blues' and that was called Clyde McCoy's. 'Dorsey Boogie' is Pine Top's, which he played at rent parties."

Saunders: "There was a pick up in business when beer came in in '33. They could go out publicly and drink. And that price was right. Beer was 15 cents and you could get entertainment. With repeal, you began to see a new light."

A good phrase, "With repeal you began to see a new light," and a prophetic one. That momentous day in February, 1933, when Prohibition was abolished, brought with it a whole new political and moral climate, and when Fiorello La Guardia, the "Little Flower," was elected Mayor of New York replacing the scandal-ridden, bootlegger-controlled administration of Jimmy Walker, conditions in nightclubs like all other phases of big city life became more decent and equitable.

Always the flamboyant actor, La Guardia was seen declaring war on the underworld in newsreels, smashing slot machines himself with an ax and ordering Frank Ericson and other previously omnipotent gamblers out of the city.

He was intent on reforming nightlife and denying organized crime this large source of revenue. When any ex-bootlegger applied for a license to run a legitimate club, they had to prove that they'd given up all their illegal after-hours locations and agree to be tightly regulated. It was in this manner that Sherman Billingsley was allowed a license to operate the Stork Club, and Jack Kriendler and Charlie Berns the "21" Club.

This atmosphere, this movement, this timing, was perfect for the entrance on the scene of three of the most unlikely individuals to ever expect to change the face of show business.

But arrive they did, and by properly using their decency, instinct and intelligence, they made an impact—particularly as it related to black performers—that is still being felt today.

The three were the aforementioned John Hammond, a tall crew-cut Wasp with a Vanderbilt bloodline, and two diminutive jews from immigrant, Orthodox families, Barney Josephson and Max Gordon. Separately, and in some instances together, they revolutionized the quality, taste and racial makeup of night life, recordings and, indirectly, movies, theater and much of American life.

Admittedly, that is an enormous statement, but these are unique men. Let's start with the most influential, John Henry Hammond, Jr.

Chapter II

John Henry Hammond, Jr.

The tall skinny white kid loped across the Harlem streets this night just as he had a hundred times before—a wide grin flashing on unstraightened teeth, the vigorous stride outlining a bulge of bills in his back pocket, his whole being propelled by an air of innocent expectancy. And along the dark streets and alleys, the word had gone out, silently, casually, but with the same mysterious thoroughness of jungle drumming—"Don't touch this kid. Don't lean on him. Maybe keep an eye out to see he's OK. Tell the brothers he's cool—not Mr. Charlie. Let him stay in one piece. He's got a lot of soul for an ofay."

They'd seen him walking up the steps from Ed Small's Basement Club jawing away with J. C. Higginbotham or buying Garland Wilson a shot in Covan's while he himself sipped a 75-cent lemonade. You couldn't really miss that kid with the lemonade! When he dug the jammin', that crewcut wagged, the eyebrows went up, the mouth opened wide, and a long drawn out "Yeah!" stressed the kicks he was getting. But no one in that uptown world could have guessed just how far John Henry Hammond, Jr., had travelled to get there.

To depict his life story fully, Hollywood would have to cast his contemporary, Jimmy Stewart, in half a dozen feature films all with varying themes. One would probe the psyche of a man born to wealth and Vanderbilt-Sloane pedigree who detested the ostentation, class consciousness and bigotry of his blood-lines, and spent his entire life seeking out and fighting for causes in the most liberal, activist manner.

Another film could highlight the instinctive talent scout who recognized the raw genius of artists before anyone else, and pro-pelled them into the creative mainstream of the U.S. by giving them the opportunity to be recorded in styles, settings, and en-sembles that would perfectly exhibit their virtuosity. The list of these performers is staggering—an endless beam of brilliance that begins in the late Twenties and continues to this very day. To name only the most famous:

Bessie Smith, Billie Holiday, Fats Waller, Coleman Hawkins, Benny Carter, Mildred Bailey, Red Norvo, Benny Goodman, Teddy Wilson, Lionel Hampton, Gene Krupa, Charlie Christian, Count Basie, Charlie Barnett, Lester Young, Freddy Greene, Helen Humes, Meade Lux Lewis, Albert Ammons, Pete John-son, the Golden Gate Quartet, George Benson, Bob Dylan, Bruce Springsteen, and Stevie Ray Vaughn.

A third scenario would be about the lowly draftee private in World War II, assigned to the Information and Education sec-tion, who tried to take on the Army brass in his attempts to shatter the status quo of segregation and persecution of black soldiers.

And then there would be the screenplay that followed the exploits of a young white newspaper reporter who in the early 1930's covered the violent Kentucky coal miners' strikes and was the driver who helped a Paramount Newsreel cameraman escape with the film that would show the entire country scenes of sheriff's deputies brutalizing strikers and breaking heads of volunteers who tried to bring food and supplies for their fami-lies.

And what of the still very young white man recruited to the board of the NAACP by Walter White, its president, who spends thirty years in this position fighting for black equality, and then has to resign years later when, under the new administration of Roy Wilkins, his views are too idealistic and uncompromising and he is plainly no longer wanted by the black hierarchy.

This has the sound of excerpts from the lives of a group of men, but incredibly it all happened to John Hammond, a person of amazing taste, principle and courage. A man who, in the period between 1930 and 1955, did more to improve the position of blacks in the United States than any other white man.

The baby born on December 15, 1910, arrived with multiple silver spoons in his mouth. His mother was Emily Vanderbilt Sloane, granddaughter of Cornelius Vanderbilt. The town house at 9 East 91st Street where the birthing took place was a gift to the young mother and father bought with Vanderbilt money. However, her father William Douglas Sloane could have easily provided it also, since he was the heir to the W&J Sloane Furniture empire.

Among baby John's relatives were Henry Sloane Coffin, the world famous pastor of the Madison Avenue Church, and his cousins were the parents of the yet-to-be-born Gloria Vanderbilt. His mother's best friend and next door neighbor, Mrs. Andrew Carnegie, Jr., came to admire the baby often.

His paternal grandfather was the youngest Union general in the Civil War, Sherman's chief of staff, and rumored to be Chief Sitting Bull's only white friend. His father's brother, Ogden, married into the Stevens Institute family and later became the U.S. Ambassador to Spain. And father himself was a graduate of Phillips Exeter, Yale, and Columbia Law School, before becoming a partner in one of the most prestigious Manhattan, Wasp law firms.

Quite a heritage for baby John. Quite a setting for someone who later on always felt more comfortable in the company of blacks than whites.

Little John's feet could get lost in a house that contained six stories, 16 bathrooms, two elevators and a private ballroom and was staffed by 16 servants and two chauffeurs. Five daughters had preceded his birth and father was already forty years old by 1910, a circumstance that robbed the boy of a close paternal relationship. He became in fact his mother's boy, and the intense, intimate bond was mutually satisfying. The activist streak in him—the strong desire to help others by means of integrity and truth—had to have come through his mother. She was an original in many ways—deeply religious from an early age as the form of relief she needed to shield her from the embarrassment of riches that constantly surrounded her. She believed it obscene to wallow in wealth when poverty and distress were so close at hand. A walk five blocks north to 96th Street and above would immediately open her eyes to the contrasts.

She didn't marry until twenty-four—late for that time. But when she started a family, she imposed on them a code of moral behavior and responsibilities, the duties of the blessed. She developed the guilt her Vanderbilt forebears never felt themselves, and so filled John with a sense of religion that at nine or ten he was sure that he would someday be a minister like cousin Sloane Coffin. When as a teenager he was turned off by the hypocrisy he faced in formal religion, he turned his missionary energy to black rights and jazz.

Mother took the Bible literally and spoke out against smoking and adultery. With little education, she was naive politically, always being surrounded by a conservative Republican circle. With her zeal she would have become a political radical if her background had allowed exposure to new ideas.

As it was, she founded the Three Arts Club, a place where good, white Christian families could send their daughters when they came to New York to pursue careers in music, theater and dance. Later on she was the financial supporter of Moral Rearmament.

She herself played the piano beautifully, studying with fine teachers, and she interested John in learning the violin at age four, and later the viola. This kept him occupied while other boys his age played sports, something he was miserable at. His total lack of coordination was another stumbling block to closeness with his athlete father. Attempts by Dad to teach his only son to ride a bike were miserable failures.

Mother was also often a problem to father. She refused to allow him to drink and smoke at home except in his study, and when Prohibition became law she took every bottle from the study and poured the contents into the street in front of the mansion. She further riled him with the pacifism she absorbed from the sermons of Sloane Coffin after World War I.

John's inability to coordinate well physically shocked people in the Swing Era later on when they realized that this "cat," who felt every syncopated beat deep in his gut, could not dance a step. And in another of life's strange twists, it was the viola lessons, the sports substitute, that in a mischievous manner opened the door to the world of blacks and jazz for John. His maternal rebellious streak appeared in many ways early on. Mother had become a Christian Scientist, and he was the only one who joined her in this faith. It made him feel special, as if he had eyes that saw what others didn't see and ears that heard what others couldn't hear.

He also had an intense desire to have a little Jewish blood in him, like in the Old Testament. Early on he heard his father mention an uncle named Louis Wolfe who was the black sheep of the Hammond clan. At different periods throughout his life, John tried to investigate whether Louis Wolfe had in fact been Jewish, but he was never able to document anything about the relative, except a tie to show business.

From the age of two on, his passion was listening to phonograph records. At three he taught himself to read or differentiate between the record labels, and at four, five and six was sneaking off at every opportunity to use the gramaphone. The grooves of the records let him enter a new world. His mother would come in to say goodnight and try to read him to sleep with passages from the Bible, but he had been given earphones so that he could listen without disturbing the rest of the family, and these were pulled out from under his pillow the moment she left the room.

He loved the classical records of Joseph Hoffman and the Scot, Sir Harry Lauder, performing "Roamin' in the Gloamin'," but soon he was wearing out a copy of the Original Dixieland Jazz Band. His allowance of one dollar a week at age 10 went entirely to the Widener Music Store for early Okeh and Columbia jazz records. He loved the sound of the blues, but it was a few years before he found out that the singers and players were black, not white—a significant discovery.

It was then that he started to break with religion and in some respects with his mother. He noticed that black servants were forced to sit in the back row of Episcopal churches and weren't permitted to take communion. He asked his mother about this and her reply upset him terribly.

"John, you're old enough to know the facts of life. I realize you're fascinated by colored people and I want you to know that everyone is born alike. But with Negroes their skulls harden when they are 12. There is a difference."

Disenchanted with his beloved religion, he buried himself more and more in his record collection and his own viola playing, cutting himself off even further from his contemporaries and his family. At the same time he started to buy the publication *Variety*, memorizing every line. Here was a 13-year-old reading and rereading theater sites, weekly grosses, vaudeville bills and reviews until he felt like an "insider." The fact that so many Jewish names were connected with the show biz items made him wish again that a few drops of Wolfe blood were flowing in his veins along with the Vanderbilt.

His father's decision to send him to Hotchkiss prep school plus the viola lessons provided a magical combination that soon led him to Harlem and the passions that would last a lifetime. Knowing of John's interest in the viola and unable to find an adequate teacher locally, the Hotchkiss administration permitted him to go to New York for lessons every other weekend.

The music teacher lived in Morningside Heights, near Columbia University, and the only way to get there from Connecticut was to take the New York Central Railroad to it's 125th Street station and cut across Harlem on foot. As John started his walk on the very first Saturday, he passed the Alhambra Theater with Bessie Smith's name on the marquee and billboards. He stopped in his tracks, magnetized beneath the big letters, unable to move because Bessie was his favorite of all the blues singers whose records he played.

Somewhere deep in this almost "too good" boy, a bit of teenage rebellion stirred, and when he joined the family for dinner at the mansion after his two-hour lesson, he very straight-facedly told his parents of an evening of string quartet playing that his teacher had arranged with his other students. Skipping dessert, he raced off to Harlem, to Bessie and to the beginning of his own individual lifestyle.

On other weekends he discovered the Lafayette Theater and Club Saratoga where Luis Russel's band played with Henry "Red" Allen on trumpet and J. C. Higginbotham on trombone. He visited every small club, always alone, always the only white in sight, and always drinking his 75-cent lemonade, which in

Prohibition days had to be particularly bad and stale since no one else ever ordered it. The boy was sure everyone around thought he was crazy. Chances are they did, but they certainly remembered this gangly, vulnerable looking youth. The bouncers at the Savoy Ballroom started to rap with him and soon were calling him by his first name.

Black musicians were having a very rough time in those days and even the greatest were willing to play in the Alhambra pit orchestra to pick up some extra cash. During show after show Hammond was seen in a front row center seat, his long body draped over the rail, worshiping Fats Waller and Louis Armstrong in the pit. Gradually the musicians began to notice him and listen for his characteristic "Yeah!" when he especially appreciated a lick. Sometimes at the end of a show they'd direct a wink at him or give him "five" in passing.

In addition to satisfying his hunger for great jazz and live contact with his recording heroes, two other allied trends were emerging at Hotchkiss that would stay with him all his life—a fine, spare journalistic style of writing, and a new political and social awareness. The latter came from his contacts with George Van Santvord, the headmaster, and John McChesney, a socialist, agnostic and Hammond's favorite teacher. Their effect on him was acknowledged by John:

"I was a changed man, I was convinced that there are no absolutes, that it is impossible for me as a human being to follow any line, be it a political line, a religious line, or a philosophical line. I recognized that there would always be points of view based on others' experience which must be considered and I had learned that dogmatism is a result of insecurity, that intolerance including my own is always suspect."

From those thoughts alone, one would have to say that Hotchkiss had provided a pretty complete education, and this makes John's decision to drop out of Yale early in his college career more understandable.

At McChesney's urging he started to read publications that he would never have seen in his home, like The New Republic and *New Masses*, all with a socialist point of view that felt comfortable to him. In the spring of his senior year at Hotchkiss, he read an article about a struggling newspaper in Maine run by a former editor of the New York *Tribune*, Ernest Gruening (who became both governor and senator from Alaska later on). Looking for some way to exercise his constructive activism, John wrote a letter to Gruening asking for a summer job on the Portland *Evening News*, a Democratic liberal paper. He got the job much to the horror of his father, who besides being a conservative Republican, worried about the disgrace for all the Vanderbilts and Hammonds summering in their second homes in Bar Harbor, Maine.

But the silver-spoon background which often rankled John just as often gave him an edge that allowed him to do his job or promote his cause in a manner impossible to someone with less financial stability. This ironic twist was to recur all through his life. In the instance of his first newspaper job, his family had given him the luxury of an Oldsmobile convertible. Because of his greater mobility than other reporters, he was assigned stories all over Maine, including a beautifully written exposé of the terrible living conditions of Indian communities being educated by the Catholic Church. Hammond visited the reservations, found grandly built churches, handsome houses for priests, no running water for Indians and not one Indian child at the high school level. He exploded internally and in print, and discovered something about himself that would again last a lifetime—he wrote better when angry, whether protesting injustice or criticizing bad music or uncaring musicians.

After entering Yale in 1929, he found his mind always on New York and music. His weekends were spent entirely at either Whytes on Fifth Avenue and 43rd Street, where hour after hour he would sit at the musicians' table, listening to the beat and hungrily absorbing their conversations between sets, or up in Harlem at the Morocco Club or Small's, where trumpeter Roy Eldridge, drummer Big Sid Catlett, trombonist Dickie Wells and singer Helen Humes began to trust him and feel comfortable with him as a friend.

John resolved to leave Yale and pursue his musical and journalistic interests, and a severe case of jaundice provided him with the way out. John's not returning to Yale was a blow to his father, who actually could have stopped his son, but in the first of many instances where he recognized the difference between the boy's convictions and needs and his own, he finally agreed to John's decision. He sent him to recuperate at a place called "The Millionaire's Club" on Jekyll Island off the coast of Georgia, where he was not only a member but president.

This recuperative vacation symbolized best the anachronisms in John's life. He was in a Wasp retreat. Blacks did all the work. Jews and Catholics were barred and this sickly guest was a young man who brought his usual reading material with him from the mainland. The eyes of the other guests and even the black waiters popped as he toyed with his food in the dining room, reading the Baltimore *Afro-American*, the Pittsburgh *Courier* and the Chicago *Defender*—all from the urban black ghettos.

For the next few years, in a whirl of constructive activity, he prepared himself by working for a radio station, three small record companies, a music publisher, an ad agency and a downtown theater; he produced two unsuccessful dramatic plays, took a job at People's Press publishing union newspapers, wrote jazz critiques for a dozen publications, and finally in 1931, was chosen to be the American correspondent for *Gramaphone*, the prestigious English musical journal.

He felt that the previous flurry of experience had brought him to the job for which he was uniquely suited, and to celebrate and symbolize a new era of his life, he left the mansion and took a tiny apartment on Sullivan Street in Greenwich Village. It was his twenty-first birthday.

Until this point his relationship with jazz was an emotional flirtation. Now he was ready to act as a catalyst in its growth and development. More important, he could see to it that musicians who had something new and exciting to play would be recorded and heard by a broader audience. He started to travel for *Gramaphone* and another English jazz magazine called *Melody Maker*. Through these sources plus an old friend, Artie Bernstein (one of the early crossover classical and jazz musicians), he met Gene Krupa, Benny Goodman and Bill Basie, all just starting out in 1931. Basie was the second pianist in Benny Moten's band. Goodman was the sub-leader and sideman in Russ Columbo's orchestra. But it was with an obscure pianist named Garland Wilson, whom Hammond heard at Covan's one night, that

John made his recording debut as a producer. Garland was black, talented, unknown and unrecorded, all the ingredients that Hammond wanted.

He always felt partial to Columbia Records because its manager Frank Walker had discovered Bessie Smith and had recorded her earliest performances, so John went to them and agreed to their conditions. John was to pay the costs involved for four 12-inch sides and was obliged to buy 150 finished records himself. Again, the affluent background didn't hurt and Hammond began his producing career modestly guiding Wilson through "St James' Infirmary" and "When Your Lover Has Gone." Columbia was so impressed that they cut four more sides for their Okeh label at their own expense.

Frank Walker and the rest of the Columbia brass decided that John was more than a nut with ready cash, that his affinity for recognizing raw jazz talent should not be ignored, and John was on his way.

That first recording session had a comical aftermath which displayed the total naiveté of the young producer. He had no idea what to pay Wilson, so decided to give him a Movado watch worth $125 in Depression money. He also failed to recognize what everyone else in Harlem knew, that Garland was flamboyantly gay. The pianist moved from joint to joint showing off his new watch saying, "Look what John gave me"—and of course it took the bewildered Hammond quite a while to live that one down.

Another amusing and yet progressive offshoot of this session was that word got back to John's social set that he had successfully produced a record, and a young deb he knew asked him to find an orchestra for the next dance at the Mt. Kisco Country Club, a restricted organization of which his father was again president. The young producer purchased a large jug of gin and sat it down next to the piano bench which supported Fats Waller, playing with a septet of Benny Carter (alto), Frankie Newton (trumpet), Pee Wee Russell (clarinet), Zutty Singleton (drums), Eddie Condon (guitar) and Artie Bernstein (bass). The club's staid timbers had never swung to jazz before and Hammond had the time of his life breaking down the barriers with seven brilliant instrumentalists, particularly since they included four blacks, one Jew, and two hungover drunks. Not long afterward, John punctuated his feelings about Wasp restrictions by insisting that his name be removed from the Social Register.

In 1932 John became deeply involved in the socio-political upheaval recounted in the chapter specifically relating to that year. But he never lost sight of the fact that usually these involvements resulted from his love for jazz and for the people who shared this enthusiasm. By 1933, "A pattern had developed in my life style centered around jazz but also reflecting an urge I have always felt to be the first to hear a great player, see a new show and find out what is going on in every town and city I can get to. . . . Like my mother I was an entrepreneur at heart, and like her I wanted to bring my discoveries to the world."

So he was very ready when the unexpected happened one night at Monette Moore's place on 133rd Street. At first he was disappointed when he was told Monette was rehearsing for a Broadway show with Clifton Webb and that a young singer named Billie Holiday was filling in. But from the first notes of "Woudja' for a Big Red Apple?" (the second lyric Johnny Mercer ever wrote) he knew he was listening to the best jazz singer he had ever heard.

Billie had come to New York from Baltimore two years earlier at age 15, but hadn't been heard around town because she had been sent to jail for prostitution. She didn't sing much blues, but took popular tunes and phrased them and colored them so that they sounded totally different from other interpretations.

She loved Louis Armstrong's sound and she often sang the way he played horn. Billie had a look and a bearing and a beauty that were ladylike, and this aura never deserted her even during her periods of degradation. John sat listening that first night deeply moved and yet elated.

"My discovery of Billie was the kind of accident I dreamed of. The sort of reward I received now and then by travelling to every place where anyone performed. Most of the time I was disappointed. But now and then it all became worthwhile."

He followed Billie from club to club—to the "Hotcha" where she found the perfect accompanist, Bobby Henderson, a stride pianist related to Fats Waller. Bobby had a similar charisma to Billie's and he made her an even better singer. John brought everyone he knew to the "Yeahman!", "Pod and Jerry's Log Cabin," the "Alhambra Grille"—wherever she moved. He had found a star and he wrote about her in *Melody Maker*. But since she was unknown outside Harlem, he knew he couldn't record her as yet. No company would take the chance. She was seventeen, he was twenty-two and he assured her that someday the record would happen. He had no illusions about the disposition that resided under her gorgeous exterior. But at least at that early time she was moderate in her use of alcohol and marijuana.

On schedule, a year later, in the fall of 1933, the opportunity came to bring together two of his musical idols, the clarinet virtuoso Benny Goodman, and Billie. If not for a trip to England six months earlier this blending might never have happened, because until then no one had ever integrated a recording session. That color line was rigid and unbroken.

But Sir Louis Sterling, the president of Columbia Gramaphone of England decided that with American Columbia bankrupt in the Depression, it was important for him to have an American who could record jazz for the English market. Because of Hammond's track record as jazz columnist for both *Gramaphone* and *Melody Maker* in London, he was the logical choice.

With great creativity, John produced eight sides by the large Fletcher Henderson Orchestra, eight by Benny Carter's big band, four by a Benny Goodman group, four by Joe Venuti the jazz violinist, and some sides with Coleman Hawkins and various accompanists. They all were tremendously successful.

The history of this first date with Goodman is worth looking into because it was the start of a very complicated and often abrasive relationship that was to last all their lives until Goodman died in 1986. Through the years Hammond spent more time and effort on the clarinetist than any other artist he recorded. Their lives became further enmeshed later when Benny became a brother-in-law by marrying Alice Hammond Duckworth, John's sister.

This first professional encounter had all the highs and lows of those that followed. As was already mentioned, John had met Benny briefly through Artie Bernstein, but when he approached

Goodman with the news that he had a signed Columbia contract to record, Benny was his usual diplomatic self.

"You're a goddam liar—and the reason I know you're a liar is that I was down at Columbia last week and Bob Selvin told me the company is bankrupt."

After John explained that this was to be for English Columbia which had plenty of money, he confided to Benny of his dream to put the greatest musicians they could find, no matter what color, under Benny's direction and just jam—swing with no arrangements.

Benny told him he was crazy—that no one would tolerate or buy records of a racially mixed band. It just wasn't done. Also jamming would be chaos with a big group. Goodman insisted that John come to hear his own new band that night—the one he was sure was right for the recording.

At that stage of his career, Benny had had a hard time making a living, underpaid as a sideman in sweet bands like Russ Columbo's. He was cynical about the record buying public's taste and understanding of jazz, and if it wasn't for Hammond's vision and persistence, he might have just stayed with "society music" and never scored as the "King of Swing."

The group Hammond heard that night was even worse than the Columbo Band—it had a rhythm section that usually played with Meyer Davis. As mild as he generally was, John did have a tough streak and he told Benny unequivocally that unless he had control of choosing the sidemen, the date was canceled. Goodman needed money desperately to support his large family in Chicago and he said OK—but, "no Coleman Hawkins, no colored guys." John asked why and Benny frankly told him what was on the mind of anyone in the business who wanted to work in early 1933.

"If it gets around that I recorded with colored guys, I won't get another job in this town."

"It can't be that bad," John protested.

"John, you know it's that bad!"

Realizing he was right at that time and place, John decided to fight another day, and with great difficulty put together an all-white band.

Gene Krupa, for instance, had had past problems with Goodman, and at first balked: "I'll never work for that son of a bitch again." But he was finally persuaded. Hammond added Jack Teagarden, Charlie Teagarden, Artie Karl, Artie Bernstein, Dick McDonough, Joe Sullivan, Frankie Froeba and Manny Klein. Manny, a trumpeter, was the only choice Goodman refused to give up because he was the leading contractor in New York for union music work, and Benny was afraid that he might need all the jobs he could get as the Depression continued.

The tunes the group did included "I Got a Right to Sing the Blues" (a Cotton Club Revue song by Harold Arlen), "Dr. Heckle and Mr. Jive," and a blues, "Texas Teaparty," built around Jack Teagarden. The record sold 5000 copies, a "smash" in 1933.

Still searching for the key to open the door for mixed race recording, John kept up his vagabond life as a talent scout. One night on his car radio he heard a broadcast from the Grand Terrace in Chicago where Earl "Fatha" Hines was playing. Hammond realized that the piano solos were not the great Earl— they were cleaner and more elegant. He stopped the car, called the station, WMAQ, and found out that Hines was ill and the sub was a man named Teddy Wilson. Knowing that Goodman was looking for a pianist, he called Benny.

"Sure I know him," Benny said, "he worked with Art Tatum in Toledo as a piano team." So John wired him $150 of his own money to go to Chicago and Teddy was signed to the Goodman Band. Through the years Hammond was unfairly accused of playing Pygmalion, of interfering in others' lives, and even profiting at others' expense.

"Not so," John says. "I never made an investment for monetary gain. As to any resemblance to that famous reformer Pygmalion, I cannot plead total innocence. After all, my mother passed on to me the urge to change the world I thought needed changing. Sometime that even included jazz . . . most of the jazz players who interested me during the Depression were given an occasional boost with some of my own money. This was in part to bring national recognition to great Negro players at a time when both the economic conditions in the country and the rigid segregation made such recognition very difficult. It was also based on my desire to hear those players, to bring together musicians who had never played together before. For instance, I brought together Red Norvo and Teddy Wilson, Norvo and Chu Berry, and Teddy and Artie Bernstein."

This talent for musical collage could now be used again since the financial success of the new Goodman recordings. Now was the moment for Benny and Billie to get together.

Goodman and Hammond were becoming close friends despite their differences and each night for a week they went to listen to Billie. Accompanying them were two of Billie's greatest fans, Charles Laughton and Elsa Lanchester, in New York for Charles's first Broadway play, *Payment Deferred.* By the end of the first evening Benny wanted to record with Billie whether she was black, brown or beige.

Timing was perfect, because American Columbia saw a certain way of bailing themselves out of debt by following the red-hot Goodman's British success with another record. So in November of 1933 Billie had her first recording date, the industry took a giant step forward and Hammond had his landmark integrated disk. In fact, doubly integrated, because one of the trumpeters was Shirley Clay, a black man from Don Redmond's outfit. The titles were "Riffin' the Scotch" and "Your Mother's Son-in-Law," and they are now collectors' classics.

Not content with having been the first to record the greatest jazz singer, Hammond set out to make his first platter with the greatest blues singer, Bessie Smith. Here, however, he had a totally different problem facing him.

Blues records were at the bottom of all record sales. The Depression left the black record buyers in even worse shape than the whites, and John's English contacts were useless because Britons bought jazz but not blues. Still, he could not forget the lady he had heard at the Alhambra that night after his first music lesson, and he talked Columbia into a deal on the Okeh label. Bessie was working as a hostess in a sleazy speakeasy in Philadelphia, singing with a bad accompanist and generally very drunk and depressed.

Hammond's approach was: "Miss Smith I'd love to get you in our recording studios. It's been two years since you've worked on a record and I'll hire the finest musicians for you."

"What would it pay?" she asked.

At that point John thought she'd say no because he made it clear that with the 35-cent label, all he could offer her was her expenses to and from New York and no more. Surprisingly she agreed, perhaps because of the financial security brought by her current boyfriend, Richard Morgan, a bootlegger who was an uncle of Lionel Hampton. Or it may have simply been the ego of an artist needing to be heard. John got Jack Teagarden, Chu Berry, Frankie Newton, Billy Taylor, Sr., Buck Washington, and on "Gimme a Pig Foot" even sneaked Benny Goodman in.

This group was impressed to be playing with the legendary Bessie. Teagarden in particular was floating. Recording with her was a dream he thought had passed him by. Initially nothing happened with those records and Columbia lost money. But later "Gimme a Pig Foot" became a jukebox standard and the entire set has been reissued many times for each successive generation of Bessie Smith fans. A close personal relationship had been established between producer and singer, and at her death in 1936 Hammond was in the midst of negotiations with Dick Altshuler of Columbia to sign her to a proper ongoing contract with their Brunswick label.

Everyone in jazz circles has a different story as to the true details of Bessie's death and there have been a number of plays and teleplays produced on the subject. From Silas Green, the producer of the tent show she was traveling with, Hammond heard that the old Packard car in which Bessie was riding was forced off the road and her arm nearly severed in the crash. Two ambulances passed her by because she was black, and she bled to death. Lionel Hampton, whose uncle Richard Morgan was Bessie's lover, confirms those details of her death, adding that the flamboyant bootlegger Morgan loved Bessie so much that he just wasted away quickly after she died. Hammond also was devastated, but there was consolation that the records would keep some part of her alive.

During this period his personal life was spartan and totally secondary to his professional interests. He was cut off from contemporaries, never dated and seldom saw the family except once a week when he carried all his laundry from Sullivan Street to the mansion to have it done properly. His "digs" in the village were shabby, the only signs of affluence being a superb record player and a good rug. But his prize possession was a dilapidated green arm chair, stained, he proudly says, by seven years of accumulation of Harlem hair grease from his musician friends' visits.

The uneasy relations with family members of totally opposite political polarity was a constant fact of life. When his uncle Ogden H. Hammond, the U.S. Ambassador to Spain during the Spanish Civil War, headed a pro-Franco committee, John joined a group of Loyalists picketing his office.

A little later, when John produced "From Spirituals to Swing" and could get no one but the *New Masses* publication to put up the money to sponsor the benefit, his father was in a dilemma. He wanted to purchase a box to indicate support for his son's venture. This purchase would be listed on the program and that listing would put him in an untenable position as a member of the National Industrial Conference Board. What could he then say to fellow members Alfred P. Sloan, Jr., and Lamont DuPont, having donated to a left of center project? He turned the box down and bought eight anonymous orchestra seats instead, telling John, "They might think I was a communist too."

But John was no communist. He certainly fought for liberal causes and favored social reform, but he would never join the Communist Party. It is easy to forget today that in the 1930's one of the many goals of the American Communist Party was the overthrow of the U.S. government. In fact, speaking of the flirtation between American blacks and the Party, Hammond, with his usual exquisite analytical vision, put this subject into the most objective perspective.

"It was important for anyone interested in the struggle for civil and social justice to understand the dangers communism had for Negroes. Considering that they had few friends among whites, communist sympathy for their cause could not be ignored. But Moscow, as many Negroes discovered, was a fair weather friend. Russia's espousal of the Negro's viewpoint, his art and his right to equal justice, coincided only with Soviet self-interest and the current communist line. The result for most Negroes who turned to communism in that turbulent decade was frustration, disillusionment and final rejection."

In the single brief governmental investigation of his politics

during the early 1950's, the F.B.I. came to question Hammond
about his connections with the Metropolitan Music School, then
listed as a possible communist front. This was the so-called "Mc-
Carthy Era" when every American liberal was suspect. The ex-
change with the very intelligent and decent F.B.I. agent went
like this:

"What are you doing on the board of the school?"

"Very simple, the school has no racial prejudice."

"How did you get involved?"

"I've been on the board of the NAACP since 1935. I've had a
lot to do with music."

After long questioning in that same direction the agent said,
"Now I have to ask you the $64,000 question. Are you or have
you ever been a member of the Communist Party?"

John replied: "I'm going to pause before I answer that because it's important to tell the absolute truth, because not only
was I never a member of the Communist Party, nor would I be a
member, nor am I now a member of the Communist Party. I
could not because I am interested in civil rights, and it is not.
Throughout the years, the communists have done flip-flops and
if I had been a member of the Party I would never have made
the waves I did."

All subpoenas were withdrawn and he was never called to
testify at committee hearings.

Hammond, however, was often accused of a different kind of
blind faith and prejudice. Critics of his writing say he is the
perfect example of reverse racial prejudice, making sweeping
statements like, "The best of the white folk still cannot compare
to the really good Negroes in relaxed unpretentious dance music." All his life he has believed that black players swing better
than their white counterparts. To him there was no white pianist
to match Fats Waller, no blues singer to equal Bessie and no
white band with the rhythm of Fletcher Henderson. And it
stuck in his craw that these artists never made a good living and
were barred from all the well-paying jobs in radio and night
clubs. To the accusation that he is a "nigger lover," his response
was, "I am."

He did, however, have some close white friends in the music
business. One was Irving Mills, an agent and enormously power-

ful publisher, who John feels did more than anyone else to help black musicians survive the Depression by providing them with income. Irving was also John's link to Duke Ellington—the only major black jazz figure who was not intimate with Hammond. As usual, the humane and yet objective nature of Hammond is enlightening when he speaks of the Duke.

"I never felt close to Duke as a person, and indeed there were few who did. For all the up-front gregariousness—"We Love You Madly"—he was a very private person. He also demanded of his friends almost total acceptance of his performance as a leader, pianist and composer. He was uneasy around critics, even those he knew admired him, and rarely read their comments. As much as possible he avoided anything upsetting.

"Duke had a feeling of loyalty to Irving Mills, who made him into a national figure in music and whose publishing company made him the best paid ASCAP Negro composer in America. I think Ellington felt it was his business and nobody else's that he would go along with whatever it took to repay Mills. He also felt that if he were ever in trouble, he could always go to Irving Mills and no one else. It was not until Bill Morris of the William Morris Agency came along to give Duke a new sense of personal dignity and to back up his advice with superior bookings, that Ellington left Mills. I give Bill Morris enormous credit for much of the later growth and success Duke enjoyed.

"My opinion of Ellington's place in jazz has not changed. I liked his band better in its early days. I was sorry to see the critics, particularly in England, hailing him as a new Delius, and a significant composer of serious music when in fact he was a jazz composer—a tribute he certainly should not have been ashamed of. That was my basic difference with Duke Ellington in the early 1930's and it still is."

Another white friend was Mildred Bailey, the best Caucasian jazz singer of the time. John recorded her through the thirties with three different groups—Goodman's band, a Teddy Wilson band in 1936, and later with an all-black band of all-stars called the Oxford Grays. The Wilson session with a small group that included Bunny Berrigan, Johnny Hodges and Graham Mansur, Sr., produced some of Mildred's classics like "Willow Tree" and "Honeysuckle Rose." The Oxford Gray Band had Mary Lou Wil-

liams on piano and had been given that name to mask the fact
that they were all black. Bailey was an original, but a mass of
contradictions and often bigoted.

Hammond had taken Mildred to hear Billie Holiday frequently in 1933, leaving Mildred impressed but jealous. She was
always fat and messy and Billie was so incredibly sexy and beautiful. But Mildred found her own way of putting Billie down. She
employed Billie's mother as a housekeeper and now and then
when gigs were scarce, Billie appeared at Mildred's house to
help Sadie in the kitchen.

Mildred admired black jazz players, and was anxious to record with them. But she wouldn't appear with mixed bands in
public places and risk loss of income or reputation, until it was
socially acceptable to do so. Strangely, Mildred and her husband
Red Norvo, the wonderful xylophonist, became Hammond's
close friends, while Billie, ethereal and undependable, never allowed that depth of contact.

Two of the greatest achievements of John's life were his roles
in both the formation of the famous Goodman and Basie bands,
and in guiding them to proper public exposure.

Goodman came to him early in 1934 complaining that he had
no important future as a sideman, and that he had to form his
own band based on a jazz style, not like the sweet ones he had
previously fronted. Hammond went all around town, including
Chinese restaurants, listening to every New York musician, and
put together a group which played briefly at the Billy Rose Music Hall. When Prohibition ended, all the various beer mobs
were looking for places in which to invest their bootleg money,
and the Music Hall became one of them. Since Benny was dat-
ing a gorgeous chorus girl from the club named Hannah Williams (who later married Jack Dempsey) he had entree to the
audition and got the job.

In a parallel stroke of luck, Willard Alexander, a booker for
M.C.A., the largest agency for bands, had dinner at the Music
Hall and got Benny to sign a contract. Willard had just been
approached by National Biscuit Company to provide the music
for one of the most unusual network radio programs ever conceived. It was to be called "Let's Dance," a three-hour dance
party every Saturday night that would allow people to try the

steps in their own living rooms. The bands hired were Xavier Cugat for Latin rhythms, Kel Murray for popular dance music and Benny for jazz.

A weekly allowance for eight new arrangements at 75 dollars each enabled John and Goodman to hire people of the caliber of Fletcher Henderson, Jimmy Mundy and Edgar Sampson to do them, and this broke the stranglehold that music publishers had on how popular songs were to be presented on the air. Instead of just "selling" the melody and the lyric, this band could now play in its own style, taking liberties with the tune and allowing for plenty of improvisational solos.

And what a rhythm section Hammond assembled. Gene Krupa on drums, Jess Stacey on piano, George Van Eps on guitar and Harry Goodman (Benny's brother) on bass. Helen Ward, the singer, had the sound and the lilt that the band's style required.

Early in 1935 John's talent as an entrepreneur came to the fore when he figured out a business parlay that would allow him to record what he considered a "dream" trio of Krupa, Benny and Teddy Wilson. Teddy was signed to Brunswick along with Billie Holiday. Goodman was signed to Victor. So he got Victor to lend Benny as a sideman for the Wilson-Holiday records and in return Brunswick allowed Teddy to join the trio that became the most famous one in jazz history.

Benny and Teddy knew each other a long time and complemented each other's playing styles perfectly. Yet they never got along and were never at ease with each other. Wilson was especially qualified to handle the delicate challenge of working with white musicians in public. He had been raised on the campus of Tuskegee where his father was head of the History Department and his mother the librarian. Teddy had the bearing, appearance and attitude that would help him to survive in a white society. Still he rejected a good part of his academic background and was suspicious of everyone.

In Benny's case his suspicions were confirmed. Even years later during the famous 1962 tour of Russia that Goodman made for the State Department, Benny continually abused him musically and personally. Bill Crow, the bass player who himself was on that tour, wrote a significant account of the vendetta in the

September 1986 issue of Gene Lees' Jazz Letter.

"Benny had just turned 53 and I asked Teddy Wilson if he thought Benny's behavior could be attributed to age. I was 34 and thought 53 was pretty old.

"Teddy snorted: 'The man is the same today as he was in 1936. You just have to ask for enough money to make it worth your while.'

"I laughed. 'Boy, your price must really be up there by this time! Why do you keep taking the job?'

"Teddy smiled. 'I have a lot of alimony to pay and besides, these jobs allow me to play with a class of musicians I can't afford to hire myself.'

"Halfway through that tour Benny had John Bunch playing with the small group as well as the big band and was using Wilson only on the opening number. Bunch felt bad about it. He considered Teddy one of his musical fathers and thought he deserved more respect.

"Benny was killing Joe Newman with kindness. He had given him most of the trumpet solos and had him playing with the septet as well. Joe was complaining that his 'chops' were starting to hurt. Mel (Lewis) and I asked Benny to give Joe a break. These people knew Teddy from his records and would like to hear him play. Why not let him do a trio number? Benny said it was a good idea and tried it on the next concert.

"Teddy played 'Stompin' at the Savoy' and 'Satin Doll' with Mel and me and the audience cheered. John Bunch, instead of leaving the stage, had taken a chair next to Joe Newman, right beside the open piano lid. He sat there beaming with pleasure, and enthusiastically joined in the applause.

"The trio numbers stayed in the program, but when Teddy was taking his bows, Benny always behaved ungraciously toward him, turning his back until the audience applause died down. He seemed to find it difficult to share applause with anyone."

Hammond himself remembers a further incident in 1975 at the Chicago screening of a television program about John called "The World of John Hammond." When Goodman joined the invited audience to great applause, John's wife Esmee remarked, "They're really rolling out the red carpet for Benny!" Teddy, sitting next to her muttered, "Yes, and it should be live coals!" It is a testimonial to the professionalism of both musicians that on wax and in public, despite the rancor, the music they made together was sheer, unspoiled perfection.

Hammond himself had an up and down time with Benny. For periods they would be inseparable and later even became brothers-in-law. But there were frustrating times when Goodman stubbornly rejected any of John's suggestions. They had numerous rows about Benny's treatment of Charlie Christian, particularly when he failed to contact the guitar genius at all while Charlie was dying of a chest disease in Seaview Hospital on Staten Island.

Their last business contact took place in 1953 when John managed a six-week tour of the original band in a co-star tie-in with Louis Armstrong. A professional jealousy feud that Benny provoked with both Louis and his manager Joe Glaser resulted in Hammond's being caught in the middle, and eventually being fired by Benny as his manager.

This feud between the Goodman and Armstrong bands may have contributed to an incident in 1954 when Lionel Hampton felt Joe Glaser pulled a fast one on him. According to Lionel, "I like being in campaigns and I went all over the country playing in rallies for the Eisenhower-Nixon Bandwagon. He won and President Eisenhower made me Goodwill Ambassador for life. Joe Glaser asked my wife Gladys, 'Let me see that plaque that the President gave Lionel saying that.' She gave it to him and when she called and said send me back my plaque, he said 'Oh I lost it in the office or someplace.' He had transferred Louis Armstrong's name and placed it on the plaque. The Cola people were going to send me on a tour of Africa as a Goodwill Ambassador, so Louis got the job instead."

None of this could ever erase the joyous memories of 1937 and 1938 when John helped Benny become the King of Swing and together they molded the most commercial and yet precisionally perfect swing band of all time.

The first step in elevating the quality of the Goodman Band to this new high level came in 1937 when Hammond found Lionel Hampton leading an eight-piece band at the Paradise Cafe, a crummy joint in downtown Los Angeles. Hampton played the vibraharp—the "vibes"—a metal-keyed resonating instrument in contrast to the xylophone which most jazz men like Red Norvo played. Lionel had received his vibraphone as a present from his bootlegger uncle Richard Morgan to add to his talents as a driving swing drummer. In fact he played the vibes almost as if he was drumming out complex rhythmic patterns and it was this style that gave the trio of Benny, Gene and Teddy a lively new dimension as it expanded to a quartet.

To be totally fair to the image of Benny Goodman, Hampton's comments about the leader have to be noted. In a recent conversation he gives a different view of Benny, defending him as the man who integrated jazz. "They should erect a statue of Benny in Times Square for what he did cementing white and colored races together." On a personal level Lionel admits that Benny liked him and always gave him special attention and leeway. None of the other wives travelled with the band, but Hampton's wife Gladys did, and Benny always saw to it that they had the suite next to his in the hotel. Through the years Lionel overheard people saying to Goodman, "Why do you need those niggers? Replace them with whites." Benny would become enraged and tell them to never come near him again.

For this band on the rise, the next rung up was the 1938 Carnegie Hall concert produced by the Sol Hurok office and fortunately recorded surreptitiously by Helen Ward's husband. John's role went no further than getting musicians for the band itself and also others from the Basie and Ellington outfits for the smaller supporting groups.

Another big step came in 1939 when he persuaded Benny to leave Victor and come to Columbia at the same moment that Count Basie did, making Hammond responsible for recording what he considers to be the two greatest swing bands. It was then that he made his last great coup as talent scout for Goodman—uncovering the instinctive genius of Charlie Christian.

Mary Lou Williams gets an assist, having urged John to travel to Oklahoma City to the Ritz Cafe where this 20-year old was playing. As with every other great musician whom Hammond has "discovered," there was never a moment's doubt about his singularity of sound. Christian had the same effect on him that Holiday, Basie, Wilson and Hampton had had—lights flashed, rockets went off and he could only wonder where everyone else was. Why didn't they hear it? In all the years Hammond has never seen anyone from the white record industry get there before him. Perhaps it was just a result of his enthusiasm for black musicians. At any rate he knew at once that Charlie Christian was now the last precision part for the Goodman small group. It only lasted two years before Charlie's death—but what a two years of music!

Lionel recently related a story about a week in Texas not long after Christian's death, when the band was booked to play at an enormous fair in Dallas. Teddy kept warning him that this trip was going to be trouble, and he seemed to be right on target when the manager at the hotel where Benny was staying followed Goodman's directive to accept his two black stars as guests, but insisted that they'd have to ride in the freight elevator to prevent potentially violent incidents.

Teddy turned that down for the both of them, and opted instead to stay with a friend in town, a Doctor Green. Lionel's wife's family came from Dennison, 60 miles away, and various cousins volunteered to drive Gladys and Hamp back and forth so that they could spend each night in family surroundings.

The daily concerts were held in a bowl-like stadium that was packed with 20,000 fans who caused a five-minute delay with their enthusiastic applause when Teddy and Lionel were introduced at the opening concert. The whole program went well and the response was warm and appreciative. Afterward a man who was a friend of John Hammond asked a guard to let him backstage to see Hampton and Wilson, and he showed him a magnum of chilled champagne that he wanted to share with them. The cop chased him away with, "I'm not letting you in there, you niggah lover." Somehow the bubbly was passed on to them by someone else. But Teddy was in a rage over the incident. "I told you what was going to happen with these people. They're the main haters of blacks."

That night they went back to stay with their hosts. Lionel told Teddy to call him and let him know when he was ready to go to the next morning's rehearsal, but Teddy was so upset he didn't call at all. Finally Benny phoned both of them, told them to get to town, and assured them that he had it all straightened out. When they arrived, Goodman had Stanley Marcus—head of

Nieman Marcus Company, and one of Dallas's most influential citizens—the chief of police, and the official who was in charge of the Fair waiting to talk to them. The chief quickly insisted that what happened the previous night was unforgivable, but he personally assured them that everyone would be respectful from now on.

Teddy decided to throw in a "zinger." "What about these signs that say 'white drinking water' and 'colored drinking water' that you've got down here?" The chief told them to go drink any place they wanted to. So Lionel and Teddy ran over to the 'white' fountain and took long and dramatic swigs.

Word got to them that the rude policeman was going to be suspended, and Gladys's family urged Hampton to prevent that, or it would only lead to more problems. Gladys's father was a high-ranking Mason and had Lionel studying to join the fraternal organization. On hearing that the policeman who was on the carpet was also a Mason, Lionel convinced him to tutor him in Masonry for the rest of the week—and the chief dropped the charges.

Hammond's happiest, most personal discovery, and the one that led to the closest friendship he ever has had with any musician, was Bill Basie. John had had a special twelve-tube Motorola radio installed in his car to keep in touch with music around the country during his long hours on the road. On a cold January 1935 night in Chicago, he picked up an experimental station from Kansas City and lucked into hearing Count Basie's nightly broadcast from the Reno Club. He remembered the name and the touch of Benny Moten's second pianist at Covan's, but here was Basie playing with a new and unusual economy of style. With fewer notes he was saying more and using a single chord or even a single note as perfectly timed punctuation to his sidemen's solos.

The horn player he was inspiring most in this band was Lester Young, at his peak. Hammond began writing about them in *Downbeat* magazine, talking the band up wherever he went and finally travelling to Kansas City for a first-hand listen. Besides Lester, the group included Jo Jones on drums, Walter Page on bass, Oran "Hot Lips" Page on Trumpet and Jimmy Rushing, "Mr. Five by Five," on vocals. It was the radio announcer who dubbed Bill "The Count" since these were the days of Duke Ellington, Earl Hines and King Oliver.

For Hammond this band played the sort of free swinging jazz that he adored—unbuttoned, never too disciplined, allowing room for improvisation. So he got permission from Brunswick to sign Basie. But Dave Kapp of Decca, using the guise of friend and emissary of Hammond, had already signed the Count to an inferior, below-legal-scale contract. Not only was Basie devastated that he had misunderstood and would not be working with his friend, but there was no provision for royalties. And so he earned nothing extra for the mammoth sales of his classics such as "One O'Clock Jump" and "Jumping at the Woodside." It wasn't until that 1939 switch that John and he were finally able to work together. Meanwhile Hammond arranged for Willard Alexander to manage the band to national prominence. He also found Freddie Greene for Bill, and for 50 consecutive years whenever Basie was at the piano there was Freddy sitting beside him playing guitar.

The first major booking for the band was at the Roseland Ballroom in New York, at that time still a segregated dance hall. No blacks were admitted and Puerto Ricans were discouraged. The gig was so important to the Count's blossoming career that he and John accepted the situation and arranged for the band to play later at the Savoy after Roseland's closing, so that blacks in New York could also dance to Basie. To compensate for the Roseland conditions, and with the courage and affrontery that an agent can muster when he believes in a client, Willard Alexander soon got the Count a gig as the first black band to play the William Penn Hotel in Pittsburgh.

Throughout the Count's life, John fussed and worried about the makeup, sound, and exposure of the band like a mother hen. Their friendship was deep and mutual, and this tie had a positive effect on the entire jazz community for five decades.

Hammond's interracial and musical contributions to the NAACP, to the World War II military and to Cafe Society and Barney Josephson are discussed elsewhere in this book. He continued to unearth musical treasures through all the decades. How much more spectacular can these names be?: George Benson, Bob Dylan, Aretha Franklin, Bruce Springsteen and most recently Stevie Ray Vaughn.

This quote from John offers the best understanding of the man and his motives.

"I have always tried to be careful about my relationship with talented people I like and admire so much, particularly in instances where I have been able to lend a hand—or to put it bluntly, a dollar. I can remember that my mother's generosities, and there were many, to many people—unfortunately had a price tag, gratitude. Lady Bountiful's payoff was thanks. I don't know how I knew, but even as a kid I knew that stank. And that eventually a sour breath of hatred leaked out of the people from whom too many thanks had been extracted.

"I've never felt I was buying anyone or putting anyone under obligation. Whatever help I've been able to give has been given freely. Money given simply represented opportunity, a chance to get something done. Seeing it happily and successfully done was all the reward I ever wanted.

"Anyone who wants anything more, anyone who wants gratitude from or credit for a talent that already exists is a pain in the ass."

Thousands of musicians and millions of jazz listeners owe a lifetime of great music to John Hammond, and the entire black population of the U.S. owes him even broader respect. The only ones who would consider him a "pain in the ass" would be the enemies of racial harmony, social justice and swinging jazz.

On July 10, 1987, after an extended illness, John Hammond quietly passed away at his house in Manhattan.

Chapter III

Barney and Max

(Or Is It Max and Barney?)

Barney and Max—sounds like a couple of vitriolic waiters who would toss the insults along with the cheesecake in the old Lindy's heyday—or at the very least, brothers-in-law who run a discount luggage store on Orchard Street on the lower East Side? In reality Barney Josephson and Max Gordon leapt into the void left by the departing mobsters after Prohibition's repeal, and became the royalty of night club impressarios. Today as octogenarians, they are still on the scene.

At Barney's Cafe Society Downtown and Uptown and The Cookery and Max's Village Vanguard and The Blue Angel they were scouts who tracked budding superstars, gracious hosts who embraced the rich and famous, and entrepreneurs whose savvy created financial success and turned both into saloon-keeper celebrities who were pestered for autographs as often as their headliners.

In the old 1930's movies, the part of the guy who ran a sleek Manhattan club was filled by Ceser Romero or George Raft or Bogart. Cut to real life, and Max is barely five feet tall, while Barney resembles the frail young man who got sand kicked in his face in body building ads. At 85 and 86 respectively, they are sweethearts anyone would be proud to show off to friends as their adorable great-grandfathers.

But sit down quickly for another of their cross-casting shockers. They were fathering children at ages 51 and 59. Max's daughters are 37 and 34 and Barney's sons are 27 and 30. As you talk to these very senior citizens today, you get the distinct impression that even now they could be providing the ladies with a little action.

The parallels in their lives from birth on are astonishing.

Max was the youngest of four children born to a Jewish immigrant from Lithuania who after arriving in this country supported his family in Portland, Oregon, by peddling wares from street to street. Max pitched in to help the family by selling newspapers as a little boy and later became a night-owl, clerking in an all-night cigar store. The family scrimped together enough to send the oldest brother to a seminary in Cincinnati to become a rabbi. Max himself eventually enrolled in Reed College, well known today but very obscure 65 years ago. He would attend classes for one year, then drop out for a year, peddling to pay for the next semester. Even then he knew he had to satisfy a creative streak in himself and wrote articles for local synagogue newspapers. When his parents sent him to New York to enroll in law school, his nocturnal prowling brought him to the Village and law school was soon forgotten. In making the rounds of restaurants, bars, and clubs he knew he had found a home. An infatuation for a young woman led him to join her in running a coffee house. When she left him for another guy, he was stuck where he really wanted to be, and soon the first Vanguard days were born.

Barney was the youngest of six children, the only offspring born in this country to a Jewish family from Latvia. The father, again a cobbler peddler, settled in a Jewish ghetto in Trenton, New Jersey. The older brothers worked in a shoe store and Barney earned money after school at the age of ten helping out in the same store. By 16 he was the super salesman, and by 21 he was earning $200 a week as the "out of town buyer" for fine shoes. On his trips into Manhattan to see the new lines, he would be wined and dined by these firms to put him in the mood to write big orders. One night when asked where he would especially like to be entertained, he said, "The Cotton Club." The elegance and style of the black entertainers had such an impact on Barney that he knew this was where he wanted to spend his life—only running a club where black and white performers entertained a mixed audience. It had to be integrated.

He had to wait a few years. But when the Depression ruined shoe sales, he borrowed $6,000, and finally late in 1938 launched Cafe Society Downtown and in 1940 Cafe Society Uptown.

Why such intensity about interracial performers and patrons in this young Jewish man from Trenton? Barney never forgot the exact day he felt so drawn to a brotherhood with blacks.

It was the opening day of school at a new junior high that was built to bring students from many districts together. Barney arrived to find all the white boys at the periphery of the room, and one black student in the middle, surrounded by a circle of empty seats. He walked up to the neatly dressed black boy on impulse, stuck out his hand and said, "Hi, I'm Barney Josephson." "Rudolph Dunston," the other boy's name became Barney's "Rosebud." The moment triggered feelings of compassion and comradery that have remained with him all his life. When the afternoon gym class began and the other boys roughed him up, he was called "nigger lover" for the first but not the last time.

How did these deep internal feelings develop? Much of it must have been instinct, something in his physiology and body chemistry, because he had no direct contact with a black until that teenager. Other liberals have traced their intense devotion for Afro-American causes to the loving care black maids or governesses lavished on them as children—or at the very least their own parents' repeated admonitions to "be kind to these poor down-trodden folk." Barney could look to neither as an explanation.

His parents were too poor for maids and had enough troubles of their own to worry much about other minorities. Father died soon after Barney was born, but his mother did imbue him with a sense of responsibility for other Jews, and this Jewish consciousness has never left him. Ironically he never has had a burning desire to help Jewish entertainers—only blacks, most likely because they were being mistreated here as Jews were in Europe.

Still, something unstated, but implicit in its insistence on decent behavior, must have gone on in that Trenton household. All the older children also developed friendships, associations and causes that were politically and socially liberal, in older brother Leon's case so excessively left of center that he was later imprisoned for his defiance of the House Un-American Activities Committee. Barney has never recovered from the results of his brother's stand.

In December 1938 when Josephson opened his club on Sheridan Square in Greenwich Village, he wanted to give it a name that would be a putdown of upper class attitudes and prejudices. Clare Booth Luce herself suggested the "Cafe Society," and some young women of the *Vogue* magazine staff proposed the famous satirical costume for the doorman—a tattered coat and white gloves with the fingertips cut out. The mood was continued by the "Chamber of Horrors" to the left of the hat check as you entered. There, a simian Hitler of papier-mâché hung suspended from the ceiling, and plaster figures of Cholly Knickerbocker, Elsa Maxwell and Lucius Beebe lounged pretentiously. The walls were covered with murals and sketches by Sid Hoff, Steig, Adolph Dehn, Peggy Bacon, Anton Refregier and William Gropper, all irreverent to high society. But lampoon was only a surface function of the club. Its main goal for Barney was the breakdown of color barriers. He was intent on having shows with the best black and white performers mixing to entertain a racially integrated audience. Josephson had heard of the trust that John Hammond had inspired in black musicians and enlisted John's help in finding the best for the club.

An incredible list of stars played at Downtown and at Cafe Society Uptown when Barney branched out early in 1940. Great piano players were featured, like Art Tatum, Meade Lux Lewis, Albert Ammons, Pete Johnson, Eddie Heywood, and Ellis Larkins. Teddy Wilson conducted the house band for seven years.

Singers heard included Lena Horne, Hazel Scott, Billie Holiday, Helen Humes, Sarah Vaughn, Georgia Gibbs, Ida James, Big Joe Turner and the Golden Gate Quartet. The most wonderful jazz musicians gave these vocalists perfect backing.

Great artists like the folk singer Josh White and dancer Avon Long were held over for extended engagements.

Of all the many styles of jazz, boogie woogie became the one most identified with the club. John Hammond had heard a recording of "Honky Tonk Blues" by Meade Lux Lewis and searched for him for two years before tracing him to a Chicago car wash. He brought Meade to New York along with a friend of his, another former taxi driver named Albert Ammons. Night after night at Cafe Society, Lewis, Ammons and a third Hammond protégée, Pete Johnson, would bring the house down with boogie played solo, in duets or all three playing at once. What was this "new-old" style that appealed so strongly that it became a craze? Jazz critic Leonard Feather technically described it as "A 12-measure blues theme with repeated rhythmic figures in the left hand in eighth notes or dotted eighths, harmoniously limited and short on melody but long on tension and excitement, with the right hand weaving complicated cross rhythms on a simple melodic structure." That erudite technical description notwithstanding, the beat came through and audiences went wild.

Obviously Barney had the right music, now he had to get the right customers. Realizing that blacks around the country were trained by rude experience to avoid the embarrassment of being turned away by the best urban nightclubs, he paid for announcements in all Afro-American newspapers extending his welcome to blacks visiting New York, and from opening night a racial ease existed on the premises that was unique in 1938.

Benny Goodman, in the club as a guest, would walk up to the bandstand to sit in for a few impromptu "licks" and pop into his mouth the clarinet Edmund Hall had just relinquished. Benny always carried his own mouthpiece in his pocket, but in the spirit of the club chose not to use it.

If a patron didn't like the fact that Paul Robeson, the actor-singer, was asking his friend John Hammond's wife for a dance, he could pay the check and leave. Barney would tell him that in no uncertain terms.

Hammond may have actually found the talent for the clubs, but Barney fostered, molded and developed them, and in some cases they were still very raw and unchanneled. He was meticulous about the manner in which they were to be presented. "I have never offered any entertainment degrading to the black race. I allow no outlandish clothing, no exaggerated Negro dialect and no Uncle Tom attitudes that have been their trademark for so long. All I want is performers, Negro and white, on the same footing."

Mothers of large families try to show no partiality, but there is always one child they love the best. In Barney's brood, he adored Lena Horne. No amount of analyzing will provide a reason. There was just something about her that reached him in a special way.

Josephson is adamant that he never had an actual sexual relationship with any black performer, and for someone so attracted to their racial characteristics that is unusual, until you understand the reasoning behind his abstinence.

"These people were so abused and exploited by whites in this country, I would have been adding to this, if I "The Boss," with my power, went to bed with them. That wouldn't have been so different from others who took advantage of them in non-sexual ways."

In a quiet moment, he admits that if he hadn't kept these desires in check, the one he might have approached was Lena. But, "I never let it develop to more than a feeling inside."

When Lena arrived for her first audition at Downtown, her appearance, her bearing and her approach to songs were very different from the lady in her one-woman shows today. Barney was struck by her beauty, but also by what he perceived to be an attempt to separate from her racial self. Her hair and dress could have given the impression of a young woman of Spanish or Polynesian background, and the tunes she chose for this audition were the type that any white band singer would have come in with.

Barney knew nothing at that first meeting of her upper middle class family or of the milieu in Brooklyn Heights that spawned NAACP founders rather than singers of low-down blues. But he wanted to see and hear the true blackness that he knew existed deep inside and he began the kind of dialogue that was to be their pattern always—a mix of great affection and patient bullying—to get her to let this all come out.

Barney: "What are you?"

  Lena: "What do you mean?"

Barney: "What background?"

  Lena: "Negro."

Barney: "Then why do you bring in these other songs that do nothing for you? Do you know 'Summertime'?"

  Lena: "Yes."

Barney: (Signaling the accompanist, Teddy Wilson) "Then try it." (She starts but with no personalization)

Barney: (Stopping her) "You have a child?"

  Lena: "Gail."

Barney: "Take it again as if you were singing it to Gail at bedtime."

And of course it came out intimately, ethnically pure and with the moving quality the song deserves.

But that night of her opening, Josephson noticed her looking only at the low ceiling of the club as she sang—not at the audience. He took her backstage and sat her down.

Barney: "Some of those people out there are used to the kind of subservient Negro who hasn't got the confidence to look them in the eye. Is that what you want them to think of you?"

  Lena: "No."

Barney: "Then pick out a couple of women in the audience and while you're singing, never lift or lower your gaze. Let your eyes burn into them."

These nuances were all part of the honing of her style that both he and Lena herself contributed to, and her performances became special. One great error Barney made in his attempts to change Lena was the brief period he had her billed as "Helena Horne," because he felt "Lena" wasn't dignified enough for his elegant star. After a few months he admitted his reasoning was ridiculous and it was back to "Lena."

Josephson never actually managed Lena as he did Hazel Scott and Alberta Hunter, but when Lena went out to Hollywood he missed her and worried about her, and would often leave the club for ten days and meet her in Los Angeles.

The very first time he picked her up at her apartment to go

out to dinner, he asked her where she would like to be taken. Her answer was a guarded, "Wherever we can go"—with an emphasis on the "can." He tried again, got the same answer and quickly realized that this gorgeous young movie hopeful was not on the Hollywood social whirl that he had expected—and her tone indicated just why. So he tried a different tack and asked her to tell him the place she'd most like to eat at if the world were totally ideal. She answered Trader Vic's, which had just opened and was the rage because of its exotic drink concoctions with the colorful wooden parasols.

They arrived and Barney asked for a table for two with great authority, staring the maître d' down. Whether it was his manner, Lena's light skin or the fact that her face was not yet familiar about town, they were seated and MGM's budding black musical star ate in a whites-only bastion that night.

After dinner Josephson again posed the question, "Where would you like to go next?" Lena was getting confident and told him the really "in" late place was then the Players Club. As they entered the club, Barney was sure their luck had run out because the manager looked up with alarm, came running over and with a hand on each shoulder was herding them toward the door, when a man from a back table rose and noisily greeted Barney. It was Bob Benchley the writer and movie humorist who always came to Cafe Society when he was in New York. Benchley never gave the manager a chance to say no, and ushered them over to sit with the "New York Gang" which that evening included some long-standing liberals like Gene Kelly. And so Lena had her unrestricted night out on the town.

Josephson was always a very reserved, self-protecting person, but when he starts talking about the old days and people he loves, he becomes as excited and enthusiastic as a kid. He has a knack for mimicry, including a very adept version of Zero Mostel's old "Casbah" routine. In 1938, soon after Cafe Society opened, this acting ability came in handy when the recently deposed gangsters sent an "emissary" requesting protection payoffs. On cue Barney reached up, grabbed the hoodlum by the tie and snarled à la James Cagney, "My best friend is the Mayor of New York. Get out of here you dirty rat and don't ever come back or I'll sic him on you!" The man left and Barney almost fainted.

Josephson only booked performers that he could feel close to. If there wasn't a certain give and take kind of friendship, they finished their engagement and weren't signed again. One of his favorites was Eddie South, a blind, black violinist who had studied the classics at conservatories in Paris, Vienna, and Budapest, was a close personal friend of European stars like Jean Gabin, and despite the cultural veneer, could "get down" and swing with the best of them.

One night, the club seemed surprisingly empty to Barney, who notwithstanding his Jewish background had forgotten that it was Yom Kippur eve. But Eddie hadn't, and stopped a particularly "hot" set to play "Kol Nidre" for the boss so sensitively, that both of them openly wept. When Barney went over to embrace South, the violinist blurted out for the first time that one of his grandfathers had been white and Jewish.

Billie Holiday was one talent with whom Barney didn't have great rapport. Like his buddy John Hammond, he found it difficult to find the right key to get close to this very moody, complicated woman. But one night they did share something that started out disastrously and ended up with a giggle.

There was only room for one small dressing room at Cafe Society and it was shared coed by singers and musicians. Most of the women would dress at home and arrive at the club ready to go on, but not Billie, who with her early bordello experiences seemed immune to modesty. She always insisted on wearing a gown when she sang, so she would walk into the dressing room in street clothes and, no matter who was there, strip down naked, pull the gown on over her bare skin, slip on high heels, fix her hair with the gardenia and go out to do the show.

She was such a draw that the club was always overbooked, and the captains, anxious to have their palms crossed, would push in more and more small tables in front of the ringsiders, so the performing space became smaller and smaller, crowding Billie in.

Barney could see she was especially upset by this one night, and to make matters worse, during her third number, somebody at one of these make-shift tables must have dropped a racial slur that she heard. She finished the song, turned her back to the crowd, bent way over, flipped her dress over her head, held the pose for a long moment, wiggled her bare buttocks in exaggerated rhythm and stormed off.

Barney followed her into the dressing room. Billie was livid, but fully ready to be fired for not finishing the show, and for the improvised strip. Josephson started to address her like a naughty child—"Billie Holiday, Billie Holiday!"—but instead of reading her the white boss riot act, he surprised her with, "Want to tell me what they said?" She shook her head no. "Well, whatever it was, you certainly told them to kiss your ass!" She giggled with him for a very long time and later did the other two shows as if nothing had happened.

But Billie was never special to Barney except as a singer. His special lady after Lena was Hazel Scott. He was her father confessor, manager, protector against the Hollywood moguls and even the matchmaker for her marriage to Adam Clayton Powell, Jr. The term manager has to be used because Josephson detests the label agent, lumping these "10 percenters" with other whites who victimized blacks. When he was running back and forth to the West Coast negotiating for Hazel and protecting her rights in her film contracts, he never took a nickel for these "agent" services. It cost him a fortune in flight fares and resulted in his neglecting the club, which was his source of income. But it suited his compulsion to right the wrongs of the white vs. black past from slavery on.

Their sympatico feelings developed early in her first engagement at the cafe. Barney was sitting at the bar when she arrived for the early show radiant in a new gown, a new hair style and obviously in an "up" mood. He paid her an especially nice compliment as she walked over to him and he gave her a fatherly good luck kiss on the cheek as she left to do the show.

A well-dressed woman farther down the bar who could only have seen the kiss reflected in the bar mirror, left her stool, glared at him, bared her teeth and spit out, "Nigger Lover! Only a Jew could kiss a nigger!"

Barney ignored her and quietly turned to the bartender telling him to give her a check and get her out. He also made him promise to hide the incident from Hazel because she also had a short fuse, and with two shows to go he didn't want her to "sass" the customers as she was known to do at any hint of discrimination.

She did the shows without incident, but afterward some employee must have leaked the news, because as she left the club, she very dramatically planted a kiss on Barney and at the door turned and threw over her shoulder,

"Only a nigger would kiss a Jew."

Hazel was the kind of woman men couldn't stay away from. Besides the talent as pianist and singer she was very intelligent and crackling with energy and pizzaz. So Barney observed one romance after another in ebb and flow. One of these was with the President's son, F.D.R., Jr., who even brought his mother to the club once to meet her. As with many other sensitive stories about the Roosevelt family, the press never hinted to the public about this relationship.

After seeing Hazel play the field for so long, Josephson decided with fatherly instinct that it was time for her to settle down and get married. He knew just the right man—good looking, wealthy, from a fine old black family—but already married! Adam Clayton Powell, Jr., a matinee idol type, soon to be Congressman, and son of the pastor of Harlem's most famous church, had been coming to the club and watching Hazel night after night from the same table. As surrogate father, Barney warned Adam that it could only come to pass if he were single again.

A while later that freedom arrived and Barney gave Hazel away at the most publicized wedding in the history of Harlem. But nice guys aren't always great matchmakers and the couple didn't stay together very many years after a son was born.

Before he negotiated a contract for Hazel to make a movie musical with Jack Oakie for Fox, Barney had heard all the rumors of great talents like Paul Robeson ending up underpaid in Hollywood. Another ploy the studios were using on black musical performers who were doing production numbers and were not too involved in the story line, was to shoot all their footage in a few consecutive days out of sequence, and end up paying them only one week in salary.

So he decided that nothing would be lost if he went in with

very firm demands. He looked the producer straight in the eye and calmly listed his terms: four thousand dollars a week, a guarantee of at least five weeks' work and no role or costume that would be demeaning to her as a black artist. In other words, no maid parts like Billie was given in "Old New Orleans," no pickaninny hairstyles like Butterfly McQueen and no bandanna like Ethel Waters. Surprisingly every clause was approved and the agreement was upheld in one test during the filming.

Hazel was doing a musical number with a chorus of ladies (not maids) all doing their families' laundry together in a courtyard—hanging wash, cleaning mattresses. That in itself was not offensive. But the art director had insisted on mattresses that looked as if they had urine stains all over them and clothing for the line that was all torn and shredded—and that was offensive. Hazel got all the chorus to agree to stop the scene until the producer came on the set. In control of her famous temper, she reminded the producer of the dignity clauses in her contract and substitute mattresses and wash were brought in.

Barney had to return to New York to mind his "store" after a week or so, but since Hazel's very stable mother was with her for the entire five weeks, he felt things would be under control. Hazel refused to fly and the day they pulled into Grand Central on the 20th Century, Josephson was trackside waiting for them. He didn't have to search very long, because Hazel came marching down the platform dressed as if she were going to a royal audience—covered with jewelry and restraining by leash an enormous Afghan dog.

After hugging both ladies and smelling the new perfume, he found out that the dog was a gift from Mrs. Jack Oakie, a famous breeder of Afghans. Jack, as star of the film, wanted to thank Hazel for her professionalism in contributing to the success of the picture. Right there on the platform Hazel kept flashing the new jewelry in Barney's face waiting for a comment, so he asked about it. She dropped the name of a famous Hollywood designer and proudly bragged that it was "a steal" at twenty-two thousand dollars. It was one of the only times in his dealings with Hazel that Josephson allowed himself to explode.

"I get you an unheard of $4,000 a week with a five-week minimum—that's $20,000—big, big money these days—Uncle

Sam is going to ask for a chunk in taxes, so maybe your take will be $14,000—and you go out and spend $22,000! You're a star lady, but you're heavily in debt."

The next night Hazel's mother called up and asked Barney to take over complete control of Hazel's personal finances. This led to a similar arrangement with other talents whom Barney managed, until the unstable Zero Mostel made Josephson vow "Never again." Zero was a comic virtuoso and a fabulous actor, but a madman to deal with personally. He had no sense of proportion about behavior offstage and he got into so many financial fiascoes—usually because of women—that Barney turned him over to other management.

Anyone who knew Barney well in 1948 was saddened and filled with compassion when he had to close Cafe Society Uptown and sell Downtown to Louis I. Louis and Max Mansch. The gentle, giving idealist became a victim of his own lifetime loyalties and the political confusions of the Cold War period. Barney's father had died in Barney's first year of life, and so older brother Leon became a surrogate parent with enormous influence on Barney's life, helping him grow up, guiding him into the shoe business, recommending investors to raise the money to buy both clubs and acting as one of the attorneys for them through the years.

Leon was also a folk hero to Barney—a man who lived dangerously and took part in emotional activist adventures, like the one in Denmark in 1935 when Leon was arrested for plotting with Danish leftists to form a commando unit to kill Adolf Hitler, still early in his career as Chancellor and not yet labelled the supreme menace. The thought always remained with Barney that if his brother's wild scheme had been successful six million Jews and millions of soldiers from all sides would have been spared in World War II.

But in 1948, Leon was subpoenaed by the House Un-American Activities Committee and was sent to jail for contempt of Congress. In 1986 when Admiral Poindexter and Lt. Col. North took the Fifth Amendment and refused to testify before another Investigating Committee, the press and public reacted quite benignly. But in the Cold War atmosphere of 1948, everyone was trying to spell out very clearly where their loyalties lay, and columnists like the powerful Walter Winchell came down hard on Barney, cloaking him in guilt by association since Leon was family and one of the lawyers for both cafes. Very rapidly the reservations phone stopped ringing and it was impossible to keep the clubs going.

It is very difficult to be objective about a decent individual like Barney Josephson, who in his lifetime has done so many positive things for so many people. Anyone close to him knows that he has always had a love affair with the United States. And it is very easy to understand that a man starting out cold in a field for which he had no preparation, would look for advice and assistance from trusted old friends whom he had grown up with.

Following this line of reasoning, he took legal and financial advice from Leon, who refused to admit Communist Party membership in front of the Committee to protect his constitutional rights, but readily admitted membership to any reporter who asked the same question.

Barney hired Ivan Black as the clubs' publicist. The same Ivan Black with whom he'd gone to grade and high school in Trenton and who had changed Sam Mostel's first name to Zero. And the same Ivan Black who later was also to take the Fifth before the House Un-American Activities Committee.

He hired another old friend from his youth to write special original material for his shows, and the friend came up with some landmark songs including the number most associated with Billie Holiday's career, "Strange Fruit," the lynch-mob metaphor. ASCAP lists this man as Lewis Allan, who also wrote the words for the superbly patriotic Frank Sinatra motion picture short "The House I Live In." But Lewis Allan was the nom de plume for Abel Meeropol, who adopted the Rosenberg boys after their parents were executed for passing atomic secrets to the Soviets. And who while teaching at Dewitt Clinton High School in New York, was subpoenaed by the Rapp-Coudert Committee, investigating teachers said to have participated in communist activities.

Barney's friends and admirers all would have defended the constitutional right of these associates to profess any political belief, but there are many who would have wished that he'd been less naïve and protected himself more from those surrounding him and using him. A few more friends and advisers like John Hammond—liberally inclined but anti-communist—might have helped prevent his loss.

Still, Barney survived the relatively short period of political confusion that we call the McCarthy Era, and for the next 20 years ran the Cookery on 8th Street in the Village, serving up great jazz pianists like Teddy Wilson and Ellis Larkins and great blues singers like Helen Humes and Alberta Hunter. Right now he is manager and part owner of the barbecue chicken and ribs place that recently supplanted the Cookery, but not a day goes by without his checking on locations for a new club that he's determined to open, featuring, exclusively, young jazz musicians—the new wave—the stars of the future—and preferably black. (Note: In late September 1988 after the first printing of this book, Barney Josephson died at age 87.)

Max Gordon is a very different psychological profile from Barney. Far from a militant, he's never been aware of having any soul-searching causes. His wife Lorraine suggests with great objectivity and affection: "Max had no goals of his own, he was just a catalyst. He lived as if he was the character he would have written about if he could really write. But he never was a writer in the true sense of the word. His creativity came in turning his clubs into salons where other talents could express themselves and interact with others.

"Yes, the Vanguard is Max's salon! He has an innate ability to react correctly to fine things. Through the years he may not have known what he was looking for and he didn't actually go out to find it, but when he saw or heard something of value, he recognized that it was good—even when its special quality was not apparent to others. Max was never aggressive enough to seek out new talent unless it went to him. He never took an act because it was something the public would 'buy.' He wasn't that kind of businessman."

Lorraine Gordon's use of the past tense is a figure of speech for a man who is still at the helm of the Village Vanguard seven nights a week. And through the years he demonstrated his fantastic taste with so many performers who had their first start at the Vanguard or the Blue Angel, later becoming star attractions in theater, movies and TV.

Though many of these were black, an equal number were white. Max never made any issue of color the way Barney did. When he arrived in Greenwich Village in the twenties, blacks were already on the scene there, and when he opened the Vanguard in that free thinking neighborhood, blacks were on stage and also were at tables. He never especially thought of it as an "integrated" club. It was just his natural manner to be surrounded by all types of people. The only issues were quality and decency.

And what quality he presented: Josh White, Maxine Sullivan, Sister Rosetta Tharpe, Butterfly McQueen in her first cabaret appearance, Thelonius Monk, Tad Jones, Dizzy Gillespie, Miles Davis, Harry Belafonte, Art Blakey, Clark Terry, Eddie Heywood, Ellis Larkins, Johnny Mathis and Josephine Premice were some of the jazz and folk musicians and singers.

One of his first cabaret acts was a group called "The Reviewers," featuring three inexperienced unknowns named Betty Comden, Adolph Green and Judith Tuvim. Comden and Green went on to write *Singing in the Rain* for Gene Kelly and *On the Town* with Leonard Bernstein, and Judith Tuvim changed her name to Judy Holliday and became a Broadway and Hollywood star through the Billie Dawn part in *Born Yesterday*.

Other unknowns getting their start because of Max were Mike Nichols and Elaine May, Orson Bean, Mort Sahl, Burl Ives, Peter, Paul and Mary, Jerry Stiller and Anne Meara, Wally Cox, "Professor" Irwin Corey, the Kingston Trio, Pete Seeger, Annie Ross, Kay Thompson and the Williams Brothers (including Andy, who danced), Lenny Bruce and Woody Allen.

To this day Josephine Premice is in awe of Max's ability to see below the surface of an audition performance. Although she later became an exotic Broadway star in *Jamaica* and then the revival of *House of Flowers*, she arrived at the Village Vanguard in so green a state that she brought no sheet music. She'd never owned a written arrangement. Fortunately, Max provided her with Ellis Larkins as accompanist and they "vamped" through a few numbers that day, and kept on vamping for two successful weeks. But what was there in Max to take such a chance with an unprepared, though talented young woman?

Max is above all a survivor. In a business where a good club will last a few years and then be replaced in the same location by another more "in" spot with a new name, new ownership and new slant, he has prevailed for 53 consecutive years in the same old haunt. No nightclub in New York history can match that. The bootlegger who gave Max his first experience in running a club ended up selling papers at a newsstand, while Max collected anniversaries. At the 50th in 1985, attended by many of his "old grad" stars, a reporter asked Max, "What makes it so great?" The reply was vintage Max!

"I don't know. We don't charge the most money, we don't have the biggest stars, and we don't serve food any more. I guess people just feel comfortable here. They feel at home."

The performers feel so at home that one big band, co-led by black trumpeter and arranger Thad Jones and white drummer Mel Lewis, started a tradition of playing on Monday nights over 20 years ago and continues to fill that slot today, even though Jones has passed away. As Lewis himself puts it, "The Vanguard to me is Carnegie Hall. I lay awake many nights thinking how would the Vanguard survive without Max Gordon and how would we survive without the Vanguard? We could move somewhere else but it wouldn't be the same. To me the Vanguard is probably the most perfect jazz club that ever existed."

Actually the place could have always been described as a basement dive—nondescript canopy and narrow entrance, steep, shadowy, claustrophobic staircase, peeling paint and seedy tables and chairs. Max chose this physical plant because it conformed to the strict codes the LaGuardia Administration set up after Prohibition repeal. For this kind of licensing, they required two exits, two bathrooms, and a distance of at least 200 feet from a church, school or synagogue. And this joint satisfied the inspectors.

But it is the performers, the acoustics and the crowd rather than the surroundings that have always made the place unique. Still, in some way, the non-threatening air of neglect keeps it casually free and improvised like a spontaneous jam session. Three hundred sixty-five nights a year it attracts patrons who are very serious about what is going on onstage.

"We get pretty good listeners" says Max. "People shush each other. They even shush me."

This Vanguard audience is often a better judge of talent than those in uptown clubs. In fact this crowd probably saved Harry Belafonte's career at its very inception. Gordon originally booked Harry into the Blue Angel, which he ran with Herbert Jacoby from 1943 to 1963. It was very elegant and in 1945, when you still had to think twice before presenting a black singer at a smart Upper East Side club, Max had given Pearl Bailey a very successful run and repeated a little later with Eartha Kitt. But Harry didn't connect well with the same audience.

Max recalls, "He sang three numbers and bowed off to light, scattered applause. That was pretty much my reaction also. A handsome black man singing three pop tunes, not bad, not good. That was the end of Harry Belafonte, I thought. Then Jack Rollins (who managed Harry and Woody Allen and today produces Woody's films) convinced me to listen to him again. Only the next time at the Vanguard. I agreed if only to get Rollins to stop bothering me." The Vanguard regulars loved Belafonte and the lines outside drew reporters and critics and a cabaret star was born who gradually expanded into a great stage, film and TV attraction.

That is a recurrent story in Max's professional life—the unknown talent getting its first modest start with him, then escalating into big bookings and big money in other media. But Gordon has never been opportunistic. Many other owners in Max's shoes would have signed Wally Cox to an exclusive contract when Wally, untried and unrepresented, walked in one day and asked for work. This would have assured Gordon of a percentage of Wally's future earnings for a certain number of years in return for launching his career. But Max couldn't get himself to deal in a way that he felt was taking advantage: "I guess I'm not a ten-percentnik."

Compute 10 percent of Cox's gross from the four-year run of "Mr. Peepers" on TV. Add to that future earnings for the soon-to-be movie star Judy Holliday, and the revenues he could have banked from the other neophytes he didn't sign, and you begin to see a fortune relinquished.

But Max, without special goals, would never think along those lines. He was content to have created his "salon" where these artistic events could happen, and later in 1980 he fulfilled another artistic urge by writing a book *Live at the Village Van-guard*, with an introduction by the erudite jazz critic Nat Hentoff. The book conveys Max's fascination with and respect for performers, but also his pragmatic way of dealing with them. Here are some of his insights on Miles Davis.

"What do you do on a Saturday night when the place is jammed and the star of your show walks off the bandstand in the middle of a set because his girlfriend is drunk in some uptown joint and phoning him to come and get her? Of all the jazz men who have worked at the Vanguard, Miles Davis was the toughest to handle. . . . I asked him once, 'Why not announce a number? Why not take a bow, at the end of a number? Why not announce the names of the men in your band? . . . '

"He looked up at me with a puzzled suspicious look as if I were crazy. 'I'm a musician. I ain't no comedian. I don't go shooting my mouth off like Rahsaan Roland Kirk. Don't get me wrong, I like Rahsaan. If you want a big mouth in your place, don't hire me. I don't smile. I don't bow. I turn my back. Why do you listen to people? The white man always wants you to smile. Always wants the black man to bow. I don't smile and I don't bow, OK? I'm here to play music. I'm a musician."

Miles in his confused, paranoid state was thrashing out at the decades of abuse of black performers at the hands of white owners. Unfortunately, here he was choosing a guiltless target.

Charlie Mingus was another tough cookie to deal with. Max wrote: "The last time I saw Charlie was in July of 1978 on the lawn behind the White House where President Jimmy Carter was throwing a party to commemorate the 25th Anniversary of the Newport Jazz Festival. Charlie was in a wheelchair, had been in one for more than a year suffering from the same debilitating disease that killed Lou Gehrig, the Yankee first baseman. George Wien, the producer of the Newport Jazz Festival, introduced Charlie as 'the world's greatest living jazz composer.'"

Max admired Charlie as a musician, but also remembered him as the leader who punched Jimmy Knepper, the trombone player, in the pit of the stomach while on the Vanguard band stand because he felt Jimmy wasn't playing what Mingus had written. And he certainly couldn't forget the night Charlie asked for an advance cash draw, and held a knife to Max's throat when he assumed the roll of bills Max handed him was not the amount he had asked for.

It was Lorraine Gordon who brought Thelonius Monk to Max's attention. Lorraine's first husband had started Blue Note Records and she had a long association with jazz musicians before she ever met Max. Once he heard Thelonius play, the pianist became one of Max's favorites. The Baroness Nica de Koeningswater, born a Rothschild, was sponsor and protector for Monk, as well as Charlie Parker and many other great instrumentalists, including Gerry Mulligan.

The baroness provided Max and his book with one of his most pungent anecdotes about the black experience as jazz men in a hostile environment. It involved her driving Thelonius through the state of Delaware to a gig in Baltimore. In Newcastle, Delaware, Monk, who was sweating profusely asked her to stop so he could get a beer or a drink of water in a motel and bar that they were passing. Unfortunately he walked into a place that didn't serve blacks, while she waited in the car. Before she knew it, a struggling Thelonius came out of the bar restrained by two policemen who were rapping on those brilliant piano hands with nightsticks as he tried to push them away. The infuriating story ends with an almost humorous, ironic twist, with Monk being released and the baroness being booked for the single reefer that the cops found in her purse.

As his book unfolds, it is almost with relief that a Max Gordon appears who can gossip a bit, be a little bitchy, and pay back for an unforgotten slight. Because in person, one can be misled into thinking he is too much the "Sunshine Boy."

Ask Max if he had unpleasant pressure from unions, the police, the mob or competitors, and his response is so benign and optimistic that he might be Jiminy Cricket sweetly warbling "When You Wish Upon a Star."

The cynics can mutter "too good to be true," "too sanitized."

Where are the sordid stains that had to rub off someplace in this particular business? Or is Max just remembering the glory and none of the "*tzuris?*"

That Yiddish word for disastrous trouble, brings up the question of what effect the immigrant Jewish background had on Max's—and also Barney's—choice of career. It's been theorized that Jews became survivors when thousands of years of oppression and discrimination taught them to be mentally prepared to escape, both literally and figuratively.

When they couldn't actually run away, they had to let their imagination fly in order to live through the troubles. This is one explanation for the high percentage of Jewish comedians, actors, musicians and artists. And it is also probably a factor in the almost magnetic pull that nightclubs had for Barney and Max.

Max isn't sure about the ethnic influence at this stage of his life. Running a club "was the simplest way of making a living. It was there! I didn't have to look further." This is the side of Max talking who "didn't have any goals."

But this same man is presenting on any given night in the eighties new fine artists like John Faddis and Wynton Marsalis with the same care as he did their counterparts in the thirties.

For a man with no goals, a very strange thing happened in 1985. The entire Kool Jazz Festival, an event that runs for two weeks and involves hundreds of the world's top-echelon jazzmen, was dedicated to—Max Gordon.

Chapter IV

The NAACP

(The National Association for the Advancement of Colored People)

To alter the path of racial discrimination and attempt to eradicate it, a minority group must have economic and political power to bolster the leverage of being morally right. Black people until very recently did not have these strengths and were dependent on the resources of whites interested in their causes. This dynamic was never more obvious than in the early formative stage of the National Association for the Advancement of Colored People. While other organizations in the fight for justice appeared on the scene and for one reason or another sputtered, the NAACP has persevered through three-quarters of a century, and certainly for its first 50 years provided the conscious continuity of black activism. Its programs have given birth to the Harlem renaissance of the twenties the nation-wide, depression-bred struggles of the thirties, the protection of the interests of black servicemen in World War II, and the preliminary groundwork for the legal revolution of the Kennedy-King era.

The NAACP germinated from the "Niagara Movement"

which was started just after the turn of the century by W.E.B. Dubois, a fiery black intellectual from Great Barrington, Massachusetts, who aimed to make blacks discontented and angry enough to rise up and fight against injustice. He could not know it at the time he made the remark, but he proved himself to be one of the most profound pundits when he predicted that "the problem of the 20th century is the problem of the color-line." His intention was also to present an alternative position that would rebel against the moderation policy being taught by his philosophical adversary, Booker T. Washington.

Dubois would settle for nothing less than equal rights at once without compromise. Washington believed that equality was a privilege his race had to earn by first learning to become good workers who would then obtain some wealth and, gradually, power. His attitude was to create hope among his people, while appeasing the whites so that they wouldn't impose stronger restrictions. His main thrust was to proceed through education, and so he started by building Tuskegee Institute. Both men were publicly critical of the other's tactics and there were sharply drawn lines set up by their followers. This fact split the black community counter-productively.

Dubois couldn't raise support money from white philanthropists whereas Washington could, so Dubois's movement only lasted four years. But it awakened reformers to the realization that a permanent civil rights organization was desperately needed, and it attracted the attention of white liberals who could help achieve this goal. One of them was Mary White Ovington, a social worker and writer who had rebelled in her own life against her upper-middle-class Brooklyn Heights background. In 1904 she had first met Dubois at a conference at Atlanta University where he was Chairman of the Department of Sociology. That trip exposed her for the first time to racial segregation southern style, and led to an assignment from the New York *Post* to cover the meetings of the Niagara Movement. There she heard Dubois resolve, "We claim for ourselves every right that belongs to a full-born American—and until we get these rights, we shall never cease to protest and assail the ears of America with the story of its shameful deeds toward us."

In January 1909 she brought together William English Walling, a southerner who had just reported on Springfield, Illinois, race riots, Herman Moskowitz, a Jew knowledgeable of conditions in New York's immigrant ghettos, and noted integrationist Charles Edward Russell. They made plans for a national conference of those believing in pure democracy, and they convinced Oswald Garrison Villard, the grandson of the famous abolitionist William Lloyd Garrison, to write the invitational "call" that would solicit a large and powerful body for the "discussion of present evils, the voicing of protests and renewal of the struggle for civil and political liberty."

Among the signers of this call were Jane Addams, the founder of Hull House, John Dewey, the famous educator of Columbia University, Mary E. Wooley, president of Mount Holyoke College, J. G. Phillips Stokes, the philanthropist—all whites—and Alexander Walters Bishop of the African Methodist Episcopal Zion Church, along with Francis J. Grimke, a militant black minister. The "call" was published on February 12, 1909, the 100th anniversary of the birth of Abraham Lincoln.

This gathering led to the foundation of the National Negro Conference that chose a committee to establish a permanent organization. Excluded from this committee was Booker T. Washington, because of what the conference felt was his posture of self-aggrandizement and appeasement of whites. In May 1910 this committee founded the NAACP—it's object, equal rights and opportunities for all. Fourteen black members of the Niagara Movement filled positions on the steering "committee of one hundred," and Dubois was hired as Director of Publicity and Research with his main responsibility a magazine called *Crisis*, which would disseminate the association's message. All the other officers were white, with Garrison Villard as chairman, Mary White Ovington as executive secretary and Walter Sachs as treasurer. Their stated credo: "To promote equality of rights and eradicate caste or race prejudice among the citizens of the U.S., to advance the interest of colored citizens, to secure for them impartial suffrage and to increase their opportunities for securing justice in the courts, education for their children, employment according to their ability and equality before the law."

The association's activist energy was directed into areas where it could influence legislation by publishing voting records in Congress on anti-black bills. All candidates campaigning for national office received questionnaires from the NAACP regarding their stand on civil rights. The Washington, D.C., branch was the watchdog for any anti-negro legislation brought before Congress or any hostile action of the government. If black railway mail clerks were to be segregated into all black units under white foremen, NAACP would mount protests until the plan would be abandoned. If separate-but-equal laws were not maintained and interstate accommodations for blacks travelling by rail were poor, the NAACP made these facts available to the Senate, the House and the public.

The organization functioned to maintain open housing, to defend blacks whose homes had been bombed in predominantly white neighborhoods, to prevent discharging of black professionals in federal jobs, to integrate union membership, to defend black servicemen in court martial cases, to rally behind those who resisted segregation and were subsequently jailed under local laws, to stimulate black voter registration, to petition the federal government to investigate lynchings and other cases involving miscarriage of justice by local authorities, and in general to get action in any situation where a black citizen's rights were being violated. No small list of responsibilities.

Violation and violence were always threatening the lives of NAACP members. In 1926 a massive white mob stoned a black home in the South. When someone within the house shot back and killed a white, the accused person was put on trial for murder. The NAACP hired Clarence Darrow, the great trial lawyer to defend, and he won acquittal by reaffirming to the twelve-man white jury that "a man's home is his castle." He also appealed to their fairness as decent human beings ruling on an obvious racial attack.

The NAACP's constant campaign against the lynching of blacks resulted in a severe assault on one of its white executive secretaries. John R. Shilady had arrived in Austin, Texas, to convince the governor and the attorney general of the state to reverse their decision to close the Austin NAACP branch and impound its records following its vigorous anti-lynching activities. Shilady was certain that merely proving his organization was legally incorporated throughout the U.S. would do the trick. Instead of the two highest ranking officers, he was interviewed rudely by the assistant attorney general who repetitively used the term "nigger" and made it clear that the anti-lynching petitions signed by several other governors would be viewed with contempt by their counterpart in Texas.

Shilady left the building dissatisfied with the progress of the meeting and was instantly seized, served with a subpoena and hauled into a court of inquiry where he was taunted by "nigger lover" remarks. But the worst was still to come, when after his release, white thugs beat him so badly that he required multiple suturing of facial wounds and had to be whisked to the train station and spirited into a New York bound train. On arrival in Grand Central Station he received a loud ovation from a delegation of red caps, but his spirit was so destroyed that he not only gave up his post but resigned from the NAACP completely.

Years later another nightmarish incident affected another executive secretary. The place was Atlanta, Georgia, the scene was an auto-pedestrian accident, and the victim was a 70-year-old man with white skin and blue-gray eyes. The motorist who struck him picked him up unconscious and rushed him to the brand new Grady Municipal Hospital, where physicians worked to save his life. Relatives were notified of his admission and when a son-in-law appeared who was obviously black, doctors cried "What—have we put a nigger in the white ward?" Still unconscious, the patient was wheeled across the street through the rain to the black ward in the old building, where he soon died. He was the father of Walter White, then Executive Secretary of the NAACP.

The logical tradition of having a black person as chief operating officer had started in 1920, but the organization moved into its most creative and effective era in 1931 when Walter White assumed leadership. To the average undiscerning viewer, Walter seemed totally Caucasian. He was blond, blue-eyed, with a mother one-sixteenth black and a father one-quarter black. Working in the Atlanta NAACP branch office as a very young man, he was a perfect double agent. In fact he became famous across the country in just that role when he filed an eyewitness account of the grisly lynching of Mary Turner in Valdosta, Georgia. The lady was eight months pregnant, but this didn't stop the mob from hanging her upside down from a tree, still alive after having been doused with gasoline and set afire. Later her abdomen was slit with a hunting knife and the baby crushed by stomping boots. Walter was rushed to New York before revenge could be taken on him for his report.

Under White's guidance and with Roy Wilkins's talent as an editor and public relations expert, a program of activism was begun that would influence legislation to improve the daily life of blacks in housing, employment, education, privileges of citizenship, and in general help them to survive the Great Depression.

Though there was never any special emphasis on activism relating to racial problems in the arts and entertainment area, when situations arose, the NAACP became involved. And in 1915, very early in its existence, just that sort of problem developed as the most ambitious moving picture of the infant Hollywood industry was being produced. The film was *Birth of a Nation* whose director was the brilliant but notoriously bigoted D. W. Griffith.

Word had gotten to the Los Angeles branch from the set that this adaptation of the novel *The Clansman*, a historical romance of the Klu Klux Klan, was particularly vicious in its portrayal of blacks after emancipation. Black reconstruction leaders were pictured as venal and vulgar, while KKK riders were put up on pedestals as noble protectors of southern honor and status quo. The obligatory scene of a black rapist in action was included, and this time had him chasing the white heroine until she fell to her death over a cliff rather than submit.

Because this was a major release that would play all across the nation in every small town, the NAACP felt that each showing could incite mob violence and racial hatred. They organized protest meetings and picket lines with moderate success. In New York, W. E. B. Dubois, Rabbi Stephen Wise and Oswald Garrison Villard staged a sit-in in the mayor's office to try to get it banned from New York theaters. A few cities did ban it and other theaters cut the most inflammatory anti-black footage. Due to pressure from the NAACP, the National Board of Review withheld its seal of approval until a disclaimer was added that read "this is a historical representation of the Civil War and

Reconstruction and is not meant to reflect on any race or people of today."

But all the important critics hailed it as a masterpiece, "land-mark" film in an emerging art form, and the campaign ulti-mately failed as patrons lined up with their money ready. It wasn't until 1942 when Walter White called a meeting of all studio heads and threatened a black boycott of Hollywood's product that the industry started to be somewhat influenced by the NAACP positions relating to increased employment of blacks in behind-the-camera jobs, and the casting of black per-formers in roles as human beings rather than stereotypes. Of interest was the off-beat choice of attorney to represent the NAACP in its Hollywood negotiations. The man was Wendell Willkie who had been known as the right-of-center conservative Republican candidate who lost to F.D.R. in 1940. Not so well publicized was the fact he had been named for the 19th century abolitionist, Wendell Phillips.

White had been encouraged to proceed with firm public rela-tions stands by the stirring success of his approach to the Marian Anderson incident three years before in 1939. The Daughters of the American Revolution had blocked attempts at presenting the marvelous contralto at a Constitution Hall Concert. Eleanor Roosevelt symbolically welcomed the singer to perform before a small but prestigious group on the White House lawn. But the NAACP topped her effort in a brilliant public relations specta-cle on Easter Sunday at the Lincoln Memorial, where an inte-grated audience of 75,000 cheered after each selection, and magazine and newsreel cameras captured it all.

Also in the thirties NAACP board member John Hammond used his influence in the recording industry to pressure all the major radio networks about their discrimination against black musicians in studio bands. He did manage to get a couple of men hired for each of the network house orchestras. But it was only a token concession, and it was to be several decades before black sidemen got the air time their talents deserved.

When blacks entered the military in World War II there were almost daily requests for aid and intervention by the NAACP on behalf of soldiers who claimed they had been court-martialed illegally or on trumped-up charges. Of course these charges were sometimes legitimate, but too frequently bigotry was the motivation for the court proceedings.

Midway through the war, the Association received an emergency request for aid at Camp Hood, Texas, from friends of a young lieutenant who was being presented with a legal problem by biased officers of higher rank. This young man would become one of the most famous athletes in the world in 1946, but at the time of this incident, he was a somewhat-recognized, ex-college football and baseball player. His name was Jack Roosevelt Robinson, and he had boarded a bus leased by the Army to take both military personnel and civilian employees to central points around the base. In this instance the lieutenant was travelling in uniform from the officer's club to a military hospital 30 miles away to have an injured ankle looked at. On entering, he chose a seat near the civilian driver and was immediately told to get to the back of the bus. When he ignored the request, the bus was stopped and the driver walked over to him and bellowed, "I said get to the back of the bus where colored people belong."

Robinson answered, "Now you listen to me, buddy, you just drive the bus and I'll sit where I please. The Army recently issued orders that there is to be no more racial segregation on any Army post. This is an Army bus operating on an Army post."

"You just let me tell you, buddy," the driver shot back, "if you ain't off this bus by the time we get to the last stop I'm going to cause you a lot of trouble."

"I don't care what kind of trouble you plan to cause me," snapped Robinson, "you can't cause me any trouble that I haven't already faced. I know what the regulations are, and I don't intend to go to the back of the bus, so get out of my face and go drive the bus because I don't intend to be pestered by you any more."

When they arrived at the last stop where Jack would ordinarily have changed to a city bus for the rest of the trip, the driver left the bus and came back with three other white men.

"Is this the nigger who's causing all the trouble?" asked one of them. A crowd of white people was surrounding Robinson. It was no time for a slugfest, but he didn't want to give ground. He put his finger in this loudmouth's face and said, "Listen, buddy, let's get a couple of things straight. You're a civilian and your job is to run this bus system. The Army decides policies on this post, and a ruling just came down from Washington that there will be no more segregation on Army posts. The second thing we want to get straight is this. I haven't bothered you, never saw you before in my life, so when you make a remark like that, you're asking for trouble."

Two MPs arrived and asked Jack to talk to the duty officer about the complaint of the driver. Captain Bear asked him: "What are you trying to do, start a race riot around here or something?" And the captain's white Texas civilian secretary said, "Well, you know you've got no right sitting up there in the white part of the bus."

Robinson objected to the secretary entering into the discussion, the captain defended her, and they were off to the races with the captain filing charges against him. At the hospital an officer gave him an alcohol test to see if he was drunk—this to a man who had never taken a drink in his life. The charges filed were insubordination, insulting a civilian woman (the secretary) and refusing to obey the lawful orders of a superior officer.

A group of black officer friends immediately contacted the NAACP and a couple of Afro-American newspapers, urging them to look into the case. A few days later, Robinson was advised that the charges including drunkenness had been dropped. Instead he was to be prosecuted on two new charges. The first, violation of the 63rd Article of War, "behavior with disrespect toward Captain Bear by contemptuously bowing to him and giving him several sloppy salutes and repeating, 'OK, sir, OK, sir.'" The second charge was violation of the 64th Article of War, "having received a lawful command to remain in a receiving room and be seated on a chair on the far side of the receiving room and did willfully disobey the same."

The board of review found Robinson not guilty of any of the charges and specifications. What seems like a trivial almost farce-like matter had much darker overtones, and was the recurrent type of situation in which the NAACP had to intervene. Later, however, in the more crucial negotiations that Branch Rickey went through in 1946 and 1947 to integrate Jack into big league baseball, he received no help from the NAACP, and instead had to call together a coalition of black newspaper editors,

YMCA leaders and the presidents of black universities for assistance.

It was to this group that he explained the delicate balance in preparing white fans and competitors for this debut that he felt could shatter discrimination in sports for all time. He begged them not to make things even more difficult for Robinson by treating him differently from other stars. "Don't spoil Jackie's chances—take this victory in stride—don't wine and dine him until he's fat and futile—don't encourage Negro fans to brag about him—don't make his white teammates jealous with too much hoopla for him." It was very hard advice to follow for a people so hungry for recognition of their race's skills. Most cooperated, and Robinson's bat and legs did the rest, and a black all-star was born into the great American pastime.

At the very time Jackie was playing his first game, the NAACP was having much success with an action to integrate the National Theater, the major outlet for legitimate plays in the nation's capital. In another of those common, ironic, but not so comic twists, members of the U.S. Congress enjoyed theater in post-war D.C. sitting in seats that blacks still could not purchase because of race. Soon after the NAACP started this vigorous campaign, Actors' Equity joined forces with them as the direct means of squeezing the theater owners until they would comply with an integration policy.

Their efforts succeeded in the case of the Belasco, a smaller less prominent legitimate house, which started to accommodate black patrons in 1948. But sadly the National Theater ownership converted it to a motion picture house, still barring blacks, rather than bow to integration pressures. As one owner said: "These people (Equity and NAACP) have given us an ultimatum—either the policy changes or we are out of business!"

What had been started in Washington, D.C., soon spilled over onto some of the hypocritical tactics of Broadway theater management. Billy Rose's spunky column "Pitching Horseshoes" of September 17, 1947, reddened some faces.

"The hullabaloo started some time back when Actors' Equity, the performers' union, insisted that its new contract with the producers include a clause giving any actor the right to refuse to appear at the National Theater in Washington as long as it continued its policy of excluding Negroes from the audience. Right-thinking playwrights and producers backed Equity in this demand and the clause goes into effect the fall of 1948.

"I think this is fine. You've got to start someplace. But now that a start has been made in one theater in the nation's capital, how about extending it to the 35 in the theater capital, New York?

"During the past week, I sent a colored man to the box office of several of the hit shows which carry the names of producers, playwrights and actors who did a lot of speechifying about injustices in Washington. In every instance the colored man was told, 'Sorry nothing downstairs.' My secretary two places behind him in the line bought an orchestra seat to every one of the shows.

"Am I accusing the high-minded playwrights and producers of setting up the color bar at their box offices? I am not. I am accusing them, however, of doing nothing in New York to lower the bar. I am accusing them of failing to instruct their box office employees to look only at the color of a man's money and not at that of his skin. Such instructions—and a little watching—are all that is necessary to get the New York box offices in line with the 13th Amendment."

By far the most publicized conflict involving the NAACP was the Josephine Baker vendetta with both the Stork Club and columnist Walter Winchell. Miss Baker was one of the many black artists who left the U.S. in the twenties and settled in Europe because they were better able to express their talent in an atmosphere more receptive to people of their race. She became a major star, particularly in France, which was her home base. Integration was one of the main goals of her life, to the point where she herself adopted ten orphaned children of all nationalities, colors and religions.

To commemorate her first, grand post-war tour of the U.S., New York radio station WLIB aired a week-long salute that joined in with festivities planned by the NAACP to honor Josephine with a "day" and a Harlem parade. Praising her and performing for her on WLIB were Walter White and Lindsey White of the NAACP and entertainers Noble Sissle, Ella Fitzgerald and Lionel Hampton, among others. The Harlem parade had an opulence and warmth unmatched by others in the past. Men swaggered in dress clothes, little girls carried bouquets of colorful fresh flowers, loudspeakers on trucks exhorted people to celebrate in the streets, and the star, who had been well publicized as a French resistance heroine in the war, beamed from her seat in an open car.

From a street platform, speakers praised her for taking a position during a recent Miami club engagement that resulted in the first integrated nightlife audience in that southern city's history. Others lauded her for her stand at Philadelphia's Earle Theater where she refused to go on unless black stage crews and musicians were integrated with their white counterparts during her run. Still others reminded the crowd how she had bombarded the National Association of Radio and Television Broadcasters with demands to rewrite their contracts to permit the hiring of blacks in their industry, how she had made the same request of the First National Bank, International Harvester and the Chicago Association of Commerce and Industry.

To quote one speaker: "Josephine Baker's life is a monument constructed by talent and courage. Future generations of blacks throughout our land must not forget that if their road is easier, it is partly thanks to her."

Soon after this unforgettable day, she canceled an Atlanta appearance at the NAACP Convention, to call nationwide attention to the fact that she had been refused lodging in three of the city's hotels. Under Georgia state laws at that time, any white hotel that granted accommodations to blacks was liable to revocation of its innkeeper's license. For that particular convention, NAACP delegates were being put up in private homes or in the dormitories of Atlanta University.

But Josephine would have none of that type of second class citizen treatment, and she told the press that in the future she would only appear in cities where integrated troupes of performers would be welcomed in housing together, and where audiences would not be segregated. Since she was no longer a U.S. citizen and was married to a white French musician named Joe Bouillon, segments of the American audience were turned off by her aggressive positions.

To her critics she replied, "My greatest desire will always be to see my people happier in America." And she made it plain that prejudice was the only reason she had stayed abroad for more than 25 years. Her militancy was expressed again in Los Angeles when she made a citizen's arrest of a Texas salesman who rose from the table next to hers in the dining room of the Biltmore Hotel and announced, "I won't stay in the same room with niggers." Police were called who told her that they hadn't heard his remark and so couldn't make the arrest, but that she had the right to do it. This daughter of a black St. Louis policeman didn't hesitate, and the judge fined the salesman for disturbing the peace.

Things came to a head one night in New York at the Stork Club when she and her husband were the guests of Roger Rico, a white singer who was starring in *South Pacific* at the time. When they arrived the doorman refused them admittance until he recognized Rico, a regular customer. Despite strange looks from the headwaiter and his assistants, they all ordered dinner. For a long time nothing happened. Finally all the others at the table received their dinners except Josephine. Customers who passed the table turned away from it pointedly, and Sherman Billingsley, the owner who knew Rico well, stayed away. Miss Baker waved to Walter Winchell who had lauded her in his column because of her Miami stand, but he looked right through her, although he was sitting nearby.

Rico insisted that her order be brought to the table. The waiter said that they were out of the crab and steak that she had requested. Instead of leaving, she went straight to the phone and called Walter White to send someone to certify that she had been refused service. When she returned to the table, Winchell had disappeared. Just then a small burned steak was brought to the table, but Rico asked for a check and they left.

Papers carried the story and her complaint the next day, and at seven P.M. that evening NAACP members picketed the entrance to the Stork Club. Walter White wrote to Mayor Impelliteri protesting the club's discrimination. Walter Winchell lied on the air, claiming that he hadn't even been there. The Stork was his hangout and he was not going to injure it. Billingsley took a stand that though his policy was to serve "the world at large," he had to consider his regular customers first.

Ten days later he turned away the son of El Glaowi, Pasha of

Marrakech. After a protest from the French Embassy, Sherman issued a letter to the press saying that given the nature of his clientele, he was obliged to turn away persons considered undesirable by the majority of his guests.

Winchell ripped Josephine in his *Daily Mirror* column and she sued him for $400,000. To the reporters she said, "Walter Winchell accuses me of being an enemy of my people and a fascist. Surely he knows that I received the Medal of Resistance for my intelligence work and was cooperating with the Allies well before the North African landings. Mr. Winchell also suggests that I'm anti-Semitic. I would like to remind him that one of my husbands was Jewish and that I have been asked to speak at the American Jewish Committee Chicago meeting later this month. . . . I must respond when Mr. Winchell accuses me of being a communist. I do not belong to any political party. He states that I have provoked previous incidents. People of color are not obligated to resort to provocation. Incidents occur on their own."

Winchell, to be fair, ordinarily fought for minority rights, but this issue was now clouded by a personal vendetta. Other tabloids started printing articles to discredit her, dredging up ugly scandalous charges. A $250,000 movie contract was annulled. Instead of acting and singing she went on speaking engagements trying to defend her position, and promoting the NAACP. Within two months all her remaining contracts to entertain in the U.S. had been abrogated. Pressures and advice from those who had her best interests at heart made her hesitate on pursuing the Winchell court case further. Federal Judge John C. Knox dismissed the action because she had failed to reopen it, and Josephine left the States to resume her career abroad.

Whether because of bitterness due to the undeserved response to her outspoken nature, or because she could not cope with the absence of public adulation, she began a course of aberrant behavior and rash, illogical statements that often results in people who have had too rapid a succession of personal defeats. While in Argentina on a tour of South America, she was quoted as telling the press that "lynchings are the order of the day," that "Negroes are treated like dogs in the U.S.," and that "U.S. laws are barbaric." In the same interview she rewrote history by de-

nying that the U.S. or Britain contributed anything to the liberation of France. "We Free French liberated the country ourselves."

U.S. Congressman Adam Clayton Powell, Jr., spoke out
against "her deliberate distortion and misrepresentation." Powell continued, "Miss Baker has presented her own wild imag-
inings as facts. She has done great damage not only to the U.S.,
but also to the cause of Negro rights and freedom. She cannot go
unchallenged." Powell agreed with a State Department report
to him that said, "The most unfortunate aspect of Miss Baker's
activities in Argentina is that she permitted herself to become
the tool of foreign interests which are notoriously unfriendly to
the U.S. and which are only interested in the causes which she
sponsors insofar as they can be made to embarrass the United
States." Still, Josephine Baker continued to perform in Europe,
and even enjoyed a farewell tour of the U.S. in the mid-60's
before she retired.

The black performer with probably the closest lifetime ties to
the NAACP was Lena Horne, who at the age of 2½ became the
cover girl of the October 1919 issue of the *NAACP Branch Bulletin.* This prophetic event came about because of her paternal
grandmother Cora Horne. Cora was an imposing lady who was a
very close friend of "Willie" Dubois, a founding member of the
National Association of Colored Women, one of the earliest
members of the NAACP and the Urban League, and a major
force in getting Paul Robeson a scholarship to Rutgers University.

A few days after Lena was born, the famous NAACP silent
protest parade against lynching was held, as both a demonstration against the killing of 40 blacks in an East St. Louis race riot
a few days before, and as a rally for support of the NAACP's
legal defense of ten blacks indicted for murder following the
riot. In one of the most awesome displays in Afro-American history, 10,000 men, women and children marched down Fifth Avenue in total silence.

Walter White watched Lena grow up as he drifted in and out
of her life, depending on whether she was living in New York in
his friend Cora's household, or elsewhere in the U.S. with her
own mother. But once Lena became a performer, he offered ad-

vice at all stages of her career. In the late thirties when the opportunity to work in Hollywood came, he strongly urged her to take it, not only for her own future but with the knowledge that her success would lead to more work for other blacks in the industry. He was also anxious to bend the color line in films still further to get black actors out of the stereotypes as servants or native chiefs in Tarzan pictures, and he obviously felt that a pretty black woman could be a weapon of leverage against the moguls to achieve these more realistic and honest roles.

Despite, or perhaps because of, Lena's family ties to the organization, she later on rebelled when she felt it acted as if it owned her and tried to use her name constantly to its own advantage. She wanted to use her position and popularity and "pull" when she thought it was important, but not when it didn't involve her personally, and not for an issue that she didn't feel was truly imperative and constructive. As she herself phrased it: "I have just learned from my father and from my grandmother not to take any nonsense from anybody. They had instilled enough of the snob in me to make me believe I was as good as any white person and I figured if this was true for me it was true for all the other Negroes as well.

"As for the Negro cause I did what I could for it by lending my name to various activities, by appearing at fund raising rallies, and so on. But I refused to be drawn out as a spokeswoman every time there was an incident. I had always insisted that any reaction I made against segregation be a personal one, a response to a situation in which I was myself involved. . . . Whenever I made a general statement of belief or commitment on some injustice that did not directly involve me, I felt as if I were reacting like one of Pavlov's pups, responding not because I chose to, but because I had been conditioned to do so."

In 1945 one instance of NAACP pressure or "advice" backfired and for a short period wrecked her career. Arthur Freed, her favorite producer at MGM, was doing a Broadway show, *St. Louis Woman*, with Pearl Bailey and Harold Nicholas, and asked Lena to assume the third starring role. Harold and Pearl realized how long it had been since blacks had a chance to star in a good show on the "Great White Way" and were anxious to do it. But the NAACP and other organizations hit Lena with a barrage of reasons why she should not—mainly because it presented black life in the same old dishonest clichés as *Porgy and Bess* and *Green Pastures*, and it was time to stop these untruthful images. She finally turned it down, and MGM, angry because they had been counting on her also to do a movie version of the show, imposed the letter of the law of her contract with them and stopped giving her permission to work in cabarets or on a Broadway revival of *Show Boat*. At Joan Crawford's suggestion, Lena went to Louis B. Mayer himself, confessed her errors, and begged for forgiveness so that she would be allowed to work again.

In the Josephine Baker "brouhaha," the NAACP wired her in Toronto where she was playing. Lena refused to make a supportive statement because she thought getting into a place like the Stork Club was an unimportant aspect of the battle for civil rights, and she told them she couldn't understand why Josephine wanted to go to such a joint in the first place. Later, she realized that she should have just fired off a statement of solidarity and let it go at that.

But Lena was not the only concerned liberal who gradually lost faith in the directions and attitudes of the NAACP once Walter White was no longer executive secretary. The administrations that followed seemed to be devoid of the energy, purpose and impact that the organization had previously exuded. It was not just coincidence that the activist surge toward the 1956 civil rights movement was ignited by newer, less prestigious groups who were able to leap into the void created by the tentativeness of the old guard. It was the Martin Luther King followers and CORE and other surging newcomers to the struggle who maintained the inertia to keep the movement going from 1956 to 1969, while the experienced NAACP played a lesser role.

One of the NAACP weaknesses at that time was its persistence in distancing itself from the white support it had always enjoyed. The transference of responsibility in leadership from Caucasian to black was constructive and positive during the twenties, thirties and forties, but it was carried beyond sensible limits in the late fifties when the ecstasy of the "Black Is Beautiful" movement, black backlash, (and a desire to be more conservative than King and James Farmer) caused the organization leaders to forget the dedicated initiative, money, prestige and impetus that white liberals had lent to not only the formative years of NAACP, but to all the other black civil rights drives.

The old friends were abandoned, and in fact forced from positions of leadership. John Hammond, after 30 years on the NAACP Board, was put in untenable positions by the actions of Roy Wilkins, Walter White's successor, and with great personal sadness had to resign.

CHAPTER V

Blacks in Hollywood

The impact of Hollywood and Las Vegas on the integration movement must be examined in consecutive chapters because both of these never-never-land communities are linked physically and emotionally for all time.

The two cities' shared existence stems from the public's deep need for escape and fantasy, and they are further linked through the omnipotent but camouflaged control by an underworld that can determine and insure success or failure.

Hollywood, with its 40-year head start chronologically, rates first attention.

During its initial decade, the displaced New York Jewish entrepreneurs who pioneered the industry from backgrounds free of artistic experience insisted on light, frothy comedies or romances for their nickelodeon-style silent films. Their instincts proved to be on target financially, and they amassed fortunes within a very few years. As they imported more sophisticated talents from the theater and the academic world, they were prodded into reaching for more ambitious and intellectual themes, which suited their own growing desires to be associated with what they viewed as art with a capital "A."

Some of the serious films that the newly imported directors made touched on the experience of blacks in the fabric of U.S. life. But in almost each instance, the on-screen version of colored life expressed and catered to the prejudices of white moviegoers, who made the difference between box office success or failure. Blacks had neither the money, nor the time, nor the desegregated facilities to make them a factor in the artistic or financial decisions of Hollywood producers.

This is in direct contrast to the present, when black ticket buyers are a very significant part of the movie viewing public because of improved jobs and income, and a product that includes subjects of interest to them. Also white patrons with fewer prejudices and more integrated contacts with blacks than previous generations enjoy films with black stars or black themes, providing they are good films.

But in the infant days of the industry, all movie characters purporting to be Negroes were played by white actors with burnt cork smeared on their skin, behaving as stupid, lazy, clownish, inefficient and inept servants and workers.

In the early 1900's George Melies described his movie *Off to Bloomingdale Asylum*, performed by an all-white cast:

"An omnibus drawn by an extraordinary, mechanical horse is actually pulled by four Negroes. The horse kicks and throws down the Negroes. As they fall, they turn into white clowns and begin slapping each others' faces, and turn black again. Kicking each other, they become white once more. Suddenly they emerge into one gigantic Negro. When he refuses to pay car fare, the conductor sets fire to the omnibus, and the Negro bursts into smithereens."

In other films of the time, these Negro stereotypes emerged: the foolish irresponsible citizen, the grinning bellhop, the inept flapjack cook, the barefoot watermelon eater, the hymn-singing churchgoer, the devoted servant who was a contented slave, and the brute African savage.

In 1905, *The Wooing and Wedding of a Coon* mocked a black marriage in comical style, and in the *Masher* a Don Juan successfully woos a veiled lady, and then goes through a Keystone Cops chase trying to escape her after he lifts the veil to reveal a black face.

Sigmund Lubin had such success with a 1909 series of *Sambo* scripts with a cast of all-black comedians that in 1910 he expanded to some *Rastus* films about a funny black who knows his place and gets the hell beat out of him by varied combinations of chortling whites.

Between 1910 and 1915 a type of film became popular that depicted characters of mixed blood, like *The Nigger* and *The Octaroon*. They all exploited the theme that even the smallest degree of non-white blood would bring a person shame and degradation, implying that there was something drastically subhuman in blackness.

The first version of *Uncle Tom's Cabin* perverted Harriet Beecher Stowe's abolitionist indictment of slavery into an accolade for black subservience. The storm that accompanied the 1915 release of *Birth of a Nation* has already been discussed. This experience did convince black self-help organizations that protest and intelligent use of public relations could be employed effectively in dealing with studios to gain racial concessions.

The earliest example of an attempt at integration on screen was seen in 1918 as a result of Hal Roach's use of the pickaninny child Farina as an equal to the other kids in the original *Our Gang* comedies. The public accepted this relationship probably because they felt there was no threat in children's playing together. Especially since these characters were essentially little clowns, a role permissible for blacks in the audience's mentality. Also, the first World War had just ended, and white attitudes toward blacks were "somewhat" softened because of even the restricted participation of black soldiers.

Sound revolutionized Hollywood, and led to a more realistic presentation of life as it was lived by all of society, not just selected segments. And this, of course, changed both the depiction of blacks and the type of black actors and actresses who were signed for roles. But in musicals, the old habit of including minstrel shows in which white actors blackened their faces and delivered Negro dialect in a manner demeaning to the Negro race still could not be shaken.

Al Jolson, a liberal in most areas, continued the blackface tradition with his "Mammy" sequence in the very first official talkie, *The Jazz Singer*. He did lend his "darkie" some dignity and humanity, but his and other versions of black voices soon became stereotypes in the same fashion as black postures and motions had in silent films. The use of blackface continued until just before World War II, with even Shirley Temple smearing it on for a dance number with Bill "Bojangles" Robinson. Fred Astaire, Charlie McCarthy and Edgar Bergen, and Mickey Rooney and Judy Garland, usually performers of impeccable taste, also resorted to the tactic of blackface!

From the minstrel figure who could be heard in addition to being seen, it was natural to progress to a new phase in the late twenties and early thirties—the black song-and-dance man with the "natural rhythm." The first all-singing, all-dancing, all-black movie was *Heart in Dixie*, but the characters were still cardboard images of plantation slaves and did nothing to present the black person realistically. The film did introduce two actors who would be featured in many other films through the years: Clarence Muse, who played the father, and Stepin Fetchit, who sang and danced and played the son. Fetchit's character's personality in this picture set the pattern that would be his stamp always— the irresponsible "nigger" who knew his place, loved his master, but continually got into trouble for which he was always kicked in the pants.

Lesser-known black actors were highly critical of the way stars like Fetchit and Bill Robinson "sold out" to Hollywood. They earned fortunes by being willing to play parts that pandered to the most demeaning myths about blacks. Robinson's answer was that he would never be given any roles if he refused these. To him it was as simple as that, "I want to stay alive." And very few black actors were finding it easy to stay alive just then. For every James B. Lowe who banked $1000 a week for starring in the second version of *Uncle Tom's Cabin*, and Fetchit who was getting $1500 a week, there were hundreds like Louise Beavers who took home between $25 and $50 a day. Salaries for extras had just been lowered from $7.50 a day to $5.00 a day.

Hattie McDaniel told a reporter, "It's much better to play a maid than to be one. The only choice permitted me is either to be a servant for $7.00 a week or portray one for $700.00 a week."

Sympathetic black characters and positive aspects of colored life were finally brought to the screen in 1929 by liberals like King Vidor. He recognized that the audible screen was a natural for the emotion and harmony in Negro spirituals and other black

music, and so for his first "talkie" he made *Hallelujah*, filming
his outdoor sequences in Tennessee and Arkansas, and studio
shots in Atlantic City.

Vidor explained why he made the movie: "I used to watch the
Negroes in the south, which was my home. I studied their music, and I used to wonder at the pent-up romance in them. It was
a virgin field then. Later the stage invaded it and plays like
Porgy were produced and made hits.

"This gave me the ammunition I wanted. If stage plays with
all-Negro casts and stories like those by Octavus Roy Cohen and
others could have such great success, why shouldn't the screen
make a successful Negro play?

"The story is based on events with which I was familiar as a
boy at home in Texas. The picture is, I hope, evidence of the
correctness of my theory that the screen can do more than just
narrate a series of events. In *The Big Parade*, we tried to catch
the viewpoint of the doughboys by summarizing many of them
in certain characters. In *The Crowd* we tried the same idea.
We've tried to do it again in *Hallelujah* with the Negro.

"I have been tremendously interested in my cast. I don't
imagine any picture ever was made with more whole-hearted
fun then was this one. We had singing for meals and singing
between scenes and laughter and play all the time. But we had
to work tremendously hard and under great strain at times.

"In the emotional scenes the players lived through the episodes. They truly didn't act them. They felt them. And I'll tell
you, it got even me at times. Some of the players, the gifted
woman I call 'Hot Stuff' for instance, will tell you that only real
tears and no glycerin ones flowed in this picture and were more
real than in any other picture with which I am familiar.

"A Negro is a natural actor, singer and born mimic. Any group
of them naturally can sing and dance in harmony. They are born
that way. It was a great experience to work with them."

The girl Vidor called "Hot Stuff" was Evelyn Pope Burwell, a
graduate of Union University with a post-graduate degree in
music from New York University. She came from the Cotton
Club shows to *Hallelujah*, but was not the star. The lead role
went to seventeen-year-old Nina Mae McKinney who had been

a chorus girl on Broadway in 1929 in *Black Birds*, and later a Paul Robeson co-star on screen.

Vidor particularly wanted to avoid showing blacks assuming the manners of white civilization. The attitudes of the characters in the picture are indigenous to the black race. In no frame was there even a suggestion of the existence of the white man.

Despite such decent motives and artistic integrity, this landmark film failed with southern distributors who just weren't interested in booking it. And although it received high praise from the well-known critics, Vidor failed to get support from some blacks in the industry like Paul Robeson, who complained in *Film Weekly*:

"In *Hallelujah* they took the Negro and his church service and made them funny. . . . Hollywood can only visualize the plantation type of Negro. . . . The Negro of 'Poor Old Joe' and 'Swanee Ribber.' It's as absurd to see that type to express the modern Negro as it would be to express modern England in the terms of an Elizabethan ballad."

Robeson himself had a very active career in films, making 11 pictures between 1930 and 1941, but the experience was never truly satisfying to him. Frustration with the studios, the roles he was offered, and the image of blacks being presented made him publicly retire from movies in 1937. But he relented and returned for *Proud Valley* in 1939 and *Tales of Manhattan* in 1941.

He had arrived in Hollywood already a major stage and concert star who had been treated with great delicacy and respect in those mediums. And so he never got used to the crass, tough approach to him by the studio bosses, or to the segregation he met with in Hollywood once away from the sound stage. It was in direct contrast to his Broadway and European treatment.

Many of the Robeson tales may be apocryphal like other bits of legendary Hollywood gossip, but Barney Josephson still tells the story of a meeting between Robeson and a studio mogul where Paul tried to negotiate a salary of $2000 per week and the executive leaned across his desk to just inches from Robeson's face and answered, "We don't pay niggers $2000 a week. You'll take $1000 and be happy it is that much."

Harold Nicholas repeats an anecdote that made the Hollywood rounds in the 1930s, about Robeson going into a bar and being refused a drink and being told by the bartender, "No niggers allowed in here." Paul came back a week later, flashed a bill of sale, and said, "Now you're not allowed in here, I own this place."

True stories, or fantasies, or whatever, Robeson did make some imposing if not commercially successful movies. The film version of his stage hit, Eugene O'Neill's *The Emperor Jones*, was the first vehicle for a black star whose supporting cast was white. The 1933 production was a financial failure basically due to its very limited distribution, and unfortunately ended the movie careers of its producers John Krimsky and Gifford Cochran. But it made Robeson a race hero to his own people, and he became the most sought-after black actor in the world. His massive presence and voice dominated the screen, as he played a man of strength and decency who possessed brains and nerve, and who could challenge the rationale of white supremacy. Robeson was bigger than life up there on the screen—the ultimate criterion of a movie star—and he opened the door for other performers, because this "star" category soon included Eddie "Rochester" Anderson, Rex Ingram, Hattie McDaniel, Lena Horne and the Nicholas Brothers.

Paul actually participated in relatively few films through his own choice. He felt he was getting nowhere in his attempts to alter the studio bosses' attitudes about the presentation of blacks.

"My reputation as a singer had misled producers into bypassing my reputation as an actor. Film producers take the attitude that the Negro must be a romantic figure or else be of no interest to filmgoers at all."

The first of his 11 films was a 1924 silent *Body and Soul*. Then in 1930 he did an experimental picture called *Borderline* in which Eslanda, his non-actress wife, played his on-screen spouse.

In 1935, he had great hopes for *Sanders of the River* as shooting started, but the producers changed it radically during editing, adding extra footage and changing the emphasis and the ending. Robeson walked out on the premiere party, refusing to make a speech. Later he said, "I committed a faux pas, which when reviewed in retrospect, convinced me that I had failed to weigh the problems of 150,000,000 native Africans."

He was happier with *Song of Freedom* about a London dock worker who longs to discover his African roots. Of this role he remarked: "This film shows him as a real man with problems to be solved, difficulties to be overcome."

But unquestionably his favorite movie was *Proud Valley*, set in a Welsh mining town. During the filming the entire cast and crew lived in miners' homes and Paul grew very attached to Wales and its people. He also was quite satisfied with *King Solomon's Mines* and *Jericho*. As to his Hollywood films, he was uncomplimentary even though they had more professional production values and big-name casts.

Show Boat was the movie he was least motivated to make. He specifically asked for such a ridiculously high salary that he thought he would be turned down, but he wasn't. Despite the small size of the role, his performance received much praise, but he personally felt that the film was infected with the usual stereotypes that hurt his race. As to *Tales of Manhattan*, the 1941 episodic film that co-starred Edward G. Robinson and Ethel Waters, he complained, "It was the same old thing, the Negro solving his problems by singing his way to glory. This is very offensive to my people. It makes the Negro childlike and innocent . . . and I wouldn't blame any Negro for picketing it."

All during the Great Depression, black actors, as those in other professions, were the hardest hit by the studios' attempts to cut back on overhead. They were the last hired and the first fired, and were always hustling for jobs. Black moviegoers had the same needs as the white community during these hard times—they required diversion to forget their troubles. To fill both of these voids, a group of black producers started to make low-budget, all-black movies, to be distributed only in black communities.

Oscar Micheaux became the best known of these, with films like *Harlem after Midnight* in 1934. His movies were purely for entertainment and never went anywhere near themes of racial injustice. To make back his investment, he may have actually been forced to be more exploitive of blacks than most white producers. He loved promotional material that showed rape scenes with much nudity. Often he would insert a lurid nude

Harlem dance sequence into a western movie with no attempt at relating it to the story. He would attempt any device to sell his product. But black audiences loved the ribald vignettes and praised them to the theater managers. So in his next film he would try to top the last with a little more "raunch" and spectacle. William Greaves, a stage actor and filmmaker, acknowledged that Micheaux was a dreadful director, but such an inspired promoter that "if he had been white he'd have been running a studio."

Even if Micheaux had been inclined to make a "message picture," his common sense would have stopped him because once black southern small towners had been shown a film of racial reform or one that commented on racial injustice, their white neighbors might have burned down the theater to protect the "status quo."

This was a period when some fine black performers had to face an identity crisis when they were asked to play far eastern or South American parts. But those actors and actresses who adapted and "made it" forced whites to take another look at the black race and admit new respect because of the taste and poise that blacks displayed on screen. One very talented actor who was in constant demand by both black producers and Hollywood during the Depression period was Clarence Muse. He proved to be eloquently prophetic when he said, "The set-up in Hollywood is highly commercial. . . . Hollywood would buy and make a best-selling book even if it featured a Negro as the central character, if the book was successful enough. I don't think politics enters into the question at all. . . . As soon as better material becomes popular with the mass American public, then Hollywood will follow the trend." And this is what actually happened 30 years later in the 1960's.

By the late 1930's it was clear that black independent producers were having a counter-productive effect on both the black image and on the artistic progress of black performers. *Sight and Sound* magazine editorialized in 1939:

"The conclusion is inescapable that independent Negro producers have lacked that special vision needed if the Negro is to be represented truly and fully in the cinema today, and if the stereotypes in which he is cast are to be discarded. The dramatic possibilities of Negro life which are so rich and varied, and the potential of the Negro actor demonstrated in the poor media accessible to him, now will reveal themselves when this social vision arrives."

By 1940 half a dozen black producers were turning out 15 such pictures a year for viewing by 13 million American blacks. The casts were black and the scripts were by black writers, but when the films were shot in Ft. Lee, New Jersey, the black Hollywood across the Hudson from Harlem, AFL film unions, where no black technicians were allowed, forced them to use white electricians, grips, and mechanics.

These movies once again did not extol or glorify the black man. On the contrary, they depicted his vices as well as his virtues. The stories and characters were lifted from everyday black life, exaggerated a little for dramatic effect. The colored hero might be a young doctor tangling unwillingly with gangsters while trying to set up a free clinic in the slums (*Am I Guilty*), or a foundry puddler who falls in love with a stenographer (*Son of Imgagi*). A high school cornetist might dream of being another Louis Armstrong and have to fight to clear the name of a minister wrongly accused of a misdeed by his congregation (*Sunday Sinner*).

A few black-produced movies were made in Lincoln, Nebraska, by the Lincoln Motion Picture Co., whose owners were George P. Johnson and Noble Johnson. The outfit tried for higher goals in its productions, but in a few years ran out of money.

Before she became a bona fide star, Lena Horne was badly advised to make a black exploitation film called *Bronze Venus*, as her feature movie debut. The black producer turned it out quickly and cheaply for a fast profit. The fact that few people ever saw it was fortunate for Lena's career, because she was the only decent element in this vulgar little musical that had poor production values. The black crew who were finally allowed to work on it had no long history of learning their craft, and so the set and lighting, mixing and editing were amateurish by Hollywood standards.

A few "B" picture producers made timid moves toward pairing black and white actors. Adventure series with sidekick heroes had become popular just then, and Frankie Darro and Manton Moreland were chosen as the first black and white side-kicks for a number of adventure stories. But Moreland still came out the servant or clown, and Darro was designated the leader of the pair who actually always solved the mystery with bravado.

Finally major studios started developing a number of black stars, presenting them with taste and dignity in integrated scripts, where they could play believable human beings even when in support of white leading characters.

One of the first of those movies was *Imitation of Life*, by Fannie Hurst, in which a young widow (Claudette Colbert) with a little daughter takes in her homeless counterpart, Louise Beavers, as her maid, with the added incentive of providing her own daughter with a playmate (Miss Beavers's same-aged little girl). Colbert promotes the maid's delicious pancake recipe into a successful flapjack stand on the boardwalk, and then eventually markets the mix commercially, becoming very rich. The maid gets a fair share of the profit.

The subplot revolves around the frustration of the maid's daughter (Fredi Washington), who is very light-skinned, to mix socially with whites once they meet her very dark and very un-aggressive mother. In contrast to the warm, loving white mother-daughter relationship, the black one is troubled and totally unfair to the self-sacrificing black "mammy." Finally the mulatto daughter rejects her mother and runs away to pass for white herself. It is only after her mother dies heartbroken that the daughter realizes that her attempt at living a lie was hopeless and cruel.

Black critics were incensed with the handling of the film's racial issues. Even *Literary Digest* of December 8, 1934, complained about the restriction of the mulatto daughter's role: "Actually she is the most important and interesting person in the theme of the book and the picture. Her tragedy is most poignant, but the producers not only confined her to a minor and carefully handled sub-plot, but also showed their distaste for her while her mother is treated with sympathy and warmth, because she is the submissive, old-fashioned Negro who, as the saying goes, 'knows her place.' The daughter is too bitter and lacking in resignation over her undeserved fate." This review and others like it failed to understand that the black mother was also a tragic figure, because though her life was dedicated solely to her daughter's happiness, she had no ability to help her out of the mulatto dilemma. Due to the financial success of *Imitation of Life*, Louise Beavers later was featured in movies with Kay Francis, Joan Bennett, Joan Crawford and Jimmy Stewart.

In 1937 Warner Brothers produced *They Won't Forget*, a tough diatribe against lynching, directed by Mervyn LeRoy. *World Film News* called it "A savage, horrifying, cynical and un-equivocal exposé of the backwardness and degeneration of the small towns in the southern states which have their lynchings, and their Scottsboro trials, and make American justice stink to high heaven."

Gone With the Wind with its Civil War setting provided many fine supporting roles for blacks. Hattie McDaniel was cast in her usual role of a "mammy," but this time played it so definitively that she became the first black to be honored with an Academy Award in 1939. (The only other blacks to ever win Oscars were Sidney Poitier as best actor of 1963 and Louis Gossett, Jr., as best supporting actor in 1982.) Some black critics still railed at her for not fighting hard enough for bigger and more varied parts. She refused to take them on, and was reserved in her answers, but Lena Horne just at the start of her career under-stood the problem, which she analyzed: "A singer is accepted, where an actress is not." And she was right. The next decade saw Hollywood make outstanding stars of a few musical per-formers like Lena and the Nicholas Brothers. But only as cameo acts in lavish production numbers without ever being integrated into the plot. And the opportunity for a black dramatic actress or actor in a leading role was still a long way off.

Harold and Fayard Nicholas were brilliant young dancers who had had a unique early life. Fame as child stars at the Cot-ton Club in its early 1930's "heyday," had led to engagements all over the world. They quickly became very poised, self-edu-cated, multi-lingual young men, totally at ease with all types of people in all age groups. In addition to their fine inherent talent, something extra rubbed off on them as they performed with the class stars of international cabaret.

Fayard, the older of the two, was acknowledged to be the

more classically pure dancer, but Harold had the pizzaz, humor, and singing and acting ability to make him more versatile. They made an immediate impression in films like *Jealousy*, Eddie Cantor's *Kid Millions* in 1934, the *Big Broadcast of 1936* and *Tin Pan Alley*. But it was in *Stormy Weather, Sun Valley Serenade* and *Orchestra Wives* (the last two featuring Glenn Miller's orchestra) and later *The Pirate* with Gene Kelly that they started "stopping the show" with dance routines that were so explosive and athletically executed that they remained in people's memories for decades. In 1987, mammoth discos in New York like the Ritz Ballroom still project their "Be a Clown" pas de trois with Gene Kelly onto the ceiling to excite their young patrons.

Sammy Davis, Jr., always looked up to Harold Nicholas. "He was the first of my generation to beat the system with his class." Sammy could never get over sitting in the Roxy Theater watching *Orchestra Wives* and seeing the entire audience in a movie house make the unprecedented move of standing up and cheering the specialty number that the Nicholas Brothers had just knocked them out with.

But these great sequences, along with Lena Horne's early MGM production numbers, had been shot so that they could be edited out of the movie without disturbing the continuity, when it was financially beneficial to cut them. In the south, the print would be devoid of these gems.

Sammy Davis, Jr., says emotionally, "Harold fought the Hollywood thing—being cut out of a movie after being put into it." And speaking of the 1950's period when both Lena and the Nicholas Brothers were not being utilized enough in movies: "Their careers were stagnant in Hollywood, they were just vacillating back and forth. They got good money but eventually said to hell with it, and went out on the road. Then California clubs like Ciro's and Broadway musicals invited them."

Harold Nicholas admits that the Hollywood period was difficult emotionally. On the one hand you were a star. On the other hand there were so many places you couldn't live in, and clubs and restaurants to which you wouldn't be admitted. One of the passions he acquired while travelling abroad was golf. He had a great set of clubs, custom-made for a short person, and he could

afford to belong to a golf club like other filmland golf nuts—
Crosby, Hope, Jack Benny.

And he *did* play on those courses, or equivalents—one day a
week, on Mondays, but never as a member. Monday was "Caddy
Day." The clubs were closed so the staff could have a day off,
and the caddies, who'd been carrying the bags and watching
"the boss" dig divots and shank shots the other six days, could
try out their own strokes. So it's true, Harold Nicholas could
play on that course, but only if a caddy friend was nice enough
to invite him to make up a foursome with the hired help.

Along with the excision of specialty numbers for southern distribution, there were other strange racial rules for movie musicals. Black and white musicians in the same band had to be
photographed as if they were not playing together. When Benny
Goodman's red hot band was signed to make *Hollywood Hotel*,
Teddy Wilson and Lionel Hampton were always seen soloing in
separate close-ups, and were never included in ensemble shots
of the band unless they were seen vaguely in the background in
an unfocused long shot. For southern distribution the solo close-
ups were snipped out. But you could hear them clearly driving
the group on the sound track.

This same form of deception was even continued in the early
days of television when white guitarist Herb Ellis was the leader
of an all-black group signed for a "Bell Telephone Hour" show.
According to Herb, writing in Gene Lees' *Jazz Letter*, the TV
executives told Norman Granz, "Now we will want to use another guitar player," and Norman said "What?" and found out
the reason, "because they wouldn't have a white and black on
camera at the same time." When Ellis refused to be replaced,
and they had to acquiesce because he was the leader, they Vase-
lined the camera lense, which so diffused the picture that viewers couldn't tell who was sitting back there in the guitarist's
seat.

Lena Horne was unquestionably the first black actress to
have the opportunity to become a bona fide Hollywood glamour
girl. By studio evaluation—she was black, but not too black! She
had a marvelous figure that was not too full. She looked like a
lady, and she had the talent to sing marvelously and yet act and
dance adequately. All the black beauties before her, like Nina

Mae McKinney, either lacked some of those ingredients or had appeared on the scene too early in the history of movie integration. So Lena became a true star even though she actually made very few films by Hollywood standards.

The list from 1942 to 1946 includes *Panama Hattie, Cabin in the Sky, Stormy Weather, Ziegfield Follies* and *As Thousands Cheer.* In *Panama Hattie* she had one brief singing appearance draped around a pillar, but her voice and sexy-but-ladylike delivery had a tremendous effect on the audience.

Stormy Weather was a true showcase for her, because in this all-black film that consisted of vignettes in the life of a pair of lovers, she was cast as Bill Robinson's sweetheart, and given decent dialogue and great songs like "Stormy Weather." Talking about these early movies years later, Miss Horne was whimsical: "There were so many stars in these films that I had little chance to be anything but a baby doll up there looking cute.

"Even so, I think those films were important. They provided a showcase for some marvelous black talent—people got to see performers like Bill Robinson, Fats Waller, Cab Calloway, Duke Ellington, and Ethel Waters, many of whom they never would have otherwise seen. I think that represents a breakthrough. We showed people that good black movies could make money. We thought we had changed things even though it didn't work out that way immediately."

In *Cabin in the Sky*, another all-black MGM film directed by Vincente Minelli, she played the devil's "emissary," Georgia Brown, a prostitute who helped Lucifer Jr. (Rex Ingram) and the boys from Hades fight the soldiers of heaven and Ethel Waters in their struggle for the soul of little Joe (Eddie Anderson). Again Lena's allure riveted all eyes to the screen, and she had some great Harold Arlen songs to sing; but she was actually too wholesome to really play such a no-good wench.

Also this production drew her into the first of her many controversies with other black actors. Ethel Waters, for one, was unreasonably jealous of how easily Lena was becoming the darling of white Hollywood in contrast to the years of rejection it had given Ethel, and she gave Lena a hard time whenever she could. Some of it was the jealousy of a woman past her prime for the newest beauty on the lot, and Waters probably thought that

Horne was being pampered without having paid her "dues."

Lena also had gotten a lead role in this picture by dealing directly with MGM, and this was not the way blacks had learned to operate in Tinseltown. Since at that time they still couldn't join film unions, a group of black performers had organized a quasi-union to prevent the studios from controlling their destinies and salaries. It was almost impossible for a black actor to get work without this group supporting and recommending him. But Lena with the help of her father and Arthur Freed had been able to circumvent them, and they resented it, claiming she was undermining their checks and controls on the studios, and would make it more difficult for other less-fortunate blacks to get fair treatment. The studio bosses loved this quasi-union arrangement because they didn't have to sign these performers to term contracts. Lena was the only one who remained on salary even when she wasn't working, due to her long-term agreement. All the rest were day or week workers.

But Miss Horne actually was always an activist for fair conditions for her race. She was a very vocal member of the Screen Actors' Guild for 30 years and was one of the first blacks to survive in Hollywood despite refusing roles she thought demeaning. Her outspokenness and her willingness to lend her support to a good cause during World War II and the post-war period was the background of attacks on her during the "Red Menace" scare, and resulted in her not being offered parts all through the 1950's and 1960's except for a cameo in the 1956 *Meet Me in Las Vegas* and the female lead in 1966's western *The Last of the Gunfighters*, with Richard Widmark.

Except for this hard-core group of contractors trying to protect their own interests, most blacks in Hollywood adored Lena, and she also had many of her bi-coastal jazz buddies who gave her loving support. Duke Ellington was among the most loyal. He considered Billy Strayhorn, his co-composer and protégé, as one of his closest male friends, and Lena as one of his closest female friends. He drew these two together in Hollywood with an emotional ulterior motive. Strayhorn was homosexual. The womanizing Duke believed in the myth that a gay man could go "straight" if his "disease" could be cured by the right woman. Lena and Billy were introduced and immediately became the kind of friends who could talk for six straight hours. Strayhorn was the one person Lena could open up to and confide her fears to. They made music together, went to movies, walked the beaches, but both knew that the Duke's scenario was impossible.

"I loved him—I would have married him if we could have married," Lena often said of Billy, who rarely gets the credit for writing songs the public ascribes to the Duke, like "Take the 'A' Train" and "Lush Life." Years later, dying of cancer, Strayhorn wanted nothing else but "to spend my last days with Lena."

Miss Horne always saw the ridiculous humor in many of her Hollywood problems, particularly as they related to her too-Caucasian appearance. MGM had been wanting to cast her opposite Eddie Anderson again in *Thank Your Lucky Stars*, this time not as a "pick-up" and a "John," but as a man and wife working as a servant couple for a wealthy white family. Lena was attracted to the idea because Eddie was another good friend, and the marital dialogue that they would deliver was funny, realistic and a step forward for black characters.

The screen test, however, showed her to be too light complected compared to Anderson, the spouse, and that was still taboo racially in those Hollywood days. Photographically they also would have been out of sync in certain lighting. When makeup people applied the standard darkening tones to Lena, she filmed as if in "blackface," so Ethel Waters got the part! But anxious to avoid this same fiasco in the future, the studio called in Max Factor, the cosmetics king, to solve the problem. He concocted a shade called "light Egyptian" which was perfect for her. It was so good, that it was perfect for anybody it was applied to. Almost any white actress could be turned into a most believable mulatto. Ironically, this put many light-skinned black actresses out of potential work. And Lena had to wait over two decades until the 1966 *Last of the Gunfighters* to have a speaking role in an integrated cast movie.

She was so fed up with this kind of nonsense that on a trip back to New York for a Cafe Society benefit, she vowed to chuck her Hollywood career. But another old dear friend, Count Basie, set her straight while escorting her home from Barney Josephson's club.

"They chose you, we don't get that many chances. You've got to go back. You've got to stay there and you've got to be good, and you've got to be right and do whatever they want you to do and make us proud of you." In this way he renewed her sense of mission.

One memory that also gave her encouragement to return involved one of the few anecdotes that illustrated Louis B. Mayer's decent side rather than his rapaciousness. Frances Edwards, the manager of the MGM commissary, told all the black performers on the first day of shooting of *Cabin in the Sky* that they had to sit at the counter, not at tables. This was being told to proven talents like Duke Ellington, Louis Armstrong and Buck and Bubbles, in addition to all the story-line stars like Lena, Eddie, Ethel, Rex Ingram and Butterfly McQueen. They were reluctant to go along with this, and requested someone from Mr. Mayer's office to come down to witness their segregation.

"Louis B." himself appeared shortly, invited them in as guests to his private dining room for that particular lunch, and assured them that the order would be rescinded. Later he blasted the originator of the order—his own brother.

Another close friend from Cotton Club times, Cab Calloway, is given credit for the depth of feeling in Lena's rendition of "Stormy Weather" in the picture of the same name that made her an international star. Lena was having a very difficult time getting down into that lyric and stripping away her cool, aloof, outer skin. After many abortive takes one day, Cab Calloway told the frustrated director, "Leave it to me."

He walked over to Lena, whispered a few words in her ear and she immediately looked emotionally destroyed. On the next take real tears flowed. A sob came into her voice and everyone on the set froze in place. After the number, she went into uncontrolled weeping for five minutes. Cab never would tell anyone what he said, but Lena claims he called her a few particularly filthy names, relating them to the divorce she was then going through with her first husband.

Lena Horne has never gotten the full credit for the leverage that her talent, beauty, and presence provided in those difficult days toward breaking down racial barriers. But in the mid-

1940's when she was playing at the black-oriented Howard Theater in Washington, D.C., the National Negro Press Association recognized it in a report on a press conference that she gave:

"This correspondent was amazed at the fluent manner in which she intelligently discussed unions, politics, race relations, social welfare . . . but here's an actual development for which Lena Horne may be given credit. At the press party were representatives of the local white press—theater critics, even editors. No other person very likely could have drawn them here despite the cordial invitation extended. Most of them had never come in contact with members of the Negro press before—or with any intelligent Negroes for that matter. A few of them were so impressed that plans are under way for an interracial press luncheon so more of the 'white' press may learn what goes on."

In this same decade of the 1940's, many fine dramatic films were made that exhibited themes and characters sympathetic to blacks. *In This Our Life* starred Bette Davis as a hit-and-run driver who blames the resulting death on a black man. The black (Ernest Anderson) is educated, and vocal in protesting his innocence in a dignified manner. Bosley Crowther wrote in *The New York Times*, "The one successful component of the film . . . the brief but frank allusion to racial discrimination. And it is presented in a realistic manner, uncommon to Hollywood, by the depiction of the Negro as an educated and comprehending character."

The Ox Bow Incident and *Sullivan's Travels*, the latter written and directed by Preston Sturges, had similarly sympathetic portraits of blacks.

World War II movies observed blacks for the first time seriously integrated into a team—the military services. Talking of *Bataan* and the character of Wesley Epps played by Kenneth Spencer, William E. Burke was interested that, "In a film in which the Negro character is supposedly treated fairly, Epps is too busy working to participate in most group scenes. When he does appear among a sizable number of comrades, he is distinctly relegated to the background in discussion."

But still, all war films from Hollywood indicated clearly that the black soldier was a comrade, shared a fox hole equally, stood in formation shoulder to shoulder, exposed to the same danger and shedding the same color blood as the adjacent white GI. And even in *Bataan*, a story of 13 soldiers given the assignment of bombing an obscure bridge in a non-strategic location, the climax has Kenneth Spencer's character saying the prayer over the jungle grave of the group's dead Captain (Robert Taylor). His eloquent epitaph for this man, symbolizing the dead of all wars, contains the movie's message.

Zoltan Korda, the producer of *Sahara* with Humphrey Bogart, allowed the first example on screen of a black defeating a white in hand-to-hand combat. Rex Ingram played a Sudanese soldier who himself has a native servant. Ingram has proved to be an especially great soldier and is treated with enormous respect by the tough sergeant (Bogart) and the rest of the platoon, who have to hold off a German tank force.

Peter Noble, a writer, describes one scene involving the black: "He uses his hands as a cup for the drinking water which quenches the thirst of the white men. Each of the whites drinks out of the hands of the Negro, and no one finds that extraordinary.

"The whites are not repelled by this contact. They admire the steadiness and dependability of those hands. Social change has been brought about by the shared experience of war."

In Hitchcock's *Lifeboat*, Canada Lee's character, a steward, performs a courageous act that the others, who are white, could not accomplish. This was a startling new theme that continued in later movies and into real-life post-war attitudes.

William Katz wrote of post-war expectations in *The Eyewitness: The Negro in American History*.

"One of the biggest problems of the post-war years was that of making America a land of liberty and justice for all. Many whites had returned from Europe and Asia believing that if the idea of a 'master race' was wrong for our enemies, it was wrong for America too."

This concept was expressed in the movie *Till the End of Time*. Robert Mitchum played an ex-marine attending a meeting of a semi-Facist group called American Patriots Association. The leader tells him "we represent all vets except niggers, Jews, and Catholics."

Mitchum shouts, "My best friend, a Jew, is lying back in a fox hole in Guadalcanal. I'm gonna spit in your eye for him, because we don't want to have people like you in this country."

Home of the Brave projected the first full-length psychological portrait of a black ever attempted on film. James Edwards played a soldier who, when he sees his friend killed, is first elated that it wasn't his own death that had occurred, and then suddenly becomes paralyzed from the waist down for no physical reasons. He only snaps out of it when the psychiatrist shouts, "You dirty nigger, get up and walk!" The doctor later assures him that the first reaction of every soldier is relief that another man was hit instead of himself.

The evolution of black roles continued in the late 1940's, moving into portraits of blacks who won over people by persevering with stable traits. These calm, self-contained professionals were often played by Harry Belafonte, Sidney Poitier and Dorothy Dandridge. This type of movie, although not sure box-office, was praised by black critics, whereas the musicals like *Carmen Jones* and *Porgy and Bess*, made in the same years and receiving broader distribution, were panned.

Although these musicals were made and directed by well-meaning liberals (e.g., Otto Preminger) and were cast with the same Belafonte, Poitier and Dandridge in addition to Sammy Davis, Jr., and Brock Peters, who were all given fine roles (and an Oscar nomination in Dandridge's case), they still perpetuated the same old myths like mulatto women being more beautiful due to their white blood and sexually permissive due to their black blood. And the Catfish Row types in *Porgy* were horrendous stereotypes. But with their major distribution these pictures served to expose white America to a whole new generation of very talented black movie stars.

Sammy Davis, Jr.'s, "Sportin' Life" portrayal in *Porgy and Bess* was praised in all the reviews as the finest conception of that role ever seen. His seductive singing and dancing and his brilliantly evil approach to the character made him the quintessential pimp. And some in the black community slapped out at the man, who is universally considered one of the finest entertainers of any era, saying that "Sam finally showed some 'soul' in this part." Davis has always been hurt when criticized by his own people, for whom he has always had the most intense love and loyalty.

But he is also bluntly honest and self-analytical, and admits that as a young performer he was always torn between commitment and having fun, and between trying to be black on the one hand and denying it on the other. He recently said during a very thoughtful conversation, "You've got to find the level of commitment you can live with so it can be a day-to-day thing—that it happens to you without it being a grandstand play. It just happens—you do it—you walk on the stage and don't take shit."

"What is blackness? Blackness is what you make of it: I can't be Smokey Robinson, I can't go that way—but don't tell me I don't have soul! I'm not James Brown with his street jive, but don't tell me I don't have soul just because I sing correctly and enunciate a lyric. You have to find your niche. Harry had to find his and settle into it. Sydney had to find where he was comfortable. Harold Nicholas was always a big irritant because he had the nerve and intelligence to say 'I'm good.' Black people loved him and white people were afraid of him, and I adored him and his talent."

On the subject of integrity, Poitier hated doing the *Porgy* role. There were threats that his career would be snuffed if he didn't, so he gave in and capitulated, but he never completely forgave himself for doing so.

Belafonte and Poitier became the first of the handsome, romantic black leading men whom the studios allowed to have roles in which they approached women and danger with charisma equal to their white counterparts, William Holden and Paul Newman.

Belafonte had come out of the jazz and calypso world and so could do both musicals and drama. Poitier seldom played comedy and was identified with films of a serious nature that still managed to be moneymakers. His career is remarkable in that he literally went from production to production making a surprising number of films over a relatively short span of years, and yet a very high percentage of these were praised for artistic quality, and also were moneymakers at the box office. Only Bogart and Holden could match him for the ratio of quantity and quality, as he starred in films like *The Blackboard Jungle, Raisin in the Sun, No Way Out, Paris Blues, In the Heat of the Night, Lilies of the Field, The Defiant Ones, Edge of the City, Cry the Beloved Country, Guess Who's Coming to Dinner?* and *Something of Value*, just a partial list of his output.

In *The Defiant Ones* he played a chain-gang prisoner who escapes with another convict, Tony Curtis, and through the interdependency of their plight, they gain respect and affection for each other, gradually losing their past prejudices. The climatic moment comes as Poitier's character sacrifices his freedom when his friend can't reach the train that will lead to escape, and Poitier jumps back off to be with him. The shared predicament made them both realize that they were brothers under the skin. This daring movie was a surprise hit with a very broad spectrum of audience.

Eventually Poitier became the top box office draw in Hollywood and also the only black to ever win the best actor Oscar.

Belafonte was really the first black matinee idol—more of a sex symbol than Poitier. His handsome features, lithe, graceful build and dazzling smile made female pulses race whether black or white. He starred in *Bright Road, Carmen Jones, Odds Against Tomorrow, The World, the Flesh and the Devil,* and *Island in the Sun*. In the latter, he was given romantic scenes not only with Dorothy Dandridge, but with Joan Fontaine and Joan Collins, and much footage was spent admiring his very masculine and very underdressed body.

In *The World, the Flesh and the Devil,* an innovative look at post-atomic war destruction, Belafonte is forced to fight the villain, Mel Ferrer, for the only woman left alive, Inger Stevens. At the end, the kind, compassionate black loses out. But this film gave Harry a multi-dimensional role to show off his skill as a dramatic actor.

There were a few other attempts to introduce attractive black performers as potential leading-man types, among them singers Nat 'King' Cole and Billy Eckstine. Cole did make quite a few pictures—*Small Town Girl, The Blue Gardenia, Istanbul, China Gate, Cat Ballou,* and *St. Louis Blues,* in which he starred as W.C. Handy, the composer. But although he was fine for character parts, he didn't ignite the screen as a potential romantic lead.

The one man who had the rugged looks, presence and raw sex appeal to become the black Clark Gable was Billy Eckstine, but strangely he never allowed himself the opportunity to succeed. He was offered the *Carmen Jones* lead before Harry Belafonte, but turned it down.

"I just couldn't go along with the treatment, the stereotyped 'dat's and dem's' the characters had to say and sing. That's old-fashioned plantation stuff. Yes, I know the picture was a big hit—but when I went to see it I walked out in the middle."

Friends say that poor management, poor promotion and unsound personal decisions undercut Billy's career and he never became the multiple-media star that was his potential. He had so much going for him and yet the plateau inhabited by Sammy Davis, Jr., and Nat Cole always eluded him.

"Mr. B," as Symphony Sid the disc jockey labelled him, started his show biz life as an instrumentalist in many excellent big bands, notably Earl Hines's quality group of the early 1930's. He was more of a musician than singer in those days, but with Hines he became a favorite when he would saunter to the mike and sing an occasional specialty number. His deep sound and amazing vibrato would have the jazz fans begging for more. So gradually singing took over and the sideman role receded.

Billy made and kept friends easily. He has always been that rare specimen of a guy who is both a man's man and a "ladies' man"—a helluva nice person to have around. And so when he decided to start his own band in the early 1940's, he attracted superb jazz men like Charlie "Bird" Parker, Dizzy Gillespie, Dexter Gordon (star of 1986's *Round Midnight*), Fats Navarro and Tad Dameron, who did landmark arrangements. This ensemble became the greatest "bop" big band ever, and for the daring pioneering musicianship, the credit must go to Eckstine for putting it together. As a bonus, Sarah Vaughan was the other vocalist and this great band gave both her and Billy beautifully shaded backings, particularly on ballads.

After the war, a combination of economics and changing audience taste caused the breakup of most of the big bands, including Billy's. But he persisted and went out as a single with instant success. For two years he was the "Great Mr. B.," filling the void caused by the dip in popularity of the white crooning stars, Sinatra and Crosby.

His interpretations of "Jelly, Jelly," "Skylark," "I Apologize" and "You Don't Know What Love Is" made him a tremendous attraction in theaters and clubs and on records. He was being paid $12,500 a week for engagements at the top of his career. Eckstine really had everything—a voice that sounded like soft cashmere and "heartbreaker" looks that featured light skin and a dashing mustache.

But gradually he watered down his style to suit what he thought white audiences wanted, instead of retaining his racial strengths. Black fans didn't like his switching more to a "pop" formula. They wanted the old "Jelly, Jelly," and he didn't help matters with quotes like, 'I hate blues, you can't do anything with them—they don't kill me.'

Downbeat magazine reviewed an Apollo Theater gig and charged that, "He didn't meet the audience half way. He gave the Apollo audience a 'Copa' show—big band, fiddles, conductor.

"It is a sad thing to see a great artist reach the stage where he has gone beyond the kind of audience who helped make him famous, has lost contact with them and their musical tastes. It is happening with Billy in his hold on Negro audiences."

But even when he played places like the Copa, things went amiss. Bob Sylvester of the *Daily News* reviewed his opening at that prestigious club, "He started out with a half-baked song by a half-baked writer, and ended with a purely dreadful piece of material by a purely dreadful writer."

Metronome magazine gave some pragmatic advice: "Mr. B. came from jazz and it is to jazz that he must return."

But Billy turned a deaf ear on this and only listened to the short-sighted plaudits of nightclub columnists like Dorothy Killgallen and Lee Mortimer who knew "Cafe Society" but didn't know music. So Nat Cole took away Eckstine's title as number-one pop singer, and Harry Belafonte the role of black matinee idol in films.

Billy is still sought after for engagements in Las Vegas and Atlantic City in 1988, even though he is past 70. And he never lost the love and admiration of friends and associates in the busi-

Young Josephine Premice arrived at the Village Vanguard with no music. Pianist Ellis Larkins saved the audition. (The Premice Collection)

Hammond and Benny. Creative harmony but frequent personal antagonism. (CBS Records)

Writer, talent scout, record producer and the most decent of men--John Hammond. (CBS Records)

Billie Holiday. Hammond discovered the greatest jazz singer, but could never condone her moods. (CBS Records)

Bessie Smith. Nobody sang the blues better. But she was literally killed by segregation. (CBS Records)

Bill Basie and John Hammond, a friendship that went far deeper than business. (CBS Records)

The producer listens to a playback with Aretha Franklin, another discovery. (CBS Records)

George Benson and his talent scout. (CBS Records)

Hammond and Hampton. The Goodman small combos integrated jazz for the first time. (CBS Records)

Barney and Max in their eighties.
They had the guts to run integrated
clubs when no one else would.
(CBS Records)

Barney Josephson at his
desk at Cafe Society in
1939. (The Barney
Josephson Collection)

Hazel Scott entertains at Cafe
Society during World War II. (Photo
by Albert A. Freeman. The Barney
Josephson Collection)

Josh White singing folk and blues at Cafe Society, with the famous murals in the background. (Photo by Albert A. Freeman. The Barney Josephson Collection)

Avon Long. From "Sportin' Life" to Cafe Society. (Photo by Albert A. Freeman. The Barney Josephson Collection)

Phil Moore leads the band at Cafe Society. Later he became Lena Horne's accompanist. (The Barney Josephson Collection)

Harold Nicholas celebrates his twelfth birthday at the Cotton Club with his brother Fayard, Cab Calloway, Ethel Waters and Duke Ellington. (The Harold Nicholas Collection)

The Nicholas Brothers in their famous "Chattanooga Choo Choo" number from *Sun Valley Serenade*. (The Harold Nicholas Collection. 20th Century-Fox)

Lena Horne and Bill "Bojangles" Robinson star in *Stormy Weather* for 20th Century-Fox. (The Harold Nicholas Collection)

Joe Louis meets with USO brass
in 1944. Second from right is
the then basically unknown
Jackie Robinson, fresh from pre-
war football heroics at UCLA.
(Schomburg Center for Research
in Black Culture)

Josephine Baker thrived on controversy
and enlisted NAACP support for her
causes. (The Jean Claude Baker
Collection)

Harold and Fayard Nicholas,
still rarin' to go today. (The
Harold Nicholas Collection)

Cab Calloway leading the Cotton Club band in the early 1930's. (The
N.Y. Public Library Collection, Performing Arts Research Center)

Marian Anderson. Eleanor
Roosevelt arranged for the concert
that the D.A.R had forbidden. (N.Y.
Public Library Collection,
Performing Arts Research Center.
Photo by Fred Fehl)

Duke Ellington with sidemen Lawrence Brown, Rex Stewart and Sonny
Greer. (N.Y. Public Library Collection, Performing Arts Research Center)

ness, many of whom are still puzzled that he didn't make it big in films and TV. It is said that he was the victim of a situation.

In 1964 when he never showed up for a "Royal Box" nightclub opening in New York due to a "situation" that deteriorated into a murky tale of a beating, and an unconscious night on park grass due to a "Mickey Finn," show business buddies sitting in the impatient audience went on stage for him and saved the engagement. "Nipsy" Russell, Tony Bennett and Robert Goulet took the early show, and Sammy Davis, Jr., Bill Cosby, Red Buttons and Jack E. Leonard filled in at the late show.

By the next evening Bill had reappeared, facially battered, but in good voice. The police never solved the mysterious attack, but all Broadway whispered the same word—"mob."

Whether the long hand of "the boys" had anything to do with the Eckstine incident or not, it is public record that they had an all-consuming interest in, and effect on, Hollywood, and that they spawned Las Vegas. Certainly, directly and indirectly they controlled both black and white performers in both entertainment capitals, and their intrusion into movie making came about as the result of the repeal of Prohibition, when the word went out to find new ways of making money.

An obscure, low-echelon punk in Chicago named Willie Bioff and Louis Lepke Buchalter, head of Brooklyn's "Murder Incorporated," got the idea about the same time of cashing in on movie dollars by controlling the power that technical unions had over both movie production industries and the exhibitors of their product. They started by taking over the stagehands' union, enlisting Frank Nitti, Al Capone's right-hand man, and Lucky Luciano to deliver the Chicago and New York votes to get their man George Browne in as National President of the I.A.T.S.E. Union in 1932. Nitti and his gang would take two-thirds of any money made from squeezing the moguls in Hollywood.

Willie Bioff was appointed as Browne's International representative. His first official move was to stick it to the Chicago Exhibitors' Association, telling them that they would need not one, but two union projectionists from then on in each theater. To save the $500,000 a year that such a ruling would cost Chicago theater owners, Bioff suggested to them that he would give them a break and withdraw the order if they would be grateful enough to slip him $60,000 a year. And they of course were very, very grateful.

Browne and Bioff started shuttling between Hollywood and New York making their imaginative deals. They threatened to close every theater in the country unless Nicholas Schenck, President of Loews, Inc., owner of MGM, and his counterparts at Warners, Fox and Paramount met Browne in his suite at the Waldorf-Astoria in New York and handed over $50,000 each in cash. The minor studios were hit for $25,000.

At the other end of the "strong arm" caper, Browne extorted 2 percent of all union members' wages as a "contribution" for a war fund in case of strikes. The war fund escalated to 1.5 million dollars per year, two-thirds ending up with the Nitti crowd, and the rest in Bioff and Browne's pockets. If anyone wondered why, or complained, a few well-muscled associates were sent to explain the situation.

In 1937 when Bioff broke the single strike called by plumbers, grips, draftsmen, and others, he did it by bringing in Chicago goons and issuing I.A.T.S.E. union cards to scabs who walked through the picket lines. Joseph Schenck coincidentally gave Willie a $100,000 personal loan, through Schenck's brother Nick, at that exact moment. There clearly existed a studio situation where, to quote Chicago Judge John Kern, the studios "knowingly and willingly paid over the funds and in a sense lent encouragement and participated with full knowledge of the facts, in the activities of Browne and Bioff."

But Willy got too greedy and wanted to take over the actors' unions also, to collect a share of the fortunes paid to the stars. Robert Montgomery, President of the Screen Actors' Guild, got his union board to pay private detectives $5000 to investigate Bioff's Hollywood dealings, and they dug up proof of the Schenck bribe. Joe Schenck was not only the chairman of the board of 20th Century-Fox but president of the Motion Picture Producers' Association. This led to the indictment of Schenck for income tax fraud and for perjury. Bioff also was indicted for income tax evasion and for an unfinished 18-year-old Illinois sentence for pandering.

Rather than go to jail, Schenck made a deal in return for exposing the racketeering. Bioff was sent to Alcatraz where after a few years he made his own bargain with the authorities and squealed about the roles Nitti and his gang had played. The gang members were put away for ten years each, but Nitti shot himself to death before he could be confined. Bioff and Browne were paroled after serving three years each, and Joe Schenck received a Presidential pardon after serving four months.

Ten years later, Bioff, living in Phoenix, Arizona, with his wife under the assumed name of Bill Nelson, started the ignition of his Ford pickup and was blown to bits. The men who patiently waited for this revenge against one of their own who had broken the code, were undoubtedly part of the group that became all-powerful in Las Vegas starting in 1946.

CHAPTER VI

Blacks in Las Vegas

Look at a detailed roadmap of the West and you'll find that even today there isn't a stop light between Los Angeles and Las Vegas. The desert oasis was originally built as an escape valve for L.A. pressures, and the straight asphalt ribbon speeded up the process of relief. Originally 85 percent of the customers were from Los Angeles and 40 years later it still holds at about 40 percent of 11,000,000 visits a year.

What is the lure? It doesn't just cater to the compulsively addicted gambler, although that certainly is a factor. But for the larger percentage of visitors it is an occasional opportunity to shed the repressions of their middle class upbringing and to un-inhibitedly indulge their fantasies in a totally anonymous atmosphere. Or if they can't allow themselves the excesses of gambling, boozing and no-holds-barred sex, then they can at least have the vicarious stimulation of observing the indulgences of others in a setting devoid of pretense.

The allegorical cliché of likening Las Vegas to a loose woman is quite apt, but in fairness to the place, she is at least a call girl who honestly labels herself a "whore" rather than the hypocritical "escort" or "companion." You gets what you see! Anything goes, and it's all up front. If you have the green you can openly buy any diversion known to man or beast. The pleasures may be grimly organized and somewhat joyless and jaded, but for a little extra cash even enthusiasm can be conjured.

One of the few things that isn't faked is the high level of entertainment in the casinos, lounges and clubs all over the town. A performer is paid higher wages here than any other place in the world. Only the most talented are invited to accept these big rewards, but he or she is expected to give 100 percent. This was always the rule, whether for the Sinatras, the Presleys, the Sammy Davis, Jrs., or whoever else had his name up in lights along the gaudy strip since 1946, when the Vegas that we know today was born out of the desert.

Los Angeles was expanding rapidly in a post-war boom, and its citizens, plush with the salaries that they were receiving in new peacetime industries, and euphoric with the relief from wartime tensions and concerns, needed to "play," preferably in a new environment. The underworld, on the other hand, had found the war years a very prosperous period by controlling the black market and dealing in "surplus" materials. But VJ Day left them with a need to once more come up with a new scheme for making megabucks with a minimum of risk.

Enter Benjamin "Bugsy" Siegel, in a tale that took on operatic overtones as it progressed. Siegel, a protégé of Meyer Lansky, was sent to California to protect the Eastern mob's position in the struggle for control of the racing wire to the West Coast. By rubbing out some Pacific Coast competitors he succeeded in this endeavor and became a force to contend with. He also deluded himself into thinking he could become a movie star with the help of buddies like George Raft, but finally settled for the power, the big dollars and the endless sex with a stable of starlets who liked his rugged good looks. Brilliantly "street smart," Benjamin saw the potential of that perennial loser, Las Vegas in the Nevada desert, and most particularly a god-forsaken strip of land seven miles out of town with not a tree in sight.

To him the set-up was perfect for a big score in gambling and all its satellite scams. Nevada, in its desperation to attract outsiders to its bleak wasteland, had legalized most of the deadly sins—gambling, prostitution (by local option), quickie divorces. But it was this very bleakness that convinced Siegel that he had found the pot of gold. Unlike any other resort, it had no distractions. No lush locations, no lure of sightseeing, no boating, fishing, tennis and golf of a Miami or a Hawaii. Absolutely no reasons to leave the building in the vicious daytime heat. Once you got the tourists there and filled them with enough to eat and drink, there was nothing else for them to do but gamble and lose their money in the comfortable, air-conditioned casino.

And so he plotted out the mechanics of a deal to build the first extravagant hotel on this strip of land and still cover the traces of its control by organized crime. He convinced a friend, "Little Moe" Sedway, to buy 30 roadside acres from a widow and transfer this property to Greg Bautzer, a swinging Hollywood lawyer type. Bautzer in turn sold the property to Nevada Projects Corp., whose largest stockholder was "Bugsy" Siegel, and in a lesser position, Meyer Lansky. Then Siegel's "backers" supplied him with a million dollars to build "The Flamingo." The builder he chose, interestingly enough, was Del Webb, a Phoenix contractor who later became famous as the one time owner of the New York Yankees, the builder of Sun City, and even the owner of some Vegas Strip hotels himself. Perhaps the strangest factor in the mob-run deal with so many twists was this choice of Webb, who later became a friend of FBI Chief J. Edgar Hoover.

Siegel wanted to build the greatest casino ever known. The illuminated pillar at its entrance would be visible for miles across the desert, and its beacon would lure players in. But there were problems facing him. The post-war economy was still stalled in wartime shortages and regulations. He wheeled and dealed, paying black market prices, pulling strings, using every cozy trick he had learned to get it done. Senator Pat Mc-Carron was "enlisted" to help provide copper, steel and other hard-to-find materials. Movie moguls came up with lumber, piping, cement. Italian Mafia connections in Italy shipped over fine marble and rare wood. Labor union associates insured a cooperative work force, and all along the way, all who helped had their palm crossed.

"Bugsy" was in a frenzy of passion and dedication to detail as this palace rose. Most of the passion was being stimulated by his great love, Virginia Hill, a redheaded siren who had been passed around from "Bookie" Joe Epstein to Joe Adonis, the king of New York gambling, before getting to Siegel. Virginia's nickname was "The Flamingo," and naturally that would emblazon the new casino.

Opening night, the day after Christmas of 1946, was a disaster. Nothing was finished or working. Planes couldn't leave Los Angeles because of a storm. Only a handful of celebrities like George Raft and George Sanders showed up to see Jimmy Durante, George Jessel and Xavier Cugat's orchestra perform. The hotel was only half full and half finished even with the extra cash that "Bugsy" had borrowed from Lansky at the last minute to get this far. The most embarrassing "shtick" came when the gambling tables lost $300,000 in the first two weeks.

Siegel closed the place down until he could raise more money to finish it properly. So far, four million had been poured in instead of the estimated one million. To top it all off, Virginia, fed up with both the desert and "Bugsy," returned to Beverly Hills, rented a mansion and goaded him by throwing lavish parties for her own friends.

Finally on March 1, 1947, Siegel felt it was really ready, but few came. Gambling losses for the first six months were $774,000, and this was something "The Boys" who were investors were not going to take. The word was put out that "Bugsy" alone had mishandled the project, ignoring cost-consciousness all along the way, and giving them a royal screwing with the balance sheet. Most damaging and unforgivable were rumors of skimming, and reporting greater losses to make up the differential.

Even before the first opening of the Flamingo, an unusual meeting had taken place at the Hotel Nacionale in Havana, Cuba, attended by Meyer Lansky, Lucky Luciano, Frank Costello, Joe Adonis, Vito Genovese, Joe Bonnano, Carlos Marcello and Santo Trafficante. On the agenda was an update of the progress of the Las Vegas project. Reports of Swiss bank accounts opened by Siegel, and wasteful expenditure of their money to impress Virginia Hill, were discussed quietly but grimly. Lansky made a desperate attempt to save his young friend by reminding the group of all the past loyal services "Bugsy" had performed for them. But according to Joseph "Doc" Stadler, one of Lansky's close friends, Luciano took Meyer aside later and told him that Siegel would have to be punished. "If you don't have the heart to do it, Meyer, I will have to order the execution myself."

And of course on June 20, 1947, "Bugsy" was hit, while sitting in the living room of Virginia's Beverly Hills house with her brother Allen Smiley. The first bullet shot through the window not only killed him, but sent his right eye skittering along the tiled floor where it was later found.

Twenty minutes after the gunfire in California, three men marched into the Flamingo lobby in Vegas. They were "Little Moe" Sedway, Gus Greenbaum, head of gambling operations in Tucson, and Morris Rosen, a Lansky torpedo. They advised the staff that they were taking over in a management change. Nobody disputed them. In the first year of Greenbaum's regime, the profit was four million.

This was just the first inkling of enormous incomes. In 1976 total revenue for Vegas gaming rooms, restaurants and bars totaled 1 billion, 800 million dollars, an increase of 34 percent over the previous year. Clubs with more than 20 million in gaming revenues per year reported net operating income as 8 percent. If this is what they reported and admitted to the Nevada Gambling Control Board, think of the figures if any more exacting and realistic audit were made of the dollars left behind in the desert during those 11 million visits a year.

So Benjamin Siegel's evaluation of the potential of the Strip was, if anything, understated. The "Bugsy" legends, some apocryphal, some true, remain a part of the mystique of the town, with his name being dropped often in the tourist traps as the newcomers pass on through. But few of them are aware of a beautiful rose garden flourishing today in an obscure corner of the old Flamingo's grounds. The flowers have been thriving spectacularly for 40 years, and rumor has it that the secret stimulus comes from the earth, fortified by the remains of enemies "Bugsy" buried there under his favored and personally tended rose bushes.

His own murder was never solved. At least no one was ever convicted. And years later, when someone broke into Gus Greenbaum's house in Arizona and cut his and his wife's throat with a butcher knife, that perpetrator also escaped detection. But Meyer Lansky lived a full life until the age of 82, and amassed a personal fortune of 300 million dollars before cancer finally hit him.

For entertainers, the code of Las Vegas when the mob took over in 1946 duplicated the one that existed in the Cotton Club days in Harlem, when the same sort of characters ruled over Prohibition night life. No blacks were accepted as guests in the Strip's hotels. No blacks were allowed to enter a casino or gamble in even the shoddiest joints downtown. The 3,000 full-time local black residents could only get an apartment in the ghetto called "Westside," and black stars, in those days including Pearl Bailey, Billy Eckstine, the Delta Rhythm Boys, Harold Nicholas and Hazel Scott, were not welcome in the hotels where they were featured, but were set up in housing for black entertainers in Westside.

In 1946 and 1947, the infant Vegas booked only a trickle of black performers. Pearl Bailey, who was the third black to play the Flamingo after Lena Horne and Arthur Lee Simpkins, was living proof that Las Vegas's strictly segregated practices had only been revived in 1946 when the gangsters took over the town, and all policies that suited their goals became the law.

Pearl and some other black friends had entertained troops in 1941 at posts in the area, and she fondly remembers a nice day they spent in the then modest-sized downtown Vegas, going from one small casino to another, playing the slots, eating and drinking in restaurants, attending an unsegregated movie house, and in general being made to feel welcome. That had all changed by the time she was a Flamingo headliner in 1947.

Pearl even had her own "Bugsy" Siegel story from that first engagement, and it wasn't all that uncomplimentary.

"I always set up in my dressing room the night before I open. If I have to wait until three or four in the morning to do it, it makes it not seem too new to me the next day. (And for the last six years I've rehearsed with the band the day before for the same reason.) So as usual I put a table cloth on the dressing table to make it a bit nicer

"Having set everything just right, I came in the next night ready for action. And wow! It looked like a magician had been in and done a magic trick. I sent for the backstage manager and asked the reason for it. He said, 'We had to take the table cloth as Mr. Siegel wants everything accounted for.' I asked for another, got it, and bless my soul, the next night the same thing happened. They removed it again. Holy mackerel! Was this to go on for three weeks? I sent again for the backstage man and once again he gave me the bit about Mr. Siegel. So I asked if I could talk to Mr. S. When I came off after the show, a young dapper and handsome man was standing by the dressing room door. Not expecting any visitor, I nodded and started into the room. But he spoke to me. 'Did you want to see me? I'm Mr. Siegel.'

"'Ah, yes, you can help me, sir.' I went into a big explanation of what I wanted—a simple table cloth. Being a user of hands, I was by now tapping him on the shoulder and pointing a bony finger in his stomach, getting my point across. Whatever struck me, I'll never know, but I remember having read this man's name. 'Are you "Bugsy" Siegel?' Suddenly I knew it—this was one of the biggest men in the underworld. He replied, 'My friends call me Benjamin, my enemies call me "Bugsy."' Now you know I had no intention of being this boy's enemy. I thought it better to be friendly. He never moved, but asked, 'Is there anything else you'd like?'"

Pearl was flustered and nervous, and just to keep talking, blurted out that she'd had her eye on a red Buick Roadmaster in a car lot down the Strip. By the next show, table cloths were piled as high as her head in the dressing room. And in the morning, parked in front of the Westside house she was saying in was the pretty red auto. The word got to her to pay the downpayment before the singing engagement was finished.

The very first black star chosen to perform at the Flamingo was Lena Horne. This sympatico, introspective human being tells as much about herself as Las Vegas when she writes:

"Las Vegas came to be a symbol of a great deal I hated in this business. It *was* and *is* where the big money is for a cabaret entertainer . . . the lure is only money, and I'm not being a snob about it, but I have not always found that when you have money you have everything. And besides, it's still a prejudiced town.

"Now a lot of good performers may think all this and they still go back. One of them said to me just recently, 'What the hell—take your money and run.' But the thing that galled me was that Vegas was the only big money channel open to Negroes. TV was closed to us, movies were closed to us, Broadway was mostly closed to us. The only place we could get the big cash was Vegas!

"That was hardly Las Vegas's fault. I know. But I had to resent it. And the resentment grew and grew until I stopped going there. In the end, it was just a personal thing. I welcomed the opportunity to go and work in physically bad, acoustically poor rooms for less money, rather than go there. Maybe it was stupid. But in those rooms, if I made it I could find me again. At least sometimes I could.

"The trouble was that throughout the decade I found it harder and harder to take pride and pleasure in my new work. I could not go forward to new kinds of expression in new media. Neither could I justify what I was doing as something that was, in my off hours, enabling me to purchase a stable, restful or luxurious home life. Quite the opposite. The harder I worked, the less chance I had to be with my husband, my children, my friends. Gradually without my being aware of it, a kind of despair began to creep over me. It would not manifest itself in a really terrible way until the late 1950's. But I know that its beginnings were in the first years of extensive cabaret touring."

Dignified, intelligent Lena does not make this unsettling incident public, but Sammy Davis, Jr., who admires her so much, wonders bitterly, "I imagine it was frustrating for Lena when her daughter went into the pool at the Sands and they drained it."

But even Lena does tell a "Bugsy" story—what else—and it derives from that first, racially pioneering engagement.

"I was playing the Flamingo, sharing the bill with a very famous Latin band. The leader was a jerk—very snide when he introduced me, and not rehearsing and not disciplining the band at all. I took it for a couple of days and then called Lennie in California to ask him what to do. I was furious and ready to walk out on the whole thing."

Her husband, band leader and arranger Lennie Hayton, knew that business at the Flamingo had been fantastic and that the owners might want to just leave well enough alone, but he called the manager anyway and got a noncommittal response.

"But then another voice came on the phone and said, 'Don't think any more about it, Mr. Hayton. I didn't know she was having any trouble, but she will not have any further trouble.' Lennie didn't recognize the voice so he said, 'Who's this?' 'This is Mr. Siegel.'

"Well, apparently Mr. Siegel sent a couple of his boys around to see the band leader and give him a little lecture. At the next show, he did not introduce me. One of the men in the band did, and it was a beautiful announcement. After that, the leader made very proper announcements, and I noticed that he and his band, who had been hanging around the club between shows and afterward to gamble, were suddenly in a big hurry to pack up and get outside when they finished work. I thought it was pretty funny, watching them scurrying around being nicer than nice. And I thought there was a kind of rude justice."

In her recollections Miss Horne tactfully withheld the name of the band leader. Las Vegas publicity records indicate that it was Xavier Cugat.

Billy Eckstine, who seems to be well liked by everyone in the entertainment world, had continual problems with the Vegas racial codes of the late forties. He could never forget or forgive having to dress in a trailer behind the Desert Inn because the hotel dressing room was forbidden to him, Dinah Washington, the Mills Brothers and other black headliners at this hotel, which was the last one to give up segregation tactics.

Finally, one day he was pushed too far and rebelliously entered the off-limits casino with a couple of white friends. The pit boss of the station and some guards converged on him, and in a rage he tossed one of them through a plate glass door. All of Vegas watched expectantly for the retaliation against Eckstine to set an example, but on the surface, none came, other than not booking him back at the Desert Inn again. One theory existed that "the boys" found his fearless, macho move admirable under the code that they understood, and decided to forgive him as long as he pulled in business. Another theory was that the loss of revenue that might follow a violent reprisal against a name performer made it not worth while. Some observers felt that they paid him back in subtler ways that caused his earning power and reputation to nose-dive in the mid-fifties.

During the same, early, bitter period of the late forties, the gentlemanly Nat "King" Cole was muscled out of the lobby of the hotel at which he was starring, when he committed the great sin of attempting to place a call at a public phone.

The first manifestation of organized protest to all this came about because of the determination of Josephine Baker. She started with the casinos and clubs, but for the long haul her aspirations went beyond the Strip to the rest of the city.

"Gaining admission to night clubs is not so important. Important, are job opportunities. You go into any of the downtown Las Vegas stores and you won't see any colored sales ladies. Why is that? The NAACP should go down and try to get qualified Negroes into this work. Maid work is honorable, but why just maid work for them? We should try to get professional people here. There are no Negro lawyers or doctors in Vegas. There is a lot to be done, and it must be done in a good way by using the head. It is most important that these things be done peacefully. Above all, it is important to be right and above criticism."

So in the fine print of her contract with the Last Frontier Hotel, she insisted on a clause that said she would not perform for segregated audiences. It also stipulated that a table for six would be reserved for her needs for every show, and she asked the Las Vegas branch of the NAACP to have six people ready as guests to fill it each night. On opening night, the six were ushered in without a problem. But from then on all blacks were turned away. She screamed at management, who countered by stating that the admittance of the blacks the first night fulfilled their obligation to her to perform before an integrated audience. She brought out the fine print clause that said she "will perform for no segregated audiences."

Her next tactic was to prove that blacks were being turned away when her table and others were still available. This was done again with the help of the NAACP. They would have a reservation for six in the name of a white person who would arrive early and hold the table. Then a mixed racial group of five would arrive to join him. When they were turned away by being flatly told that the captain had misunderstood the pronunciation of the name of the early arrival, and that no reservation had been made under that name, Josephine would have her evidence of discrimination. She would then enter through the lobby door, personally ushering the same group to her table successfully. This charade had to be repeated each night to insure the integrated audience she had sworn to have. Her spokesman issued this statement to the press:

"Miss Baker's purpose is to let people get used to seeing Negroes in places. When people see that Negroes know how to act and hotel officials find that their customers are not going to walk out, there'll be no need for such discrimination."

To fully understand what Josephine was driving at and to get a feel for just how depressed entertainers must have been under 1947 Vegas conditions, we have to listen to the man who is considered by most critics to be the most talented black entertainer since Bill Robinson. Sammy Davis, Jr., has played Las Vegas more times than any of the others, but he wrote about one particular evening in November of 1954 that changed his life. This night had such an impact on him first, because after all the humiliation he had experienced during the segregated period, his present "gig" coincided with the lifting of most of the barriers, and second, because he was about to leave for the automobile trip to Los Angeles that led to the horrible accident in which he lost an eye.

Sammy had just finished his last show at the New Frontier and was still flushed with the gratification of having been good and having been appreciated.

"As I stepped out the stage door, the glow from the casino was lighting up the desert, and as the doors swung open and people came out, the sound of money, laughs and music poured past them as if there was just too much hilarity inside to stay bottled up. It was out of my way, but I felt like walking through there for the sheer joy of knowing I could.

"The deputy sheriff standing just inside gave me a big 'Hi ya Sam.' I waved and kept moving through all the action, past a wall of slot machines, the dice tables, blackjack. . . . 'Hi ya Sammy'. . . . 'Swinging show Sammy'. . . . 'Here, make room for Sammy.'

"'Thanks, not tonight, gotta run to L.A., catch ya' tomorrow.'

"I loved the way the crowds opened up for me and I circled the room twice getting loaded on the atmosphere they'd kept us away from the other times we'd played Vegas, when there'd been a law against me. When it had been 'Sorry Sam, but you're not allowed in the casino—you understand.' But now we didn't have to understand and the joy of it swept through me every time I walked through that door."

Despite the casino segregation in the past, the Frontier had treated him differently from other black headliners in giving Sam and his entourage accommodations in the hotel itself, and he probably was allowed the first black patrons ever out front during a show, when they saved a table for his own family one opening night. But it was frustrating after the last show. He felt like a conquering hero trapped in the security of his own fortress, since his suite was the only place on the Strip where he would be allowed to party and unwind. This star just couldn't get into other hotels to see other acts, and this led to the all night "wingdings" in his apartment, for which he was often criticized.

The ban by other lounges was put to the test after one triumphant opening night. A new white assistant just couldn't believe that Sammy would not be welcome anywhere in Vegas, and in front of the jubilant dressing room crowd of well wishers, he made a very public telephone call to attempt to get a table in Sammy Davis's name at the Desert Inn Lounge. The look on his face as he got the "put down," turned the party into a wake. So Sam called up for a case of champagne, invited the entire line of white chorus girls up, and another potential orgy was about to commence.

Sammy's father and his uncle, Will Mastin, were getting increasingly unhappy with these brawls and the crowd that was surrounding their star partner, especially when Afro-American papers started joining the white tabloids in providing spicy copy about Sam. One night, Dad pushed him into a bedroom, locked the door and took a clipping from a black San Francisco paper out of his pocket. The headline read, "Is Sammy ashamed he's a Negro?"

"Sammy Davis, Jr., who recently sparkled like a 14-carat gold star on the stage at the Fairmont (a hotel in San Francisco) was a rare pleasure to us as a reviewer and a pride to us as a Negro, but unfortunately persistent reports of his off-stage performances leave much to be desired. During his stay in San Francisco, he never once came by the neighborhood where he stayed in days before he was able to make the move to the less dark, more glittery side of town. Clearly, Mr. Davis is doing nothing to discourage rumors that success has erased his memory for friends who knew him 'when.' His all-night, all-white, orgy-style parties are the talk of Las Vegas, where he is currently appearing. We are sorry to be the ones to remind Mr. Davis of his obligations to the Negro community, but even sorrier for the necessity to do so."

His father added coals to the fire already blazing, with his own remarks, until Sammy exploded, reminding Dad that all his black San Francisco friends had been with him at the Fairmont. When Sam Sr. pointed an accusing finger in the direction of the crowd that was in the living room right then, Sammy Jr. agonized:

"Dad! Where in the goddamned hell am I going to find colored people in Vegas? Ya want me to invite Mrs. Cartwright? Should I go over to Westside and find cats I don't know and invite 'em to a party just to dress up the room? Or maybe you'd like me to send a plane into L.A. for buddies, so the paper'll be happy."

But it was inevitable that other blacks would jump on performers like Sammy and Lena who so detested racial segregation that their instinctive response was to integrate their own lives. As a result they constantly were attacked from both sides.

In Sammy's case there was such a choreographed assault on him in the black press that even when playing clubs with no discrimination at the door, black patrons started to stay away. Finally he tried to meet the problem head on by arranging an appointment with the owner of *Jet* magazine.

"Mr. Johnson, why are you turning my people against me?"

The faint smile disappeared, "We're not trying to turn anyone—"

"I didn't say 'trying.' If I thought it was deliberate, I wouldn't be here. But you're *doing* it. Not so much *Ebony*, but your guys on *Jet* have been bum-rapping me with little zingies in nearly every issue. I've been convicted of taking turn-white pills, but I was never invited to the trial. Between your magazine and the papers like the *Defender* and the *Courier*—all of them—you've been holding America's first all-colored lynching. Now what I want to know is why?"

"Mr. Davis, you are the one who makes the news. All we do is print it. When you don't like what you see published about yourself, please try to remember that it's only a reflection of the image which you have created."

"Well, there's been a little distortion folks, a little crack in the mirror."

He laughed unpleasantly, "Can you seriously be telling me that you haven't gone out of your way to indicate a complete disavowal of racial ties, to disassociate yourself in every conceivable—"

"Mr. Johnson, I didn't come up here to do two choruses of nobody understands me! You've been printing your point of view. All I ask is that you listen to mine . . . a few weeks ago a Broadway column ran an item saying I turned down $25,000 a week in Miami Beach because I refused to live in the colored section of Miami. Now the fact is I *won't* live there. But that's not why I turned it down. We were offered our own suites in the hotel that was trying to book us. We turned it down because my father, my uncle and I have one firm rule—we don't play where they won't open their doors to colored people. The columnist obviously didn't know about the suites, so the item came out sounding like I hate colored people so much that even for $25,000 a week I won't live with them."

"Mr. Davis . . . How do you, a prominent Negro, justify the use of a white man when you know how scarce good jobs are for Negroes?"

"Mr. Johnson, Morty Stevens is one of two white men out of seven people who travel with me. He's the best man I know of for the job. He's arranged three hit songs for me. . . . Should I be prejudiced and do exactly what we hate when people do it to us?"

"You bought a house in a restricted area of Los Angeles."

"Right, I've got one of the best houses in Hollywood—and incidentally, the neighborhood's not restricted any more. I'm a liberal and I decided it would be wrong of me to boycott one of the best neighborhoods just because the people who live there are white. I'm taking extra glory in the fact that I'm a Negro and I beat the odds. . . . I made them the hard way. I'm not so damned thrilled over the unnecessary problems I've had because I'm a Negro, that I had to work harder because I'm a Negro, and that I had to be better at what I do than if I were white. Sure, I've suffered because I'm a Negro, just like you've suffered and a lot of us have, but I have never for one breath of my life been ashamed that I'm a Negro."

Gordon Parks, the Renaissance man, was in the midst of filming *The Learning Tree*, serving as producer, director, screenwriter, adapter of his own book, and composer of the background score, when he had his first puzzling confrontation with the same inscrutable Mr. Johnson.

"What a joy it was to watch day by day *The Learning Tree* unfold right before our eyes. By this time the entire crew was caught up in the drama, it was as much their film as it was mine. To a great extent, each of them had been picked with great care. For the first time blacks were working beside whites behind the camera, for the first time a black man was in charge as director. Much was at stake, and we knew we were adding a new chapter to the annals of the American Film Industry. The white crew members made great efforts to teach the black crew members as much as they possibly could. It was indeed a beautiful thing to experience. Although my book and my life was being filmed, as far as I was concerned *The Learning Tree* belonged to all these black technicians who, like me, had aspired so long to work behind a Hollywood camera.

"Yet, despite the general state of happiness surrounding us, Vincent Tubbs, our public relations chief, seemed terribly upset about something. One morning I asked him what was wrong.

"Frowning, he answered, 'For the life of me I can't figure out why *Ebony, Jet*, or any of Johnny Johnson's publications haven't been out here.'

"'Were they invited?'"

"'Of course, just like everyone else.'"

"I urged him not to worry about it. We were getting wide coverage from the media and *Life* magazine had commissioned my son, Gordon Jr., to photograph everything happening on location. But Tubbs couldn't stop worrying. He put a call through to *Ebony*'s managing editor in Chicago. After dinner one night he played me a tape of the conversation which went something like this."

"'Hey, aren't you guys coming out?'"

"'Nope, sorry Vinnie.'"

"'Why?'"

"'Johnny's orders. The staff held a couple of meetings about it, but he won't budge.'

"'What's his trouble, man? This is the first time in history that a black man is directing for a major Hollywood studio. Even if he hates the guy, it's his obligation as the owner of a responsible black journal to report the event.'

"'You're right. We argued that point with him, but his order stands. And anybody who goes against it is going to be fired.'

"'Has he got something against Parks?'

"'He denies that. In fact he says he's quite fond of him. We're as puzzled as you are. All of us wish we could be there. It's a hell of a good story.'"

Johnson's strange attitude toward Parks and his film has never been properly explained to this day, and somehow he and Parks remained good friends after the incident.

Sammy Davis, Jr., wasn't alone in his frustration over his own race's misunderstanding of his desire for an integrated lifestyle that included integrated friendships and relationships. Harry Belafonte was also the recipient of an onslaught of abuse from blacks, and Las Vegas played a pivotal role in this confusing phase of his life. Like all the other performers of his generation, he had gone through the standard, but never forgivable, early humiliation of having come to Vegas flushed with success in New York singing at clubs like Birdland, the Village Vanguard and Cafe Society, only to get second billing at the Thunderbird on the Strip. He was put through all the horrors of being lodged at a grimy black rooming house, unable to use the Thunderbird's pool, gym, casino or restaurants, and confined to an "isolation booth" next to his small dressing room where he was forced to eat his meals and entertain his visitors.

But three years later when he had become a bona fide cabaret, recording and film star, he was top-billed at the Riviera Hotel, lodged in a lavish in-house suite, treated with dignity, and flattered by the manner in which life-sized posters of his torso were being pilfered from the lobby by white female guests as fast as they were replaced. Still, there were a few other major problems in his life.

His wife Marguerite and his children were there with him, but Marguerite's presence was merely to provide her with the six weeks of resident status to fulfill the terms of a Nevada divorce, and Julie, the woman he had left Marguerite for, was two months pregnant in L.A., awaiting the signal that the divorce was final so that Belafonte could remarry.

Marguerite was black, very cultured, highly educated and the darling of all their joint friends. Harry himself had looked up to her throughout their marriage, as she helped support him with her own career while he struggled to catch on in show business. He had been insecure, she had been strong and controlled, and their marriage had followed more of a mother-son relationship than a union of lovers. In Julie, Harry had found his passionate romance. For the weeks between the Las Vegas divorce and his new marriage, Harry had kept the wedding secret, ostensibly to protect his children, but probably more to camouflage the timing of the new pregnancy. Close friends were so in the dark that two of his buddies, Adam Clayton Powell, Jr., and jazzman Illinois Jacquet came to Vegas to urge him, throughout a long night, to reconcile with Marguerite. Neither of them knew that there was already a brand new Mrs. Belafonte.

When it heard the news, the black press and most of the black community dumped on Harry. The fact that Julie was the only white member of the Katherine Dunham Dance Troupe, and had shared with them all the indignities and prejudices of blacks touring in the South and abroad, meant nothing. She may have looked dusky and Indian, but she was white and Jewish, and the *Amsterdam News* was up in arms.

"Many Negroes are wondering why a man who has waved the flag of justice for his race should turn from a Negro wife to a white wife." Accompanying photos established the point of Belafonte's racial pride a shot of him with a piece of African sculpture, another holding a copy of Langston Hughes's *Pictorial History of the Negro in America*. But then they turned bitchy and undercut this praise by dredging up an old saying that was once applied to heavyweight boxing champ Jack Johnson:

"Give a Negro man fame and fortune, and he's got to have a

white woman, a Packard and a bulldog." The article ended with "Harry Belafonte's popularity with his own race is hanging in the balance at the moment."

The singer insisted on making a statement in *Ebony* magazine. "I believe in integration and work for it with all my heart and soul. But I did not marry Julie to further the cause of integration. I married her because I was in love with her and she married me because she was in love with me."

Julie was quoted in the same article. "I just fell in love that's all. Sure we talked about the problems, especially about children, but for me it was easy. The years I spent as the only white dancer in Katherine Dunham's Company gave me an insight into Negro culture and I am proud to be a part of it."

Still many prominent blacks criticized Harry. Not so Louis Armstrong, who commented sincerely, "White men marry Negro women and we don't squawk, why should anyone get hot when it happens the other way around?"

This pattern of notoriety was to baffle and confuse Harry always. Neither money nor celebrity could soften the shock of the contrast between adulation on stage and criticism and backbiting off stage. And whether the applause or the brickbat was being dispensed by blacks or whites didn't alter the effect.

On this particular issue of his homelife, it should be noted that at this writing over three decades later, the Belafontes are still married.

The irony of being unable to satisfy the black press no matter how much of an effort was made, and yet being constantly bolstered by white show business friends, was not lost on Sammy Davis, Jr., a man who never forgets a kindness. He speaks of an emotional debt to Mickey Rooney who invited him to make a tour of RKO theaters with him in 1945 when they had both just come out of the army, and who made sure Sammy and Dad and Uncle Will stayed at the same hotels he did. Mickey also touted him to nightclub owners and saw to it that he got decent work. One night Sammy was with Mickey at the Flamingo at a time when the casino was still restricted. Rooney wanted to play blackjack and asked Sam to stand behind him at the table and just kibbitz. A Texan sitting opposite, loudly made it known that he wouldn't play at a table with "niggers" around. The tiny

Rooney jumped up onto the table to gain enough height to start choking the bigot, and after they were separated, he made the pit boss apologize to Sammy.

Davis's most supportive friend has always been Frank Sinatra, who affectionately calls him "Smokey" because of his chain habit with cigarettes. Frank not only cast him in the first integrated "buddy" movie, *Oceans Eleven*, filmed at the Sands in Vegas, but he insisted that Sammy get top billing at the hotel over Dean Martin, Joey Bishop and Frank himself during their famous all-star club act that played there evenings, while during the day they shot the film. Unsolicited, Frank, as the producer of the movie, gave Davis a higher salary than he had ever gotten before in Hollywood. Both the cabaret act and the flick exhibited the special chemistry all these performers had together personally and professionally.

Sinatra's track record in his defense of racial equality has always been above reproach. During that same Sands hotel engagement, word had gotten back to Sammy that certain security guards were turning away black casino patrons, and one day when he and Frank were sitting in the lounge having a drink, they both saw an incident where two well-dressed and well-behaved black couples were being escorted out. Sinatra flew into a rage, called top management to the scene, and invited both couples to stay at the hotel as his guests. Frank was a vice-president of the Sands in this period and strict enforcement of a non-segregated policy was insured from then on at the hotel.

Although mob control of Las Vegas is not as obvious as it was in 1946, it nevertheless is a deeply rooted condition of the functioning of the city. So there is no way that the progress of racial integration can be a major concern in that town, except with the performers. Management is still at the other end of the spectrum from the compassionate liberals like Barney, Max and Hammond, and it must be kept in mind that their prime interest is in the making of enormous profits and the maintaining of strict control of the system.

But good things do still happen today, and all the progress in the last 40 years in Vegas should be cherished. On Saturday night March 20, 1987, at the Bally Hotel, Sammy Davis, Jr., had just scored one of the greatest triumphs of his career. At the age of 61, when most singers have lost the power, reserve and control of their voice, he had sounded even better than during any of the previous decades, as his energy and artistry syncopated him through a new arrangement of "Any Place I Hang My Hat Is Home."

The crowd was magnetized, and the Bally owners beamed because he had fulfilled the quintessential service of any Las Vegas star—the house casinos were reporting record-breaking figures of the amount of money in play at the tables during his engagement. True, he was sharing the stage with Jerry Lewis, but it had been plain from the audience responses whom they had come to see and who was providing the special draw.

After the late show, up in his suite with a small quiet party of family and friends—still "up" from the joy of the special give and take with his audience—his performance continued as he personally and lovingly cooked a light meal for people whose company he enjoyed. A newly reissued and reengineered record of some of Sinatra's finest 78's from the 1940's played with exquisite fidelity on his sound system. Periodically Sammy shushed all conversation to a standstill, and with the intensity and awe of a knowledgeable groupie, urged his guests to share in the subtleties and nuances of his buddy's approach to the lyric. And when the fantastic breath control allowed for an effortless and soaring sustaining of a note, his eyes closed, his body swayed and he "quelled" with the pride and appreciation of a Jewish mother.

This complex professional, still taut and tingling from the great reception to his own performance, was celebrating his personal hero to help himself unwind. Later he took a guest by the arm out onto a terrace, chill with the pre-dawn Nevada air, and pointed out where the perimeters of the sandy desert had been in 1947, and far off across the lights to where they had now receded. This was a man whose pride told him to keep remembering how much he had contributed to this town's growth, and how the purity of his talent had made it easier for other blacks right here on the Strip, and all the way over to Westside. There was also the knowledge of how his effect on white audiences had made them return to their own home towns with a more understanding and sympathetic approach to the concerns of their black neighbors.

He probably never expressed it better than in this quote from memories of his bigotry-filled stint as a soldier in the U.S. Army, when opportunities to perform in camp shows sometimes came his way.

"I lived 24 hours a day for that hour or two at night when I could give it away free, when I could stand on that stage, facing the audience, knowing that I was dancing down the barriers between us."

And a few years after the war when other performers like Sinatra and Jack Benny and Danny Kaye started telling people in Australia and Europe, "Wait 'till Sammy Davis gets here—you'll really see something," and all the major overseas concert halls and theaters rushed to book him, "My goal was to knock down every fucking wall I could, because there is no place for those barriers in this world."

Sammy Davis, Jr., is a very complex man and to prove that the best of us are never completely satisfied, and that there is always a dichotomy of the human heart, he expresses pleasure with the progress of integration on the one hand, but can't avoid a post-script of sadness as he says today, "We lost something very valuable to us [when integration succeeded]. We lost linkage with each other. There were only three or four major black performers in Vegas in 1945 when I first came here. All the rest of us played in little joints downtown. But everyone lived in one section—it was segregated but boy did we communicate together, and we hung out together. We made our own fun. You know, I was angry about the fact that we couldn't stay on here at the hotel, but when I was playing the Flamingo with Mickey Rooney and Frances Langford, I'd go back to Westside to the little black clubs like El Morocco and the Cotton Club and there would be guys there like Billy Eckstine and Paul White and Elroy Peace, who was with Ted Lewis, and this was our own and we controlled it.

"As things progressed and got better on the social scale and economically, we lost that. Integration took away something of value and didn't replace it with anything from the black culture—it's what Robert Ruark said in his book—you're fighting for this and striving for that then you have to go back and say I want my roots! For example there are no black barber shops anymore—to sit around and talk—and I miss that."

CHAPTER VII

Blacks in Radio and TV

Radio was an infant in the early 1920's. People were becoming fascinated with this new science-fiction device whose operational theory was too complicated for them to fathom. "How does it happen?" "How does the sound travel to us?" They marveled at it as they fiddled with their own home-assembled crystal sets, trying to make connection with a voice or a musical instrument. A joyful shout of "Eureka!" might be heard when the circuit was successful, and the magic finally reached their ears from the ozone.

Just as motion pictures presented blacks as stereotypes for its first two decades, radio did the same early on. And just as films presented its black characters in the beginning by using white actors in black face, radio took it one step further, asking the white actors to attempt a black dialect.

It was impossible for blacks to get a foothold in this new industry, and the situation was to repeat later at the inception of television. Sammy Davis, Jr., puts it best: "We couldn't do it ourselves because we were outside the system. It's always someone in the system that has to say 'Let's open it, let's let them in.'"

The first black entertainers to be heard on radio without white "stand-ins," or more aptly "sound-ins," were the great jazz musicians. When everything else in showbiz collapsed during the Great Depression, jazz flourished because it was the perfect escape from the fears and concerns of hard times. Up-beat rhythms and dancing with abandon were an antidote for feeling mighty low. And radio jumped in on the craze.

Every major nightclub and hotel had a network "remote line" through which local or national audiences could listen to the Big Bands they were featuring, and even smaller joints were tied in if they had booked groups that had a special sound that would attract jazz devotees. In this manner Duke Ellington, Fletcher Henderson, Louis Armstrong, Cab Calloway, Count Basie and Jimmy Lunceford developed cross-country followings of fans long before they arrived in person to play a town on theater or ballroom tours.

The Mills Brothers' harmonizing at a club were picked up as early as 1925, but it would be a full ten years before they would be heard on guest shots on the Friday night Elgin Hour. At one point Calloway was on the air three times a week, because all three networks had the Cotton Club "wired" for a scheduled broadcast on different nights.

Actually Cab became the first black to have his own nationally heard and sponsored network show in 1936, presented by the Shell Oil Company at nine P.M. each Saturday night. In general, big business felt it was a bad investment to sponsor black entertainers, but Cab had become the type of cult figure comparable to what happened later with Elvis Presley and the Beatles, and Shell couldn't pass up his commercial possibilities. Starring in a "hidden" medium was particularly bizarre for Calloway, because if ever there was a visual performer, he was it. Cab was a whirlwind, and his strengths were his mobile face, outrageous suits, flying hair and wild, agile, unpredictable moves, as he half-flew, half-danced all over the stage while leading his musically excellent band. His rich tenor voice was well trained and well controlled, and the material that he sang was unique and tailored to his extroverted personality, especially when he threw in some scat choruses. But he really had to be seen for full effect, and it is ironic that he became such a radio star after many years of well-received club and stage antics.

Calloway's rise before this 1936 breakthrough had been explosive. He had arrived in New York from Baltimore via Chicago with a band he was leading called "The Missourians," to sub for

Duke Ellington at the Cotton Club in 1930, when Duke went to Hollywood as the first black orchestra to appear in a major feature film.

Very rapidly "The Missourians" title became "The Cab Calloway Orchestra," which started to split the year with Duke at the Cotton Club because flamboyant Cab was just what its lavish shows needed. Besides his personal magnetism and his "Hi-De-Ho" scatting, he always hired the most musically disciplined sidemen for his orchestras. Through the years, the caliber in evidence included Ben Webster, Milt Hinton, Benny Payne, Benny Carter, Don Redmond, Illinois Jacquet, Doc Cheatham, Cozy Cole, Dizzy Gillespie, Jonah Jones and Chu Berry. Cab himself, admittedly, was a journeyman drummer and sax player. In fact, one of the conditions set by Chu Berry before he would leave Erskine Hawkins and join Cab's band was that Calloway would never play his sax during a performance—and Cab gave in.

The country finally got a chance to see, not just hear, the band when Al Jolson insisted that they be cast in his musical movie *The Singing Kid*. Film audiences had never before been exposed to anything like Cab's "jivin'" and he became an instant favorite. Walter Winchell, who could make or break performers, hired him as a guest on his "Lucky Strike Radio Show" and, very soon after, Rudy Vallee featured him on the Fleischmann Hour. Shell Oil analyzed audience response to his guest shots, and decided to take a chance and give him his own show. This perfectionist came through for them, even on radio.

Calloway has always been the consummate professional, whether very early in his career when he joined Louis Armstrong in "Connie's Hot Chocolates," or in the movie phase in the 1940's that included *Stormy Weather*, or during the Broadway period that saw him play Sportin' Life in a revival of *Porgy and Bess*, and co-star with Pearl Bailey in the black version of *Hello, Dolly*—and even up to the present, when on New Year's Eve 1986-87, the octagenarian drove a New Year "Limelight" disco crowd of yuppies wild showing them what real swing and real charisma are all about.

For most of his life Cab played down any discussions of racial discrimination. In an interview in the New York *Sunday News* on

January 28, 1968, he was quoted as saying that in all his decades of show business life, he couldn't recall a single instance of bias. "Being a Negro hasn't made the slightest difference in my career. I believe the Negro has been given a fair shake in show business all the way down the line. Look at Bill Robinson, Fats Waller, Ada Brown and Sidney Poitier. There's always been integration from the time I started in the entertainment world." Again, in 1972, he told the New York *Post*, "I never felt discriminated against. I've never been in any marches or demonstrations. I prefer to make my contributions silently. I contribute to NAACP, Red Cross and the Urban League."

Why he preferred to take this stance may be attributed to his personality, that of an on-stage extrovert and an off-stage introvert and loner. But in 1976 he wrote a very frank autobiography with the help of his son-in-law Bryant Rollins, and this time he discussed his exposure to bigotry. He talks about a pioneering trip in 1932 as the first Negro Big Band to tour the south, a type of gig that black performers gave the code label T.O.B.A., "tough-on-black-asses." Here's Cab on the subject of that circuit:

"This may seem strange; after all, jazz originated in the south. But it was always played there by the small combos hidden away in whorehouses and speakeasies, or on the riverboats. This was to be a big public tour with all the publicity and fanfare. They couldn't get us into some of the concert halls, the south wasn't ready for that. After all, we had just broken through the color barrier in the white theater circuit around New York City. . . . We played in all kinds of places. In Durham, North Carolina, we played in a tobacco warehouse that was as big as Madison Square Garden, and they put a rope down the middle of the warehouse, and the whites danced on one side and the Negroes on the other. In Atlanta and a couple of other places they had a white dance first, and all the Negroes sat upstairs in the balcony and waited. Then they had a Negro dance, and all the whites sat upstairs in the balcony and waited."

On one stop in Virginia Beach, he and his pianist Benny Payne had gone ahead in a car, and they got word that the bus carrying the rest of the band had broken down. After the M.C. announced the band would be an hour late, the all-white crowd started drinking heavily and getting restless and ugly. To stall for time, "Benny and I went out there and started singing show tunes and pop tunes like, "Ain't Misbehavin'" and "St. James Infirmary." People were hollering and stomping, and somebody shouted, 'Let's take this nigger out and lynch him.' All this was going on while I was trying to sing, and I could see Benny sweating, and I was sweating like hell too. I was just waiting for somebody to jump up on the stage and start something. Around 9:15, the band got there. Jesus, was I relieved . . . we weren't used to that kind of treatment. In the Cotton Club we were the cream of the crop, and we were used to being celebrities . . . now all of a sudden we were forced into small broken down buses and kept out of restrooms and restaurants. The hostile white audience was the last straw.

"The worst incident of the whole trip occurred in St. Petersburg, Florida. . . . We were playing to an all-white audience in a tobacco warehouse. As the evening went on, the crowd got louder and drunker, until at around one in the morning, some drunk threw a Coke bottle and it hit Leroy (Maxey, the drummer) square in the side of his head. When the bottle splintered it cut a huge slash in his head and he was bleeding like a stuck pig. We stopped playing. Some of the guys were pissed as hell, they wanted to make a ruckus, but with about 2000 whites in there, I figured it wasn't the time to take a stand, so I cooled everyone down. But Leroy was in bad shape. We took him to the back and the other guys were ready to call it quits. Leroy said, 'Hell no, we came here to play music and we're gonna finish. These folks are not going to run us out of this town with a Coke bottle, man.' We wrapped some bandages around Leroy's head and went back out and finished the dance."

And after one gig, where they were paid by cash in a sack: "It was Easter Sunday morning. Lord, I will never forget that morning. Here we are on the highway between Raleigh and Durham with all this money. Nobody's slept for a couple of days, and since we left Raleigh in such a hurry, nobody's eaten. And of course it's hard to find a place that will serve Negroes on an ordinary day, but on Easter Sunday morning, it was impossible. . . . Finally, we sent one of the white bus drivers into a hamburger joint and he brought back a sack of them. We stood on the side of the road, eating hamburgers and washing them down with Dr. Pepper. Then we got back in the buses and drove on to Durham—a bunch of guys each with two or three hundred dollars in his pocket, who couldn't buy anything to eat or drink because we were Negroes. We were not what you could call docile Negroes. We were tough guys who had played in the whorehouses and gambling houses, and it took something out of us to accept that kind of crap."

So when a European offer came, Cab grabbed it. English producers were always keeping their eyes open for anything new and different that was scoring with the American press and public, and they offered large amounts of money for this exotic act to do concerts. Blacks weren't asked to play for dances in London. The fans were captivated by the band, but a London newspaper critic wrote an article accompanied by two pictures, one of Cab and the other of a famous opera singer who wasn't drawing the crowds that Calloway was. The caption read, "What's the matter with the English people, that they will not go to hear this great opera voice, but they will pay money to hear this octaroon yell!"

In 1935 Cab and his first wife Betty tried to move into a house in a white section of White Plains, New York, and with all his status and fame it took a vigorous campaign of pressure by the Urban League for the neighborhood to accept him peacefully.

But the racial incident that most aroused his considerable temper, and his legendary, quick-reacting fists, took place in 1944.

"One time in the forties, I had my band in Kansas City playing a theater. Whenever I was in K.C. I would stay with a friend, Felix Payne, a Negro politician. Well, on this trip, Felix's son, Felix Jr., was home on vacation from Lincoln University in Jefferson, Missouri. I had run into my friend Lionel Hampton in the street one day, and he had invited me over to the Playmore Ballroom there in K.C. to hear his show. So Felix, Jr., and I went over one night. I walked up to the box office and bought two seats. But when I got to the turnstiles, the usher wouldn't let us in. This was an all-white audience. Well, I started to argue with the usher, next thing we were fighting. Came to find out, this guy was an off-duty cop. He pulled out his revolver and busted me in the head. Felix jumped in and the place was in pandemonium. I was bleeding like a stuck pig, so they took me to the hospital, bandaged my head, and then Felix and I wound up in jail. We were bailed out in a few hours. Felix, Sr., was quite a well-known politician, but the wire services carried this story and it made headlines all over the country. Felix and I sued the city and the ballroom, but it was one of those courtroom situations where the judge is looking out the window and an all-white jury is sitting up there knitting. It cost me personally about $15,000 in lawyers' fees, but nothing ever came of it. The point is that I wouldn't stand for that kind of treatment. Hamp was a friend of mine, and he had invited me to see his show, and there was no way that usher was going to keep me out of there without a fight."

Calloway's most famous radio exposure had come in 1941, when WOR aired him coast-to-coast in "Quizzicale," a satire of all the other quiz shows that were the rage of that period, like Kay Kyser's "Kollege of Musical Knowledge." On "Quizzicale," "experts" selected their question with a roll of dice, and their comical answers proved they were frauds. Cab played "The Doctor," leading his band, handing out cash prizes and kidding around with his stooges—mainly Brother Treadway, played by one of his sidemen, Eddie Barefield. In fact, all of the speaking stooges were from his band, including Milt Hinton. There was total disregard of the script, ad libbing was rampant and hilarious, and the dialogue purposely sounded as if it had been written by impostors trying to sound like Harlem hipsters. It was the very first all-black radio show, and even those who had maintained that this type of program would never be successful nationally, admitted it was a "natural" and had clicked. The public's reception of Calloway's frenetic use of musicians' jive talk led to the eventual incorporation of many of these "in-house" words into everyday white conversation. This was particularly so after 1944 when he wrote a *Jive Dictionary for Hipsters.*

Not everyone in the jazz world was happy with either Cab's "Quizzicale" put-on or the dictionary's attempt to commercialize on musicians' slang. They felt that this respected "pro" had exposed his own image, and those of blacks in general, to ridicule, because both the radio program and the book were not based on the honest spontaneity of good jazz, or musicians' natural "rappin'," but were pure affectation—white people learning to dabble in phraseology that had evolved spontaneously from jamming. Years later Dave Frishberg made the point with his brilliant send-up, "I'm Hip!"

The credits for early radio show writing never officially contained a black writer's name. Even programs like "Amos 'n' Andy" which portrayed black characters, was solely acted by whites and listed 10 white writers, Freeman Gosden, Charles Correll [Amos 'n' Andy], Bob Connely, Bill Moser, Bill Fischer, Bob Moss, Paul Franklin, Arthur Slauder, Harvey Helm, Shirley Illo, and one token black—Octavus Roy Cohen. So white performers were masquerading as blacks speaking dialogue that white writers hoped would catch the correct racial vernacular. And still, it was the most successful long-run comedy show in radio history, because despite the dialogue that was exaggerated for the milieu it portrayed, it had universal and pan-racial humor. Sometimes when its creators were stuck on a particular script they would import a black writer to fill in a situation or "doctor" a plot. Sammy Davis, Jr., a tremendous radio and "Amos 'n' Andy" fan as a youngster, has researched the subject:

"You couldn't get a black writer to sit down unless he had a black artist he was writing for. Most of 'Amos 'n' Andy' was written by white guys, and then black artists like Flournoy Miller of Miller and Lyles wrote stuff for Freeman Gosden and brought it in to him. Freeman would say, 'Oh, that's funny!' and Miller would say, 'Of course it's funny—we invented it—you guys are impersonating it, but we invented it!'"

A ridiculous situation arose when drama replaced jazz music as the radio staple, and black actors started auditioning for parts. For the first time the networks chose them for servant roles rather than use a white performer as a mimic, but only if the black sounded "Negro" enough on the air.

Actress Maidie Norman complained, "I had been told repeatedly that I don't sound like a Negro." And Johnny Lee agreed, "I had to learn to talk as white people believed Negroes talked." Even a few years later when "Wonderful" Smith was cast in a role on the Red Skelton show, he confessed, "I had difficulty sounding as 'Negro' as they expected." Smith played Red's chief comic antagonist, and reviewers hailed him as the "Negro comedy find of the year (1941)."

Jack Benny was one of the first from within the system to properly weave a black character into his radio family, and let a black actor play him. In the 1930's, Benny, along with Fred Allen and Edgar Bergen, was tremendously powerful and involved in the total control of his hugely successful show. He personally monitored every phase of the radio production, and was the overseer of the development of his cast of offbeat characters, who provided the familiarity and running-gag type of recognition that made listeners tune in religiously week after week. Fred Allen also used the neighbor format with the residents of "Allen's Alley," and Bergen had his roster of dummies friendly with Charlie McCarthy.

Jack was a liberal politically and socially, and had the backbone to insist on ethnic characters that might appeal to the first and second generation Americans who made up a high percentage of his listening audience. But he also was a hard-nosed, pragmatic businessman, and if a character did not work out commercially, he would see to it that it was dropped. The ratings of the show came first, his melting pot philosophies ran a definite second.

Benny loved the screwball neighbors he talked to on the program, like Mr. Kitzle. But he spent the greatest effort and thought on developing the part of his servant "Rochester," played by Eddie Anderson. At a time when all black movie servants were grinning, shuffling, obsequious characters, he showed courage in insisting that Rochester be an arrogant, sometimes abrasive and meddling, chauffeur-butler who would often infuriate Jack's "Boss" character, but who would prove himself to be actually a loyal, affectionate member of the family when the chips were down.

Benny even let Rochester have an emotionally full social and personal life, by writing in a girlfriend part—the maid of the neighbors next door. Eddie Anderson had been featured in many Hollywood movies already, but was best known for the raspy, squeaky radio voice that capitalized on entrance lines like "Coming Boss!" to Benny's shouts of "Rochester. Oh, Rochester." Anderson became a star on this radio show because Jack let him become one, and as he shaped the character, more and more program time was allotted to Rochester's antics, and the listeners loved it. Benny let him do jokes with him and also gave Anderson permission to say to the writers, "Can I change this? That's just not the way it should sound." And the writers often went along with it, because he was on target.

Jack so loved the Rochester image that he took Anderson along on projects in other media, giving him a juicy part in the movie *Buck Benny Rides Again*, and later on for his weekly TV show in the late 1950's. On radio, Rochester's arrogance might not have offended white listeners—to hear it is one thing—but again on TV Benny insisted on showing it in black and white. And he also gave Rochester an attractive, sexy TV girlfriend.

There were other instances of black film performers playing servants or workers on radio shows, but never with the latitude that Anderson had. Ruby Dandridge, of the Dandridge Sisters (but actually the mother of Dorothy and Vivian), played the maid "Geranium" on NBC's half-hour "Judy Canova Show" in 1945, and Willy Best had the role of a worker who bantered with Jimmy Gleason, the owner of a diner, on the "Jimmy Gleason Show" on ABC in 1946.

As early as 1939 Rex Ingram had played Mr. Fullerton, a neighbor in an NBC soap opera "Against the Storm," about a young woman refugee from central Europe, as she struggled to adjust to a new life in the U.S.

There were also some early musical shows that utilized blacks. *Show Boat* even had a radio life in 1932 as a pioneering variety program. In the cast were Hattie McDaniel and Jules Bledsoe, but even here a supposedly black comedy team of "Molasses 'n' January" was played by the white act of Pick and Pat who did a sort of Amos 'n' Andy routine. And from 1930 to 1949 the "Horn and Hardart Children's Hour" featured a small percentage of talented black youngsters on its shows. Billy Daniels and the Nicholas Brothers used it as a springboard for broader exposure. As announcers, this show had two very young men who went on to much greater fame. One was Paul Douglas, who became a stage and screen star with *Born Yesterday* on Broadway and *A Letter to Three Wives* in Hollywood, and the other was Ralph Edwards of TV's "This is Your Life." Billy Daniels also appeared on "The Little Betsy Ross Variety Hour," to which most of the better Horn and Hardart acts graduated.

CBS is the network that deserved plaudits for a concerted effort to employ blacks during the 1940's. "Beulah," a show about the misadventures of the colored maid of the Henderson family, ran on radio from 1945 to 1953 and then became the basis of a TV series. Through the years Beulah was played by, first, Hattie McDaniel, and later by Louise Beavers. Beulah's girl friend "Oriole" was interpreted by Ruby Dandridge, and so for a while the show employed all three Dandridge ladies after Dorothy and Vivian had smaller roles written in for them. In the later years of the series Butterfly McQueen took over as Oriole. Beulah also had a steady boyfriend who turned out to be Marlin Hart in some years and Ernest Whitman in others. So this long-running program provided work for many fine black talents.

Producers at CBS particularly admired Ruby Dandridge and Butterfly McQueen. Butterfly became a regular on the "Danny Kaye Variety Hour" in 1945, and Ruby also played Ella Rose, a funny lady on "Tonight at Hoagy's," which was a series that simulated an old-fashioned jam session at Hoagy Carmichael's house. She also appeared later as Belinda the housekeeper in the "Father of the Bride" series. The network seemed to be on a kick with piano men, because in 1943 they cast both Teddy Wilson and Herman Chittison in the roles of alternating Blue Note cafe pianists on the "Casey, Crime Photographer" crime drama serial.

But the most daring move CBS made was to take the basically white 1942 soap opera, "We Live and Learn" (in which Juano Hernandez played one of the few black characters) and turn it into an all-black soap called "The Story of Ruby Valentine" in the 1950's. They set the serial against a Harlem background, with the story centering about the experiences of a beauty parlor owner. Juanita Hall was cast as Miss Valentine and Earl Hyman (today Bill Cosby's TV father) and Ruby Dee were in support. Luther Henderson did the background music and many of the off-screen production jobs were handled by blacks.

Mahalia Jackson was another performer whom this network

tried to promote, but her gospel singing, however brilliant, did not catch on with broad audiences.

With all this comedy and musical activity, radio was still very unsure as to what to do with black contributions to American life when it produced documentaries, or docudramas, like Du Pont's "Cavalcade of America." This program's main intention was to idealize U.S. history, portraying its course through somewhat glorified biographies of a different American hero each week. It didn't have a very large audience during the 1930's, gaining only a rating of 7 while the Jack Bennys and Fred Allens were scoring 30 or more. But the show was nurtured, because it was both patriotic and educational, as a form of public service. At the same time its subjects were extremely limited. The labor movement, for instance, was never mentioned, and for a dozen years it had not portrayed a black hero, or even made mention of one.

John Brown, the abolitionist, had received favorable treatment, but when Brown told the court that had just sentenced him to death, "Had I interfered on behalf of the rich, the powerful, the intelligent, the so-called great . . . it would have been all right." The script omitted the word "rich" from the quote. And when the series finally presented a biography of a black on November 15, 1948, it specifically chose Booker T. Washington, the man who preached that the black should "keep his place until better educated."

Again, at the start of World War II, radio was in a dilemma as to how to handle the situation of the black GI. The War Department recognized the dangerous morale problems that were cropping up, both as a result of the terrible discriminatory practices facing blacks training in southern military camps, and in the divisive and false rumors of black GI incompetency that were being circulated as an attempt to poison the white public's attitude toward the colored race.

The method of approach in helping the black GI image was mainly turned over to Louis G. Cowan, the producer of the very respected radio program "Quiz Kids," and a public relations expert who since the war broke out was performing his specialty for the War Department. He decided to use radio as the best means of reaching the largest number of decent American families in 1942. First he convinced the producers of the "Our Gal Sunday" series to write in the character of a young Negro named Franklin Brown. Brown was in military service and only appeared on certain installments to coincide with his fictional furloughs home. But even on other episodes, mention of his name stimulated conversations between other characters on the show that discussed loyalty of blacks to their country, and Franklin's obvious success in performing his military duties.

"The Romance of Helen Trent" was likewise peppered with bits of propaganda that would help ease the integration process in the services and so strengthen the total war effort. Cowan arranged for an episode in which a truck loaded with strategic goods, and the heroine, Helen, were rescued by a black doctor, who later was given a job as staff physician in a war factory. This episode continued for weeks, discussing "the capabilities of the Negro, his unflagging loyalty, and his patience with persecution." Louis Cowan went back to producing in post-war radio and came up with another hit, "Stop the Music."

When TV threatened to bring about the "death" of radio (which to this day has proved to be a nonsensical theory, since radio continues more successfully than ever, albeit changed in its directions and programming), networks, advertisers and sponsors started to look for new markets. They studied the growth of the phenomenal black magazine *Ebony*, and its buying public that was essentially not touched by white media, and realized that a market of 15 million blacks had virtually been overlooked. So the years 1948-1952 saw the burgeoning of black radio stations aiming at the same constituency as *Ebony*, with programming built around Rhythm and Blues music. These stations presented black recording talent, but in 1951 were all white-owned except for WSOK in Nashville, and WERO in Atlanta. That same year the Atlanta station had a staff of 122 with only six of them white. Twenty percent of the listeners were white.

WLEW in Louisville, Kentucky, in 1948 had already been concentrating on black programs, using black announcers and black copywriters to handle advertising from black-owned sponsors. And many white stations with white programming were starting to hire black disc jockeys like Joe Adams of station KOWL in Santa Monica, California.

But not all blacks agreed that the progress of integration of radio was moving with any real hope for the future. In 1949, the classical actor Canada Lee complained that "a virtual iron curtain exists against the entire Negro people as far as radio is concerned. Where is the story of our lives? Who would know us if he had to know us only by listening to 'Amos 'n' Andy,' 'Beulah,' Rochester and minstrel shows?" Lee stated that CBS's "Suspense" radio series had employed Lena Horne in 1944, but had not cast a black in the show since then.

The New York Times of July 10, 1949, reported that Lee, who repeatedly denied that he was a communist, joined with Paul Robeson, William L. Patterson of the Civil Rights Congress, and white author Howard Fast to violently attach American radio station owners for their efforts to distort and conceal black problems, and their refusal to hire qualified black workers. They spoke at a conference of the Committee for the Negro in the Arts, held at the Theresa Hotel in Harlem, attended by 300 black workers from radio, TV and the theater.

The meeting was a carefully planned demonstration, particularly Robeson's speech that was totally political and never addressed itself to the broadcast issues at hand. The one dissenting voice to the others' came in a speech by Lambert B. Beenwkes, a black general manager of Station WDAS in Philadelphia, who suggested that blacks forego the "militant struggle" advocated by Mr. Lee, and concentrate on qualifying themselves for positions in radio and TV. He said "radio station executives are interested in talent and do not care what the color of a man's skin is." Mr. Beenwkes, who arrived without prior authorization from the sponsors of the meeting, was denounced by subsequent speakers. It never occurred to the gathering that Robeson, sitting there massively on the stage, whose talents had provided him with open opportunities in concert halls, theater, films and records, was the living example of the point of Mr. Beenwkes remarks.

This is not meant to infer that bizarre and upsetting racial incidents were not still occurring in radio. Lena Horne, rehearsing for her second appearance on "Duffy's Tavern," was told that listeners supposedly objected to her calling Archie, the manager, by his first name, and the suggestion was made that she put a "Mr." in front of "Archie." Gardner went to the program's higher-ups and had a stormy meeting that "solved" the problem. The decision was to have them not call each other anything. That must have made it difficult for the writers doing the continuity.

But Norman Corwin more than made up for this slight, when he invited Lena to perform in one of the most prestigious radio plays of all time, "Document 1777." Corwin, who is in a class by himself as a respected, intellectual, writer-director, produced this for the Mutual network as a plea for an International Bill of Human Rights. The drama took place during a UN roll call, with behind-the-scenes vignettes that illustrated man's inhumanity to man in the countries involved in the UN vote. Lena's co-stars, to name a few, were Charles Laughton, Laurence Olivier, Edward G. Robinson and Robert Young. Corwin's first major directing assignment had been the CBS premier of "Ballad for Americans" with Paul Robeson in 1939.

Sammy Davis, Jr.'s road to TV stardom was eased by the kindness and friendship of black entertainers and by white liberals already established in the business. After World War II had ended and he was discharged from the Army, it took a little while for his career to get a foothold on the West Coast. Things happened gradually. He and his uncle and father used the Morris Hotel as a home-base in L.A. It was a nice, old hotel in what used to be, and is now again, the Japanese section of the city, and he knew it was sure to be comfortable because it was where all the Pullman porters stayed. Los Angeles was already a pretty open town racially then, and Davis was getting to be a familiar figure because of his spectacular success during a long engagement at Ciro's. People he knew from the vaudeville days would invite him to watch a number shot at a movie or TV studio, and the behind-the-scenes crews started to accept him as one of the "in" boys. He was such a film and TV buff that he hung around as much as they would let him.

The feature of his act in those days were uncanny, on-target impressions of white singing stars, and Johnny Mercer's newly formed Capitol Records signed him to do a recording of these,

which immediately won a *Metronome* magazine award. In the
Capitol Records building was a place called "Coffee Dan's" on
Sunset and Vine where all the record and TV people hung out.
It became Sam's home away from home, and everybody in the
business was talking about "the kid who works with his uncle
and father." The columnists started to pick up on him, with rave
mentions of the all-black show he was doing at the Million Dol-
lar Theater, with people like Nat Cole and Louis Jordan. Billy
Eckstine was a supportive loyal friend, along with Count Basie,
"The Duke" and Dizzy Gillespie. They were, as Davis puts it,
"The people who kept bread on my table because they said,
'Hey, we got 10 weeks to do, you want to go work with us? And
they got us bookings—Lionel and Gladys Hampton were marvelous.

"Black performers were so generous in terms of 'Hey, go out
there and do what you do!' Nat (Cole) said to me, 'You M.C. the
show.' I had never M.C.'d a show before, but I learned it, and he
said, 'Go on out there and do something' and so supportive! 'Do
more, show them what you can do.' Count Basie was always
there with 'Go out, dance some more, do the impressions.' I was
tentative, but they were opening doors for me. A lot of white
performers would say, 'I won't book that act!'—Danny Thomas,
Tony Martin. Danny said at Slapsy Maxies, 'I don't need them on
the bill with me—too strong an act.' They weren't being bigoted. They were just afraid it was too strong a colored act. 'That
kid goes out there and he's talking. He thinks he's fucking white,
goes out and says 'Good evening ladies and gentlemen.' He
thinks he's from England."

Finally, in 1949, Spade Cooley, a Texas swing band leader
who had a TV show emanating from the Santa Monica Pier, invited Sam to do his first guest stint on the tube. Among those
tuning into that show were some of Ed Sullivan's staff and one of
Eddie Cantor's NBC producers. Sullivan signed him first but, in
a wild incident of bad luck, just as Sammy came on the cable
broke down. During his impressions, the sound was working
and listeners thought he was a new, white talent.

But the following week, on Eddie Cantor's program, after
Sam had a show-stopping five-minute routine, Cantor was so
moved by his brilliance that he embraced him on camera—the

first integrated hug on a TV screen. And then Eddie took his own handkerchief, wiped the beads of sweat off Sammy's face, put the handkerchief back in his pocket and asked, "Would you come back next week again?" That exposure, and that kind of acceptance by a star of Cantor's magnitude, got the executives to offer him a slot on "The Colgate Comedy Hour" series, and he became a national attraction, which in turn led to the Las Vegas bookings, nightclubs like the Copacabana in New York, and eventually motion pictures. Sammy says that TV executives always treated him well because of Cantor's example.

Later in the 1950's, both Dick Powell, who was one of the stars and the major producer at Four Star Productions, and the people connected with the General Electric Theater, gave Davis the opportunity to be one of the first blacks to play the parts of believable human beings in a number of dramatic teleplays dealing with important controversial subjects.

The first one for General Electric took on the problem of the brown babies left behind in Germany by post-war GIs. Sammy played an Army sergeant in Berlin, trying to relate to a little brown boy who only spoke German. Sam calls it a "heavy piece," but he was nominated for an Emmy Award that year for this, his first attempt at a TV dramatic role.

Dick Powell, a close personal friend, knew of his hobby of collecting guns, and at parties had seen his awesome dexterity doing gun tricks and fast draws. He also knew that Sam had made a study of the under-publicized role of black cowboys in the development of the West and had heard Sammy's tales of the black who had invented bull-dogging. In his nightclub act the diminutive Davis often did jokes about wanting to play the first black movie cowboy, and that is exactly what Powell allowed to happen on TV. He got his writers at Four Star to come up with an exciting, dignified portrait of an early black cowboy in a valid dramatic conflict that gave Sam the chance to display his flashy moves with six shooters.

Although Sammy cherished the opportunity to do these individual dramatic parts, no black actor was cast in a weekly dramatic series until Bill Cosby became the sidekick of Robert Culp in "I Spy" in the middle 1960's.

Red Channels was a small newsletter in 1947, purporting to list communists and communist sympathizers so that the radio and television industries could protect themselves from being soiled by any contact or employment of creative artists who had these political leanings. By the early and middle 1950's, its power had inflated, in both broadcasting circles and Hollywood, to the point where it became a final blacklist that could destroy a career by pure innuendo.

The misguided standards and paranoia of the times are perhaps best symbolized by the fact that Lena Horne was deprived of TV work in 1952 because of her Paul Robeson connections, and yet someone like Billy Daniels was cleared for his own local ABC show to be aired just before Walter Winchell's national ABC-TV show on Sunday nights. Winchell was one of the powers who could make or break a performer with organizations like *Red Channels.* He was also a big fan of Billy Daniels, a very light-skinned singer with a seductive, insinuating, spellbinding type of delivery, who had made a tremendous success of Johnny Mercer's "That Old Black Magic."

Billy Daniels had no Red ties, had never been a member of a front organization, and so was declared fit and proper to host his own TV show regardless of his less-than-exemplary private life. In those days morality had one standard—your position on the Cold War. And so it was not a deterrent that Daniels had an insatiable desire for white women; that even though he married a few, he had multiple affairs concurrently with other white women throughout those marriages; that two chorus girls at El Rancho in Las Vegas staged a knife fight over his sexual favors with one requiring hospitalization; that another woman, Ronnie Quinlan, slashed his face and neck 35 stitches wide when he tried to ditch her; and that a few years later, an intoxicated Daniels pulled out a pistol and shot another patron, James Jackson, in the after-hours Seventy One-Ten Club. Jackson survived, Daniels was tried, but the case was dismissed. These events are just one example of the confused standards in judgment of who would work and who wouldn't during the *Red Channels* period.

In the middle 1950's Nat "King" Cole became the first black to have his own weekly series on national network TV, in contrast to Daniels's show which was local to the New York area. The producers and the network were willing to take a chance on giving him the slot and spending the time and money to develop and promote the still-unsponsored show, because they felt that of all the black performers, he had the personality, the class, the attitude and the career history to win over white audiences and white sponsors, and to neutralize the liability of his color with even southern viewers.

After all, this was the man who five years before had become the number one male singer of romantic ballads, both in record sales and in *Downbeat* and *Metronome* magazine polls, taking over the spot from the temporarily declining Frank Sinatra, who had not yet made the comeback with *From Here to Eternity*. Nat's style and diction were unique. Billy Eckstine said, "He's one of the two guys who took a style and made a voice of it. The other was Louis (Armstrong)." It was logical that if a black had the charisma and acceptability to become the country's foremost crooner of love songs, he certainly should be expected to be a winner on TV. And this man, by his grace, had already contributed so much to the American blacks' image. But the fate of his program is both a commentary on the executives who didn't fight to save it and the performers of all races who did.

It was a time when black performers were standing up more militantly and taking activist positions in the emerging political civil rights movement. Cole was not prominently involved in this for many reasons, but still his rapport with his race was such that he was never attacked, like other non-participant celebrities.

A few days after the civil rights violence in Birmingham, Alabama, he said: "I've always tried to set myself apart from controversy or from anything political. I've never known any kind of violence because of race. I was raised in a Christian family (father a minister). My father had the respect of the community, and I never had contact with trouble. For this reason I never did get a complex about the business of being colored." He knew that artistry could erase prejudice, and often made the point, "Some of the worst bigots in the world own my records."

In a quiet discussion with friends, he explained, "I'm a performer, not a professional agitator. I don't believe in lip service. I'm not for talking, criticizing, blasting—I'm interested in doing something positive." Positive to him was being a life member of

NAACP and anonymously giving large donations to that organization and others important to black self-help. But he was adamant about principle. "I don't allow myself to be exploited in any way. Being of a minority and a performer, I'm careful what I do and say isn't taken and twisted."

And the mere acceptance or idolization of black performers by whites was not sufficient for what he wanted to see his race attain: "We can be something special, little dolls. We're no threat to anybody. When people see us they're relaxed, unworried. If Harry Belafonte or Sammy Davis walk in some place, then they will be recognized and concessions will be made. That's no good. Let a brilliant doctor or lawyer, or educator be recognized as a worthwhile man—then we'll be doing something."

Despite his seemingly gentle, pacifist approach to bigotry, Cole had been exposed to his own share in the years before the inception of his TV program. When he bought an $85,000 house in the Hancock Park Section of L.A. in 1948, neighbors started to leave signs reading, "Get out!" or "Nigger heaven" on the lawn at night. A lawyer for a neighborhood association told Nat, "We don't want undesirable people coming here."

"Neither do I," Nat responded, "and if I see anybody undesirable coming into this neighborhood, I'll be the first to complain."

And just before his signing by the network, during an appearance at the Municipal Auditorium in Birmingham, in the Alabama where he was born, six white men rushed on stage and brazenly tried to attack him. He was unhurt except for a slight back injury and the affront to his sense of decency. He canceled an Atlanta appearance, saying he "Wouldn't sing in the South for a million dollars"—and he never returned to Birmingham for the rest of his life.

No sponsor ever materialized for his TV show and the story of how it was kept alive for almost a year by the desperate determination of some super-star friends to keep the ratings up and not let the program die is a credit to the business. Frank Sinatra, Bing Crosby, Sammy Davis, Jr., Harry Belafonte, and others appeared for minimum scale, hoping that some conglomerate would see the quality and sign to support a proper budget. And a tremendous audience tuned in each week—who wouldn't, to watch the incredible duets of Cole and Sinatra? But finally the show had to go off the air when big business continued to turn its back.

The usually reticent Nat explained to any reporter who would listen, "Sponsors don't have any guts; they pay far too much attention to cranks."

And, "There is a lot more integration in the actual life of the U.S. than you'll find on TV. But I notice that they always have integration in the prison scenes on television."

He also told the entertainment world that he would never forget how they had rallied to help him.

"Real show people are democratic. All performers have something in common. They understand talent. The trouble is with people who run show business. The people who are in charge of the TV industry are not a part of that show business."

And he made it plain that he felt "advertisers are shortsighted in their attitude towards Negroes. What they might lose in sales by sponsoring a Negro, they would more than make up through the goodwill of the millions of Negroes who watch television. The trouble is that the people who run these shows do the thinking for the American people before the people get a chance to think for themselves."

Nat recalled the comments of a famous cosmetics manufacturer when approached to sponsor his show: "Negroes can't sell cosmetics!" Cole snapped back: "What do they think we use? Chalk? Congo paint?" And what about companies like the Telephone Company? A man sees a Negro on a television show. What's he going to do? Call up the telephone people and tell them to take out his telephone?

Unfortunately, cancer of the lung caused Nat's death in his mid-forties long before the Redd Foxxes and Bill Cosbys scored commercial successes, with advertisers fighting for their services. But that was another era in the evolution of entertainment integration.

Redd Foxx's early professional and personal life made him the most unlikely candidate to become a favorite of middle American viewers and conservative advertisers. But that is the role he filled later with his "Sanford and Son" series. By that time he was already well past middle age, and rather than having come out of "nowhere," he had come out of 25 years as an underground comic in vaudeville and nightclubs. At first, his claim to fame was a series of big-selling "party" records that were so dirty that those in the "know" used to call Lenny Bruce "the white Redd Foxx." He took credit for having started the sexual revolution with his records. They may have been kinky, but they were also extremely funny, and soon he became the most bankable X-rated star in Las Vegas—which was quite a feat considering the Strip deals in more "X's than O's."

In 1976 after six straight years of being ABC's number-one sitcom star, and 20 years after Nat Cole couldn't even find a sponsor, Foxx bitterly protested that the TV industry was still riddled with racial discrimination. He claimed that he wasn't allowed to produce his own show as white network stars did, that he was refused the opportunity of his own "special," and that his failure to win one Emmy nomination despite his high ratings was because of an industry conspiracy against blacks.

Foxx's biggest dream "is to establish a shrine, a museum of black accomplishment," in Taft, Oklahoma, a small black community that he has aided financially in the past. "It'll show what blacks in all walks of life have done throughout the history of the country—Jackie Robinson, Nat 'King' Cole, Ralph Bunche."

This concern with blackness and its niche in history is not surprising in a man whose closest buddy in their young adult years was the man later to be known as Malcolm X. They were struggling to stay alive sleeping on the streets together, and scrambling for jobs as short-order cooks in Greenwich Village "greasy spoons." This was during a period that preceded Malcolm's prison sentences, but even then they were so poor and desperate to survive that any anti-social action was permissible in their minds. Malcolm's attitude, as he himself describes it in his book, was that he was so contemptuous of the whole social scene that he would take advantage of anybody and feel no guilt about it.

They even had their first superficial political experience together, but they actually were looking for anything but "isms." As Redd describes it in a 1971 *Penthouse* magazine interview with Leonard Feather, "Yes, I remember one time Malcolm and

I joined the Communist Party—maybe not joined it, but signed something or other—because they had white broads and food, and I hadn't had a broad in a year and hadn't had real food in two weeks. So here was this basement in St. Nicholas Avenue in Manhattan with the white girls, and Malcolm and I went there. We signed some papers and they gave us a whole stack of litera-ture, and you'd dance with the chicks, smell the perfume, and eat the sandwiches. You just couldn't avoid being part of things like that because there was food, man—stacked high cakes and lemonade, even bologna you could put in your pocket. I would have joined anything. I'd have joined the KKK if they had some sandwiches."

Malcolm went on to some petty, and not so petty, crimes, got caught, and during his prison stay, started educating himself for his future role as one of the most significant though controver-sial black leaders of his time. And Redd, encouraged by the laughs he got in street rappin' sessions, began the long slow climb from sleazy cellar joint shows to fly-by-night record pro-ducers and finally the gradual progression in Las Vegas from the Castaways, to the Aladdin, to Caesars Palace, before TV fame and the big bucks.

He feels that he and Malcolm didn't really end up with very different goals for their people. "I believe in fighting prejudice in my own way. When people have heard my act, they may go out with a better attitude. I have faith in the power of humor." But being passed over for an Emmy really stuck in his craw. As with most performers, the applause, the money, the notoriety weren't enough. He wanted the brass ring also.

"When 20 years from now they mention the Emmys, my name won't be among the guys who had something to do with American comedy. It means that I'll be eliminated from the his-tory of my own profession. I didn't do nothing. It's like I wasn't there."

Ten years later Bill Cosby did all the things Redd Foxx wanted to do. He produced, he had "specials" and he won Em-mys.

It would be constructive to go back to a more detailed look at "Amos 'n' Andy," a program title that embodies almost all the history of broadcasting, starting in the earliest days of radio, continuing as the longest-running comedy hit of the medium, then having a second life of success on TV, and finally in the 1980's becoming a cult vehicle through nostalgia programming.

Because its characters were black, and its setting a black ghetto, it also served as a microcosm of all the changing attitudes of networks, sponsors and viewers toward blacks over that span of time. And lastly, it provided a battlefield for skirmishing between opposing factions of the black community, and exposed their varied expectations of the media in presenting images of their race.

As in so many other instances, the originators of what is still to this day the most famous program pertaining to blacks was conceived, written, produced, and in its radio life acted by two white men. One, Freeman Gosden, was a bona fide southerner. The other, Charles Correll, was a northerner one generation displaced from the South.

Gosden became interested in radio when he was trained as a wireless operator on a U.S. Navy Patrol Boat during World War I, in the Atlantic looking for signs of German submarines. While fingering his wireless key, he started receiving one of the earliest radio broadcasts when a voice clearly said, "Hello Navy, testing." He shouted for other crew members, "People can talk to each other through the air without any wires."

Correll was a bricklayer in Illinois who taught himself to play piano and one night helped out a friend who was the producer of a cross-country circuit of amateur theatricals that raised money for local charities. Both Gosden and he met and became friends in Durham, N.C., in the course of doing managerial work for this firm.

In 1921, in Chicago, they decided to give show business a fling themselves as performers, and for five years they just about made a living doing comedy and song in small country clubs and obscure theaters. But in 1926, Gosden suggested a routine largely based on black characters from his southern childhood, Correll added some ideas from blacks with whom he had had contact, and "Sam 'n' Henry" was born. The comedy played off two blacks of opposite personality and their resulting conflicts.

Gosden had had a colored "mammy" at home, and his mother had a young black boy named "Snowball" in her household when Freeman was growing up. He used these familiar old friends' speech patterns and outlook to structure the characters of "Sam 'n' Henry." The idea impressed the Chicago *Tribune's* radio station WGN so much that the two young men were signed for a fifteen-minute spot five nights a week at a salary of $125 each per week. And the public loved the funny little black community they built in listeners' minds through the magical effect of radio on vivid imaginations.

Within a few months they were number one of all Chicago programs, and they were truly pioneers since it was before the time of Fred Allen, Fibber McGee and Molly, Jack Benny and all the later "name" shows. Gosden and Correll proved that radio could build new opportunities for show biz performers.

But after two years they wanted to join a new phenomenon that had just been developed—a national hookup. This couldn't be achieved through the Chicago *Tribune* outlet, so they signed with another station to go coast to coast, and because there was a legal question about the rights of the *Tribune* to the title of "Sam 'n' Henry," they became "Amos 'n' Andy" without basically changing their format. An institution had been born, because five nights a week from 1928 to 1942, all America could tune into 15 minutes of Amos 'n' Andy, and after 1942 once a week for 30 minutes.

All the actors were white, but even blacks had trouble finding fault with the comic accents and delivery. Gosden played Amos, Kingfish and Lightnin'. Correll played Andy and often some lesser characters. Publicity photos of them for magazines or newspapers showed them in minstrel blackface. And they became one of the great success stories of American entertainment history. The white public embraced the characters like family. When Amos 'n' Andy and the affairs of the Fresh Air Taxi Company were on the air, the Telephone Company reported that calls fell 50 percent. And to try to avoid losing customers, some movie chains would follow the practice of stopping their film, piping in the 15-minute radio show, and then resuming the projection of the movie.

Blacks listened to the program also, recognizing in the situations a broader version of idiosyncrasies they were familiar with in their own friends and relations. And no black organization complained then on the images being presented. Everybody just laughed from deep in the belly.

But in the late 1940's CBS decided it was time for Amos 'n' Andy to move on to TV as a series, and potential problems arose, first because of Gosden and Correll's concern in maintaining the integrity of their now-visual cast of friends, and later because of attacks from the NAACP and other black organizations.

Naturally, all of the radio cast including Gosden and Correll would have to be replaced by black actors for the TV version. But it took two years of preparation and careful searching to find their visual counterparts, because 20 years of listening had implanted a definite image of the looks and demeanor of the cast in the public's mind.

Andy had to be a big blustering fellow—romantic and extremely gullible about Kingfish's schemes. Amos needed to have the look of a gentle, practical, hard-working family man, struggling against Andy's follies and the wiles of The Kingfish, who had to have the stamp of a lovable rogue with a twinkle in his eye and the devil in his heart. Kingfish's wife Sapphire would have to own the energy and gall of a "battle-ax" from the moment she came on screen.

Flournoy Miller, the author of *Shuffle Along*, a famous black review, spoke to friends at the Negro Actors Guild and they reminded him of an actor he used to know, Spencer Williams, as being the perfect Andy. Williams had gone on to become a screenwriter and producer, but Miller remembered him as a hilarious performer, and so CBS traced Spencer to Tulsa, Oklahoma, but had no address. Their local radio outlet broadcast requests for information on his whereabouts, and after Williams's pastor heard one of these and contacted him, he soon was muttering the classic, "I'se regusted" for TV.

An actor named Alvin Childress auditioned for Kingfish, but when Freeman Gosden saw him he knew he *was* Amos. Tim Moore, an ex-boxer and ex-vaudevillian from the old Broadway *Blackbirds* cast, became Kingfish. Gosden and Correll worked with these actors for two months so that the radio voices would be matched and perpetuated as closely as possible by their TV successors. The program opened to great ratings and great reviews.

But Walter White and the NAACP had been waiting all during the preparation years to deliver an attack. White issued press releases calling the show, "a gross caricature of the Negro which had done much harm." And he threatened the sponsor, the Blatz Beer Company, with a boycott by blacks. "We could not conceive of your sponsoring similar distortions of Jewish, Catholic, Irish or other minorities."

White obviously was blocking out his knowledge of fantastic long-run hits like *Abie's Irish Rose*, *Tobacco Road* and Gertrude Berg's "The Goldbergs" that had all set the precedent for the success and acceptance of exaggerated comical views of minorities on both the Broadway stage and radio. *Abie's Irish Rose* at that time held the record for longest-running show in Broadway history, and it benevolently kidded both Jews and Irish in the same manner that "Amos 'n' Andy" lampooned blacks. Miss Berg's writing for "The Goldbergs" radio hit was cuttingly satirical about Jewish habits and speech patterns. White's campaign created a massive split in the black community, and on this issue turned many black performers against him.

On August 8, 1951, *The New York Times* reported: "Negro actors voiced fear that the charges levelled against CBS-TV and the Amos 'n' Andy show would ruin chances of Negro actors for work, and they stressed that the NAACP does not speak for the majority of blacks. They claimed the NAACP action has actually threatened the 'greatest opportunity given Negro actors in recent years.'

"In a move to set up a positive program to help Negroes in show biz, the group formed a new organization, the Coordinating Council for Negro Performers, which immediately voted a resolution commending CBS 'for its statement that it is continuing its improvement of the Amos 'n' Andy series, and its guard against the casting of Negro performers in unfavorable light on radio and TV programs.'

"The Council, comprising mainly members of the Negro theater guild, will operate as a separate body. Lester A. Walton, former U.S. Minister to Liberia, is Chairman, and one member from each show biz guild and union took part in its formation. Noble Sissle (the band leader and composer), who was the Authors' Guild rep on the Council, asserted that the approach taken against the CBS show by Walter White was all wrong. 'People can always switch the dial if they don't like a certain program. But we can't tell the American public what to like.' He claimed Negro actors were particularly responsible for the situation since they never formed an organization to protect themselves against such outside groups. The new Council will stress the necessity of a balanced program to prevent the perpetuation of stereotyped roles."

The cast of "Amos 'n' Andy" wired congratulations to the Council asserting that the opportunity given Negro thespians by the show "is being threatened by ill-informed people of our own race who have irresponsibly threatened to boycott our sponsor (Blatz Beer) and have unfairly characterized the show, its producers and ourselves."

Walter White's campaign failed and the program ran until 1966. In 1958 it was still number two of all programs running on station WPIX.

But the NAACP was not finished with their mission. In 1954, White tried to get the BBC in England to change their minds about buying the program. He told them the show, "Which has done harm in the U.S., may be even more harmful in England." But the BBC resisted his pressure and it was telecast in Great Britain.

The program has continued to be a focal point of controversy even in the modern era. In 1985 episodes of the radio show were rerun on a nostalgia radio format in Boston, and were criticized by the black clergy.

And a few years before that, there was a debate on the subject that included Charles Woods, Flo Kennedy, the Civil Rights activist, and A. Peter Bailey, a critic. Woods co-founder of the Black Films Research Committee, supported the series, saying "it is pointless to discuss whether 'Amos 'n' Andy' involved stereotypes . . . the actors were caught in the middle. They had a talent and wanted to express it. . . . Once we know who we are, we should be able to enjoy the whole gamut of our entertainers. I love 'Amos 'n' Andy.'"

But A. Peter Bailey, editor of *Ascent of Man*, said, "it worries me when people in other countries only see something like 'Amos 'n' Andy,' and to them *that* is what black people are like. .

. . I would not mind it if there were some counterbalance. I don't oppose the program because it is untrue, but because it is one-sided."

The general public, black and white, who spent a lot of their lifetime arranging their schedules so that they wouldn't miss an episode of "Amos 'n' Andy" on radio or TV can only respond to this long, repetitious fuss about a classic form of comedy with the even more classic line, "I'se regusted."

Chapter VIII

Blacks in World War II

In 1940, with all the indications pointing to the entry of the U.S. into the European War, the Roosevelt Administration, the military services and black leadership were all very concerned with the role Afro-American men would play once conscription arrived. The racial situation in World War I had been a disaster from everyone's standpoint. Blacks had been treated horrendously in uniform and they, in turn, had not performed as well as they could. Despite the increases in education, job preparation and general assimilation into the main stream in the black community between 1918 and 1940, everyone realized that this progress nevertheless had been inadequate considering the time span. And everyone was nervous about what would happen this time around.

On September 22, 1940, Walter White, T. Arnold Hill and A. Phillip Randolph, the most prestigious black leaders of that time, met with President Roosevelt to discuss this entire subject. As a result of this conference, Assistant Secretary of War Patterson released a statement to the press that included these provisions:

1. "The number of Negroes in the Army would be maintained on the general basis of the proportion of the Negro population of the country."

2. "Negro organizations would be established in each major

branch of the service, combatant as well as non-combatant."

3. "Negro Reserve Officers eligible for active duty would be assigned to Negro units officered by colored personnel."

4. "When Officer Candidate Schools are established, opportunity will be given to Negroes to qualify for Reserve Commissions."

5. "Negroes are being given aviation training as pilots, mechanics and technical specialists. This training will be accelerated."

6. "Negro civilians who are qualified will be given positions in arsenals and Army posts."

7. "The policy of the War Department is not to intermingle colored and white enlisted personnel in the same regimental organization."

The three black leaders were pleased with the gains that had been made but bristled at the #7 clause and felt they had been sold out. They also wondered whether there would be a large gap between the intentions and the word of the War Department.

As reassurance to them, Colonel Benjamin O. Davis, the senior black officer, was made a Brigadier General, and William H. Hastie was appointed Civilian Aide to Secretary of War Stimson for black affairs. His role was to plan the organization of Afro-American units and investigate complaints regarding their treatment. He immediately suggested using soldiers without racial separation.

General of the Army George Marshall responded to Hastie's suggestion saying that such a directive "would be tantamount to solving a social problem that has perplexed the American people throughout the history of this nation. The Army cannot accomplish such a solution and should not be charged with the undertaking. The settlement of vexing racial problems cannot be permitted to complicate the tremendous task of the War Department, and thereby jeopardize discipline and morale." But Marshall, a brilliant man with great vision beyond merely military matters, did order the formation of a black division.

To further honestly express the Army's dilemma, the Adjutant General's office issued a statement that stressed that the Army did not create the problem, that the Army consisted of people with individual views, and that orders could not change these views. The Army would not be "made the means of engendering conflict among the mass of people because of a stand with respect to Negroes, which is not compatible with the position attained by the Negro in civilian life . . . the Army is not a sociological laboratory."

The first issue of *Crisis* magazine (the publication of the NAACP) after the U.S. entry into the war declared, "Now is the time not to be silent," and continued to reaffirm the loyalty of black Americans while contending that the sacrifice should be for a "new world which not only shall not contain a Hitler, but no Hitlerism. And to 13 million Negro Americans that means a fight for a world in which lynching, brutality, terror, humiliation and degradation through segregation and discrimination shall have no place—either here or there."

But whatever the decent intentions on both sides, the Stateside training period of black troops repeated the disasters of World War I. The pain, sadness, fear and frustration are best expressed in letters that black soldiers wrote about their situation. The first two were trustfully sent to the President of the United States:

"Dear Sir, Your Negro soldiers in the Army serving for this country are treated like dogs. I know this outfit will fail because any soldier here will either go over the hill or fail. We have 1/3 in jail now. Mr. President, if you have to pay for the sins against Negroes, well you would burn the rest of your life because we are being treated as if we are the enemies. I haven't wrote this in big words because it all come down from the depths of my heart. But in the end, I am ready to die for Old Glory because I love the Stars and Stripes."

"Dear Sir, There is no describing the indignities to our spirits imposed upon us by the mediocrity of so many of the officers under which we serve. The majority are ignorant of our background, psychology and indifferent to our aspirations along any lines."

The following incidents reported in letters from southern camps were not the exceptions. They appear so numerously and so repeatedly that they must have been an almost daily happening.

Eugene Gallard speaking from Gordon, Arkansas:

"Around the 14th of August we were hiking from our encampment at Gordon to a new area further away. We had been marching about two hours when we were stopped by the State Police and white Military Police. They approached the white officer leading us. One of them said, "You officers get those niggers off this white road. Yes, I mean you niggah lover!" One of the officers didn't move fast enough and a deputy walked over and hit him on the side of his head knocking off his glasses. Lt. Carey retaliated with a few well thrown punches, which I regret to say didn't help his situation. They almost beat him to death.

"I was in the front line of the march and a deputy stuck a Thompson sub-machine gun under my nose and told me, "Get the hell up in the rough niggah, I mean you." I rolled down fast into the gully which was full of water. We had to walk in the ditch, being forbidden to put our black feet in the white man's highway."

Discrimination was not just dispensed to enlisted men. A black lieutenant talks of a long wait in a Texas train station. "I had to walk down an alley to the back of an eatery to ask for something to eat. Yet there were white M.P.s with German prisoners of war inside enjoying each other's company over a steak dinner. It sickened me so I could not eat a bite after ordering. I was a civilian soldier in the uniform of my country and I had to go through an alley to the back door while some of Hitler's storm troopers lapped up the hospitality of my country. I think the Army, government or white people, which in the end are the same thing, purposely humiliated blacks in uniform to attempt to make them feel they were less than men."

By 1942 the situation was so bad and relations between black soldiers and civilian and Military Police were so explosive that riots were anticipated. It was doubtful that black troops, having been exposed to continual abuse and flagrant discrimination at the camps and in adjacent towns, and with access to ammunition, would remain quiet.

Hundreds of soldiers and civilians fought in Alexandria, Louisiana, after the clubbing of a black soldier by a white M.P. in front of a theater in the heart of a black district. In Little Rock, Arkansas, large crowds brawled while M.P.s tried to arrest a black soldier who was finally shot by a white civilian policeman. At Tuskegee, Alabama, Negro M.P.s took a black soldier from the custody of a white city policeman at gunpoint, only to have 15 armed white auxiliaries join the deputies to take the soldier back and beat and disarm all of the Military Patrol. Black soldiers on the post expected the townsfolk to attack the base.

The New York Afro-American paper, the *Amsterdam Star-News*, expressed a bristling view of these conditions: "They (Negro soldiers) cherish a deep resentment against the vicious race persecution which they and their forbearers have long endured. They feel that they are soon to go overseas to fight for freedom over there, and when the comparative, new found freedom is challenged by Southern Military Police and prejudiced superiors, they fight for freedom over here."

To attempt to improve morale in these Stateside training camps and defuse the tensions, sports and entertainment programs were developed by Army Special Services and the USO Camp Shows. At first any sanction for matches between black and white teams was denied, but as the war progressed this became more acceptable and contributed to improved relations. Inter-post leagues were formed in large bases like Camp Lee, Virginia, Ft. Lewis, Washington, and Fort Dix, N.J., utilizing well-known ex-college and ex-professional stars of both races, playing on integrated teams.

The Army-wide exhibition tour of world heavyweight camp Sgt. Joe Louis in 1943, sparring with local unit champs, both white and black, broadened the base of athletic competition in many posts.

For arts and entertainment, most bases had separate buildings for separate viewing of shows by black and white troops. But often a "special arrangement," consisting of a block of reserved seats, was made available to black troops in the main post theater if a performance by an outstanding "sepia" celebrity was scheduled. "Special arrangement" or "regular arrangement," problems usually arose.

Lena Horne concluded a camp show tour in anger at Ft. Riley, Kansas, because of insensitive scheduling. She and her accompanist Horace Henderson (brother of Fletcher Henderson) looked out from backstage, and as usual saw all the officers sitting down front in the best seats. She accepted the fact that rank has its privileges, but behind them were only white enlisted men. She knew black troops were at this camp because Joe Louis had been stationed there for a while, and Lena and Joe still kept in touch after a brief but torrid love affair that ended the summer of 1942. Henderson told her that the next day at noon they would entertain black troops in their mess hall because they weren't allowed in the main theater. Lena wanted to walk right out. "I won't do it. I won't do it," she shouted at Horace, who calmed her and reminded her that the white GIs shouldn't be penalized for discrimination policies that they didn't make themselves.

After this show she made an unsolicited trip to the black USO where she sang and then listened to all the "Jim Crow" stories from the troops. She promised herself that she had to do something, had to say something. When she arrived at the black mess the next day, all her soldiers were there, but the front rows were occupied by white men. "Who the hell are they?" Lena asked, only to be told that they were German prisoners of war. She marched down off the platform, turned her back to the Germans and sang to the guys in the back of the hall. But by the fourth song she was so choked with anger and humiliation that she went backstage and couldn't continue.

Furious, she called a private cab and had it drive her to the local NAACP office, where the young woman in charge happened to be Daisy Bates, who years later was the driving force behind the dramatic integration of Central High School in Little Rock, Arkansas. Daisy urged her to do something the national media would pick up, so Lena wired the Hollywood USO telling them she was quitting the tour in protest. When she returned to Hollywood, two of the organizations sponsoring the tour reprimanded her publicly. The word was passed down to keep "that big mouthed woman out of southern camps."

But she returned to the south many times during the war, not under USO auspices, but paying her own fare and her accompanists' expenses herself. And much later, to smooth things over with the USO, she joined Bill "Bojangles" Robinson as co-chairman in charge of entertainment for a luncheon in Harlem at the Hotel Theresa, to raise funds for the organization which did so much good, and was really not responsible for military policies.

Most of the black entertainers appearing in camp shows were jazz stars, since there actually were few black movie, radio or vaudeville names at that time. Very naturally, this brought John Hammond onto the scene for his own personal exposure to military racial problems. Drafted into the Army in 1943 and stationed first at Ft. Belvoir, Virginia, he inquired about entertainment at the camp and was told that there had been none that year. Through Lincoln Kirstein, the Assistant Information and Education Officer (a man long associated with ballet troupes and the Shakespeare on Avon Theater) he arranged for his friend Count Basie to play a concert. Actually it had to be two separate concerts—one for white and the other for black troops.

This event led to his making his first Afro-American GI friend and his first southern white cracker enemy. The friend was a young college graduate, a piano player named Rufus Smith. The enemy was a young sergeant who had been a straw boss in a Georgia prison camp and who boasted of the number of "niggers" he had killed. The sergeant overheard Hammond telling another enlisted man that his grandfather had been a northern general on Sherman's staff in the Civil War, and hated John from that moment on.

One night Hammond invited Rufus to meet him at his barracks, and at that exact second, the sergeant, drunk and looking for trouble, arrived. Hammond's first threat of a court martial resulted from this, and his own private war with Army discriminatory policies had begun. Soon after, John's captain delayed delivering a Red Cross message summoning him to New York on emergency leave to be with his wife and their dying newborn baby. Hammond always wondered whether this had been done spitefully because of his attempts to help black soldiers, or whether it had just been carelessness on the part of the officer.

In 1944 he was assigned to the Port of New Orleans Embarkation Center for duty in the Information and Education Section, to help with special projects concerning black troops at segregated Camp Planche, where their morale was very low. Whites had three excellent service clubs, a good library and other luxuries. Blacks had one miserable PX, a class C service club where they could buy ice cream and sandwiches, but not eat a regular meal, and they were deprived of Afro-American newspapers because of the editorials critical of racial policies in the armed forces. All mingling between white and black soldiers, particularly in sports, had been banned by a new commanding officer.

Hammond wrote a letter to his wife telling her of these conditions and also of his intention to write to his friend Walter White of the NAACP about what was going on. John had been a member of the board of this organization since 1935. During a telephone conversation, Mrs. Hammond reported that his letter to her had been opened and stamped by the camp censor. On cue, he was called up first by his lieutenant and then by his captain. They knew he had gotten his present assignment through the intervention of his politically powerful cousin General Osborn, and so didn't put him down as firmly as they would have liked, but he entered further into the doghouse by turning down a post in G-2 Intelligence to make weekly reports on conditions of the black troops, a role that would in practice make him a stool pigeon who would uncover troublemakers and malcontents.

Instead John approached old friends, the Minsky burlesque family, to sponsor an all-black package show that would start at Camp Planche and continue on to other posts. They helped him get Ella Fitzgerald, the Ink Spots and Cootie Williams's Band that included a very young piano man named Bud Powell. John insisted that either all the soldiers would see this show at the same time or there would be no show, and he got away with it.

Once a week he repeated this practice, featuring at different times Orrin Tucker, Jan Garber, Ada Leonard, an ex-Minsky stripper whose all-girl band had a couple of blacks passing as orientals, and Louis Jordan and the Tympanny Five.

He also sought out a new recreation officer, Lt. Ralph Metcalfe, the Olympic sprinter, to help him start an integrated sports program. Segregation at Camp Planche was demolished by sports and music. Flushed with success, Hammond started open house jam sessions for all troops, bringing in white and black Air Force musicians from the Lake Pontchertrain Air Base like Mundell Lowe, the guitarist, and Jack Green, the trombonist. This enraged his captain. It was the last straw and he put in a request for John to be transferred. On January 17, 1945, Ham-

mond's most prestigious service concert went on while he rode
a train to Camp Gruber, Oklahoma. But as he thought of the
Billy Eckstine Band that featured Dizzy Gillespie, Howard
McGee, Charlie Parker, Gene Ammons and Sarah Vaughan
swinging away at Camp Planche, he knew that he had left it a
different place than he found it.

The military was not the only place where bigotry was incit-
ing violence. Civilian uprisings were taking place in major cities
of the North in the summer of 1943. Detroit, with a population
of 1,600,000 including 500,000 southern whites and 210,000
blacks, mostly from the South and working in the auto industry,
was pregnant with racial unrest. Many of its churches headed by
white southern evangelists, were basically fronts for the Ku Klux
Klan. These Evangelists like Frank Norris from Alabama who
preached the standard "Sulphurous Gospel of Southern Tradition," Gerald L.K. Smith from Louisiana and Father Coughlin, a
Catholic with a wide radio following, were rabble-rousers who
thrived on interracial strife. The war had intensified job opportunity problems, housing shortages and blacks' disappointment
with their roles in the auto unions.

On a 90-degree Sunday afternoon in June of 1943 about
100,000 minority people left the ghetto to cool off in a park on
Belle Isle in the Detroit River. A fight broke out between whites
and blacks in the park, with the result that 25 blacks and nine
whites were killed. Word spread to Paradise Valley on the other
side of the bridge and the riot spread there until actual fighting
involved 5,000 people. Black roving mobs attacked individual
whites. Stores were broken into and looted. White groups retaliated. It took 36 hours before the governor of Michigan asked
President Roosevelt to send in troops, who arrived just as the
rioting spent itself.

In a very different situation with a different ending, New York
City erupted in August of 1943 as a fight, transformed by rumor
into an unprovoked murder, set off a riot. A black soldier inter-
vened in a Harlem hotel when he saw a white policeman argu-
ing with a drunken black woman. The soldier grabbed the
rookie policeman's night stick and the officer shot him in the
shoulder.

Rumors spread that the soldier had been murdered and a riot

ensued on this searingly hot day. Walter White wrote about it: "To be understood properly, what took place Sunday night should be divided into two wholly separate time units, the first lasting three or four hours, saw the blind infuriated smashing of store windows on 125th Street. For no other reason than that they symbolized a bitterness which had grown among Negroes all over the country. The second began sometime after midnight when looters took advantage of the disorder to pillage."

Mayor La Guardia, on very good terms with black leaders, called Walter White and Roy Wilkins, ordered all available police to Harlem, and called the Military Police to get military personnel out of Harlem. At Walter White's suggestion Fiorello asked for equal numbers of black and white M.P.s. La Guardia and Mr. White personally drove to the area but were forced to leave. A soundtruck was driven block by block announcing that the soldier had not been killed, and pleading for the rioting to end. But it took all night to control it. Black leaders did not support it or condone this uprising. La Guardia had also acted quickly and efficiently and, through this example, the police acted objectively to protect the peace, rather than as biased onlookers.

And of course, La Guardia had handled it without state or federal forces being called in. Black leaders backed him. Lester B. Granger wrote, "It took race riots in five great cities to wake up white America to the dangers of racial conflict. It took a riot in Harlem to teach Negro Americans that all racial intolerance is not on one side of the fence and that a Negro riot in action is every bit as bestial and blindly destructive as a white mob." Adam Clayton Powell, Jr., told Harlem, "The police have proved themselves New York's finest."

By 1944 racial matters started to turn in a definitely positive direction, due to many variegated factors. Firstly, there were strong personal influences exerted for the good by Franklin and Eleanor Roosevelt, General Eisenhower, and others with the power and charisma to impress the populace. Secondly, Adolf Hitler's vicious campaign of racial genocide made average decent Americans take stock of their own attitudes and prejudices, and thirdly, and most important, blacks were overseas, getting into combat, proving their excellence and illustrating vividly that while a battle rages, segregation is forgotten.

Franklin Delano Roosevelt had a strong track record since 1934 of repeated progressive legislation and policies to improve the status of Afro-Americans, and although he was an active Commander-in-Chief in the political and military tactics necessary to achieve victory in World War II, he did not interfere in the day-to-day running of the military branches. And so he seldom seemed to directly influence the plight of the black soldier, sailor, airman or marine.

He was such an aggressive President and took such a positive position in contributing to "the second reconstruction" period for blacks during the New Deal, that many were puzzled about his "laissez-faire" attitude toward the internal racial attitudes of the military services. Whether the fact that he himself was an ex-Under Secretary of the Navy played a part in this hands-off policy was never clear.

Roosevelt started his first term in 1932 as the northern leader of a Democratic Party dominated by southern control of influence and power. And so despite a black unemployment rate around 50 percent, two-thirds of the black voters went Republican in 1932. They voted for the party of their hero, Lincoln, as opposed to the Democrats who still were remembered as opposing emancipation and reconstruction, and who still defended racial segregation and disfranchisement.

The new President's need to work harmoniously with a largely white southern-controlled Congress and a white southern-styled federal bureaucracy, plus the party's tradition of advocacy of states' rights, made him move very timidly at first in racial areas during 1932 and 1933. Initially the "New Deal" was just the "old deal" for black people. The famous National Recovery Administration was almost indifferent to their needs, if not actually hostile. Many disadvantaged minority entrepreneurs had to close shop. Black workers, who were essentially without union organization, earned a lower wage scale, and the Agriculture Department allowed large white landowners to dominate county committees, keeping black sharecroppers and tenant farmers from receiving their proportionate share of crop reduction payments.

But F.D.R.'s humanitarian instincts should never have been in doubt, and gradually in 1934 he surrounded himself with liberal advisers like Harold Ickes, Harry Hopkins, Will Alexander and, most important, his own wife Eleanor. He listened to their counsel plus that of protest organizations calling for racial reform.

Blacks started to register and vote in greater numbers, forming a bloc that national politicians could not ignore. F.D.R. sent them aid via programs of the Farm Security Administration, the National Youth Administration, the Public Works Administration, the U.S. Housing Administration and the Works Progress Administration. And gradually, the gap between white and black benefits in employment, income, education, housing and health narrowed significantly. Roosevelt also tripled the number of black federal employees, and desegregated work facilities in U.S. agencies and departments. Thousands of black professionals were hired for high-level positions. He even had 100 black administrative advisers so close to him daily that they were referred to as the Black Cabinet or Black Brain Trust, and they made the federal government aware of their race's needs.

This group included Mary McLoed Bethune, the Director of the National Youth Administration's Division of Negro Affairs and an extremely close friend of Eleanor Roosevelt, Dr. Robert Weaver, Adviser on Negro Affairs in Public Works, and William H. Hastie, assistant solicitor in the Department of the Interior.

The President's appointments to the Supreme Court championed the rights of minorities, and formulated constitutional guarantees to protect civil rights, in essence the first steps in the demise of the separate-but-equal doctrine. F.D.R. also charted a new course for his party when in 1936, for the first time, the national party accredited blacks as delegates to its convention, invited black reporters to the regular press box and selected blacks to deliver welcoming addresses, invocations, and a seconding address for F.D.R.'s nomination.

But it was in more subtle personal acts that the President and his wife repeatedly set an example to the nation as to how to act toward minority groups. And in the main, the friends and associates they surrounded themselves with continued and broadened these object lessons.

At the very moment that Adolf Hitler was imposing his own personal hatred of what he termed Jewish and impure races on the German nation, a very small but significant social incident was taking place between the Roosevelt and La Guardia families. At an official function in New York that both couples had attended, Mrs. Roosevelt spontaneously leaned over to Marie La Guardia and invited them to lunch at Hyde Park the following weekend. Marie hesitated, saying that no one was available to take care of the children that day. Eleanor replied that of course the children were included in the invitation. Marie again hesitated, explaining finally that their children included Richard, the son of their long-time cook who had been named for Fiorello's brother and was being brought up as a member of the family—and . . . "And what?" Eleanor waited. "And he is colored," said Marie.

Mrs. Roosevelt beamed. She was a woman who never passed up a chance to live out her commitments, and she told the La Guardias that they must bring Richard. Afterward part of the national press corps criticized La Guardia for putting the President in this position. But just the honest reporting of the facts set a tone that reminded readers of the decent behavior of their leadership.

Eleanor Roosevelt from the very beginning of the New Deal became the champion of concerns for people who needed special attention. She became the clearing house through which proposals relating to these groups would pass. With Harry Hopkins she called a White House conference on the emerging needs of women and within a year the Federal Emergency Relief Administration and the Civil Works Administration were employing 100,000 women who had previously been without jobs.

Fearful that the youth of America might be turned against democracy by the Depression as others had been in Italy and Germany, she urged the President to form the National Youth Administration. It came to being in 1935 and employed high school and college students so that they could continue their studies. Black women and black youths received their fair share of benefits from these programs.

Mrs. Roosevelt actually was the first person connected with the White House since Lincoln to take an uncompromising public stand on the question of civil rights. At times both the personal and official actions antagonized segments of her husband's political supporters. Still, she plodded on in the directions that she felt were necessary to her own conscience and her country's. In 1938, while attending the Southern Conference of Human Welfare in Birmingham, Alabama, she saw delegates seated in two separate rows according to color. She took a seat on the side marked "colored" and refused to move. Finally when police threatened to break up the meeting, she took her chair to the platform, facing the audience, but definitely placing it closer to the black side.

Her most famous act of protest came in 1939, when she resigned her membership in the Daughters of the American Revolution when that organization refused to allow singer Marian Anderson to perform in Constitution Hall. To publicize further her feelings on the issue, Eleanor arranged for an Anderson concert to be held on the grounds of the White House.

F.D.R.'s sympathies lay in the same direction as his wife's, but as an executive leading all segments of the population through very difficult times, and needing broad support for many of his priorities, it was more prudent for her to "run interference" in her semi-official manner. To quote the pragmatic F.D.R., "First things come first and I can't alienate certain voters I need for measures that are more important to the movement by pushing any measures that would entail a fight."

During World War II, Mrs. Roosevelt constantly used the war as an opportunity to drive home the interrelationship between national defense and domestic reform. She saw the global conflict as a test of democracy, trying to protect the reforms already achieved and using the emergency for leverage to pressure further social advances. Working with the NAACP she helped bring about an executive order banning discrimination in war production industries. After her husband's death, her concerns were demands for desegregation in housing and education, and championing all civil rights movements.

The tone of conduct from others in high places as the U.S. entered combat in Europe was reflected in this order sent by General Eisenhower to all officers in his command as the Supreme Allied Commander of European Operations. This letter in the firm, no-nonsense style of "Ike" was issued on the arrival in London of the first U.S. black troops:

"Undoubtedly a considerable association of colored troops with the British population, both men and women, will take place on a basis mutually acceptable to the individuals concerned. Any attempt to curtail such association by official orders or restrictions is unjustified and must not be attempted. Further it must be realized by all ranks that it is absolutely essential that American officers and soldiers carefully avoid making any public or private statements of a derogatory nature concerning racial groups in the United States Army. The spreading of derogatory statements concerning the character of any group of U.S. troops either white or colored must be considered as conduct prejudicial to good order and military discipline and offenders must be promptly punished. I am taking this means of bringing the matter again to your attention because I feel that it must not be handled in a routine or perfunctory manner. It is my desire that this be brought to the attention of every officer in this theater."

The other side of the coin was the racial images being aggressively disseminated by Adolf Hitler and other German leaders. Only those who lived through those times could appreciate the extent of the ideological bombardment that came from the Nazi propaganda machine and was picked up and emblazoned on the headlines of newspapers and magazines, and, perhaps most vividly, in the newsreels of the U.S. and England since the early 1930's. No political figure in world history was so quoted and so photographed as Adolf Hitler, to the point where every citizen in every city and town in the western world was clearly aware of his controversial beliefs.

And the most controversial of those were his insistence that the Aryan race was pure and all others were fouled—most particularly those with Jewish or black blood. Although his diatribes had started appearing in the international press a few years before, most Americans took full notice of him for the first time during the bombastic theatrics he exhibited at the 1936 Olympic Games in Berlin.

Richard D. Mandell in *The Nazi Olympics* wrote:

"As the 41st Olympiad of the modern era opened, the masters of national socialist Germany were tense. They had told the German people that their athletes were going to win the 1936 Olympics. Now everyone knew that German athletes as a group had never done well in international competition. Since the first modern Olympiad in 1896, Americans had dominated the games."

On the first day of competition the American track and field team consisting of a high proportion of blacks, including the multi-talented Jesse Owens, breezed to one medal after another to the embarrassment of Hitler and his staff. They scrambled to devise some sort of scoring system that would hide the size of the U.S. lead. One official proposed the disqualification of all medals won by "Negroes" since the Nazis considered them sub-human.

Jesse Owens put on one of the most versatile displays of athletic talent ever seen. He won four gold medals, and in each of his finals, he either equaled (100 meter dash) or set new olympic records (broad jump, 200 meter dash, 400 meter relay). Reporters, photographers and fans followed him everywhere, making him an instant media star.

Hitler, who had ordered the most supreme extravagance of pageantry ever seen at the games, put himself on display daily in the Grand Box and saluted the athletes with great pomp, but he never congratulated Jesse Owens, and also snubbed Cornelius Johnson, the black American high jump winner and David Albritton his racially related runner-up. Hitler choreographed this insult by leaving the stadium the moment the last of the German high jumpers had been eliminated.

Ultimately Germany did capture the largest number of medals due to their strength in events like gymnastics, yachting and marksmanship. Baldur Von Schirac, a German olympic official suggested that the impression of amiability that was the theme of the games might be strengthened if Hitler were to be photographed with Owens, his rival in popularity. The Führer blew up and screamed at what he considered an insult. He ranted to Von Schirac, "The Americans ought to be ashamed of themselves for letting their medals be won by Negroes. I myself would never shake hands with one of them."

Since Jesse wore the colors of their country and had represented it in such a valiant manner, even bigoted whites in the U.S. objected to these remarks and, as was the case with Joe Louis later on, Jesse became a black recipient of Caucasian respect.

Although anti-Semitic propaganda had been ordered toned down for the foreign visitors during the games, American newsreels carried pictures of the front page of Julius Streicker's *Der Sturmer* hate sheet with a vicious cartoon of a Jew and a banner slogan "Jews are our misfortune." These blatant examples of racial hatred abroad made many Americans examine their own prejudices more objectively, perhaps for the first time and perhaps only superficially—but a start had been made.

And as the years passed between 1936 and 1945, the German step-by-step annihilation of the Jews of Europe brought with it further deep repercussions in the U.S. regarding its own racial attitudes.

Americans had to take stock of their own feelings during the early Nazi anti-Jewish measures which bore some resemblance to southern segregation statutes toward blacks. Of course within a few years the solutions to "the Jewish question" escalated to such inhuman and maniacal levels that completely separated it from even the worst bigotry that had ever gone on in the U.S.

After the D-Day invasion, American black soldiers were starting to enter into combat experience on European soil, and the rules and results were diametrically opposite to what had gone on during training in the U.S.

Horace Evans assigned to the tank corps led by the often lionized, often criticized General George Patton, remembers the day the general personally praised the 761st, a totally black outfit.

"Patton let us know he had asked for us. He said he sent a mother-fucking message asking for more tankers. The answer was the best tank unit they had was black. The general replied, "I only take the best. Who the fuck asked for color. I asked for tankers.""

And Eddie Donald of the same outfit: "One thing is obvious—whatever happened overseas, good or bad welded us together because to this day we are all friends and meet yearly somewhere in the country. . . . David Williams was the only white officer who stayed in command of a company throughout, always meets with us. He is the blackest white man you would ever want to know. He is one of us. His men, all black, would follow him to hell and a few steps beyond. So you see, it's not color that Negro soldiers respond to, but the leadership exerted, and the trust, respect and confidence the officer can engender."

At sea, similar changes were taking place. Ray Carter was in the Navy where black men could only have jobs as mess boys. He had always complained of being a "house nigger, cooking, waiting on tables, shining shoes." But he had to make these remarks after his ship was sunk and he was among 70 survivors picked up by a raft:

"I really must inject the no-segregation bit while we were floating and swimming around in the warm waters of the Pacific. Talk about togetherness, we were straight out of the 'three musketeers'—all for one and one for all. Brotherly love just oozed all over the place."

Statements by white enlisted men and officers make an even stronger impression as to the battle on human relationships.

A white platoon sergeant from South Carolina:

"When I heard about it, I said I'd be damned if I'd wear the same shoulder patch they did. After that first day when we saw how they fought, I changed my mind. They're just like any of the other boys to us."

Another white staff sergeant from Alabama: "I didn't want them myself at first. Now I have more trust in them. I used to think they would be yellow in combat, but I saw them work."

And this is the official report of the white Division Commander, Major General Edwin F. Parker of the 78th Division on the performance of his black platoons at the Remagen bridgehead in Germany:

"Morale, excellent. Manner of performance—superior. Men are very eager to close with enemy and destroy him. Strict attention to duty, aggressiveness, common sense and judgment under fire has won the admiration of all the men in the company. The colored platoon, after initial success, continued to do excellent work. Observation discloses that the people observe all the rules of the book. When given a mission, they accept it with enthusiam, and even when losses to their platoon were inflicted, the colored boys accepted their losses as part of war and continued on their mission. The company commander, officers and men of Company 'F' all agree that the colored platoon has a caliber of men equal to any veteran platoon. Several decorations for bravery are in the process of being awarded to the members of colored platoons."

A white commander of another infantry regiment to which two black truck companies were attached, was startled by the derring-do of his truck drivers who had not been trained for combat.

"It was early morning that I first became aware of the fact that our Negro truck drivers were leaving their trucks and going at German soldiers all over the landscape. I personally saw it over and over, but in addition to my own observations many reports reached me throughout the day of the voluntary participation of these troops in battle, and their gallant conduct."

Ollie Stewart, a black war correspondent who stayed close to the hottest action all through the war, sums it all up in the most eloquent manner.

"There is no color line in fox holes. No one can predict the attitude of the soldiers when they return to America after the war is over, but each month I noted a change overseas. The common foe, the common danger and common hardships of battle are bringing American troops closer together.

"Soldier after soldier has told me he can never be narrow minded again after seeing such widespread human suffering.

"Technically our Army is separated by racial lines, but actually every man in our uniform has been brought together by our job. Freedom for all is our aim, and even the most rabid hater of a different race has been forced to admit that to gain victory and freedom for himself, he has to share some with every comrade in arms.

"There is no color line in fox holes, or when a landing barge is being shelled, when an airfield is strafed or when a convoy is divebombed. I have seen colored and white who have glared at each other before a bombing, get quite chummy after death whistled by in big hunks of shrapnel."

CHAPTER IX

The Aftermath

(Blacks in the Cold War and the McCarthy Era)

The aftermath to World War II was understandably a complicated period considering all the adjustments that the average man in the street had to make. Service in the armed forces had caused careers and education to be interrupted, marriages had been severely strained, families were still mourning the death of loved ones, little children were having to trust and become acquainted with fathers who were virtually strangers to them, and the chaos was accentuated by the mood of discharged servicemen suddenly free of the confining regimentation of military order. The non-conformist was finally able to express himself. There were no more "Articles of War" to fear, or violations of company commander's orders to be penalized for, or buddies depending on your back-up performance. A free spirit was permissable again.

This was symbolized by what was happening in the latest progression in jazz. The perfectly blended sax section of Glenn Miller as it pulsed and throbbed through "Moonlight Serenade" had been in harmony with the ensemble effect and precision teamwork required for successful pinpoint bombing teams, or the launching crews on aircraft carriers. But with peace came a need to get out from under the mechanized regimentation necessary for victory. The year 1946 brought an intense desire for individuality of thought, action, dress, comportment and music.

For jazzmen, especially the blacks, it meant a rejection of the ensemble and a return to the solo, but a solo so personal that nothing from the past could provide a guideline or pattern for the sound or the feeling as you blew it. It was eccentric, it was non-conformist, it was *bop*.

Bop's roots were in the ghetto and were nourished in obscure nightspots. Swing had been developed at first by under-appreciated bands like Fletcher Henderson's, Jimmy Lunceford's, and Count Basie's, and then copied and turned into commercial success by white bands, where it appealed to mass white audiences, but lost its spontaneous excitement. After VJ Day, young black musicians went through a deliberate, self-conscious rebellion against that sound, threw away the rigid arrangements and started again from the gut. They took chord progressions of traditional blues, along with some standard pop tunes, and metamorphozed them into jagged, multi-noted improvisations, played at either breakneck tempo with furious intensity, or slow ballads bending the notes and staggering the beat to the bop drummer's polyrhythms.

You couldn't really dance to bop or scat-sing the riffs. There was something neurotic and spaced-out about it, like reality gone beserk, and it never condescended to commercialism. But it did suggest the violence that had just been encountered in the war. Charlie Parker, Dizzy Gillespie, Thelonius Monk, Miles Davis, Kenny Clark, Max Roach, Gerry Mulligan and others took it to the clubs like the 3 Deuces and Birdland that were springing up in post-war New York to entertain racially mixed audiences. Billy Eckstine even started a big band exclusively devoted to bop arrangements. These men were somehow tuned into the chaotic, socio-politics that would agitate the world for the next three decades.

Most of this agitation was taking place in the labor market. Working people were restless, providing the U.S. with more union strife than at any other time in its history. In 1946, 4-1/2 million workers went out on strike at a loss of 113 million work days, four times the number of days lost during 1937. Even right-wing California towns like Oakland suddenly found themselves paralyzed by general strikes. This militancy of rank and file workers planted the seeds of paranoia in Congress, which feared that Americans might be vulnerable to a spread of ideology from Russia as the Cold War began. The struggle dominating American post-war politics was again between conformist and non-conformist—but here it was no contest. There was no way the conformists would lose. The patriotism of a victor was on their side. In late 1945, the U.S. had just experienced the relief of anxiety, the joy of peace, the exhiliration that comes with a sense of having pulled together to accomplish victory following a long uphill climb from devastating early defeats.

Patriotism was endemic, pride was understandable, pleasure and self-indulgence were necessary to the healing of the many wounds. Memories of betrayal were so fresh—particularly the Japanese attack on Pearl Harbor, and the knife in the back that Russia had delivered when Germany offered her Poland as a prize.

The fact that Russia switched sides later in the war and re-aligned herself with us when it became more expedient to do so never really erased the feeling of betrayal that the American public felt toward her. Russia was on everyone's mind. We had been propagandized to respect the Litvinovs and the Molotovs in the *Mission to Moscow* days before the war, then to become furious at the fickleness of a trusted friend and compatriot, and finally to admire and root for her as Russia strangled the German Panzer Divisions so far from home and supply lines during the frigid winter of 1944.

It was all very confusing. How could the nation which had just become the natural leader of the capitalist world get along with its economic antagonist, the leader of the Communist world? The wartime menace of "Fascism" would quickly be replaced by the Cold War "Red Menace" in the minds of the American public and its leaders.

In the words of Winston Churchill in Fulton, Missouri, on March 5, 1946, "From Stettin in the Baltic to Trieste in the Adriatric, an iron curtain had descended across the continent of Europe. The dark ages may return the stone age." He further said that communism was on the move world wide, and no one could know what Russia and its "Communist International Organization intends to do in the future or what are the limits, if any, to their expansive and proselytizing tendencies."

Neither President Truman nor his advisers considered domestic communism as a political or internal security threat, but in order to protect the policies they believed necessary for the post-war role of the U.S., and in order to maintain their power, they were willing to sacrifice the freedoms of domestic communists to satisfy the appetite of the Right Wing and so protect American liberals like themselves from conservative attacks.

There has always existed a delicate balance between individual freedom and the perception of national security. Martin Dies, the First Chairman of the Special House Committee on Un-American Activities, retired in 1944. But in 1946, he approached Truman and urged putting into effect seven recommendations made a few years before by the committee, saying that the public climate was correct for action now.

The recommendations were:

1 .Deport alien communists.

2. Require registration of members of all communist organizations.

3. Refuse to recognize unions having communist officers.

4. Fire communists holding public office.

5. Bar alien communists from entering the U.S.

6. Cancel citizenship papers of every naturalized communist.

7. Compel the CIO to get rid of its communist leaders.

Dies was correct about his assessment of the political atmosphere, because at another moment in U.S. history this program would have been laughed at as the rantings of an angry, professional anti-communist. Soon others of his leanings picked up the crusade. Joe McCarthy had just been elected to the Senate in 1946 so at this early stage his contribution was minor, but the head of the F.B.I., J. Edgar Hoover, more than made up for him by going on a cross-country speaking tour, calling for a holy war against this rising "Red Menace." Hoover called it a "godless, truthless philosophy of life" and stated that communists were infiltrating every aspect of life in the U.S. He described internal communists as "panderers of diabolic distrust."

"The danger of communism in America lies not in the fact that it is a political philosophy, but in the awesome fact that it is a materialistic religion, inflaming in its adherents a destructive fanaticism. Communism is secularism on the march. It is a mortal foe of Christianity. Either it will survive or Christianity will triumph, because in this land of ours, the two cannot live side by side."

Martin Dies believed this rhetoric from Hoover and others would provide the atmosphere for the public to accept domestic anti-communist programs and investigations. President Truman answered Dies through his Attorney General Tom Clark, who talked of statutes to deal with "persons who advocate the overthrow of the government by force and violence."

In the next five years all seven of the recommendations of Dies had been put into effect. In that time span, the U.S. had moved from a Soviet-American wartime alliance to a Cold War, then to a Hot War in Korea, and an internal struggle between forces trying to protect democratic principles and freedoms, and those who were ready to bend them as a means to an end. The balance between individual liberty and the right of the state to protect itself was the equation at stake here.

The principal legal weapon against communists was the Smith Act of 1940, under which they could be indicted for conspiracy to teach and advocate the duty and necessity of overthrowing the U.S. government. But it was a new coalition of segments of the F.B.I., the Justice Department and other federal agencies that really expanded the anti-communist program. They helped what was later to be known as "McCarthyism" to flourish, and they used the legislative branch of the U.S., the media, the courts and sometimes a reluctant presidency to achieve their goals.

Elected officials did not apply the brakes that were available, and were drawn along on the ride. And to maintain objectivity, it must be assumed that most of the super-patriotic bureaucrats honestly believed at the time of their actions that their techniques were the only way to protect American democracy. In their own minds they were constructing a mechanism to erase traitors on the inside, and deflect the related foe on the outside.

Hoover bypassed his own superior, Attorney General Tom

Clark, and sent letters to Truman via Harry Vaughn, Truman's old World War I buddy and military aide. One of the earliest of these marked "personal and confidential" concerned a meeting held at the home of Frederick Vanderbilt Field, described by Hoover as "a financial angel to the communist government in this country."

Most of the report consisted of quotes from Paul Robeson who was a guest at the party. The meeting was not labelled illegal or conspiratorial, but the significance of the letter is how much time and effort Hoover made his bureau spend to monitor it with electronic equipment. It was one of the first examples of excessive use of F.B.I. power, and a hint of what political repression could be expected later on.

Soon Hoover began to operate totally independent of the attorney general, who in 1943 had ordered the end of the detention list that Hoover had started compiling in 1939. This list included aliens and citizens whose presence at liberty in this country would be dangerous to the safety of the U.S. in times of war or national crisis.

In 1946 Hoover ignored the intentions of the attorney general by simply starting his list over again, this time changing the title to "Security Index." Reports and investigations were initiated without notifying either the Justice Department or the attorney general. By late 1946, 10,763 names were in this index.

Hoover often leaked material to his friend Senator Homer Ferguson of Michigan, so that he would pressure the Justice Department to use the Smith Act against the communists. Richard Nixon said the Smith Act would be of no value, since "the communists have developed techniques for taking over governments without using force or violence" and he pushed for his own Nixon-Mundt Bill which would make it possible to outlaw specific types of political parties. But President Truman attacked that bill during a press conference:

"I never make comments on bills that are pending until they come before me, but as to outlawing political parties in the U.S., I think it is entirely contrary to our principles. I don't think the splinter parties do any harm, and if there is a conspiracy to overthrow the government, we have laws to cover that," and so the

Smith Act was utilized to indict 64 leaders of the American Communist Party.

And the attacks and accusations spread rapidly to those not actually in the party, even to those suspected of communist leanings. As if playing into the hands of the conservatives, those in the party seemed bent on self-destruction as they became more and more overtly subservient to Russia. All this was pushing the Democratic Party into a stronger anti-communist pose to support their goals of an internationalist anti-Soviet foreign policy, and to ward off Republican attacks. And when Henry Wallace started the Progressive Party as a third party and attacked Truman, new dealers like Walter Reuther of the United Automobile Workers, Eleanor Roosevelt and Hubert Humphrey, formed the Americans for Democratic Action with ties totally to the Democratic Party. Liberals were moving away from the left.

Truman went along with internal repressive policies like Executive Order #9835 in March of 1947, establishing a Federal Loyalty Program and authorizing the attorney general to compile a list of tainted organizations. Association with any group on this list would subject a federal employee to dismissal. Two thousand of them actually lost jobs and countless others were harrassed. Minor "crimes" like owning books on Marxism, supporting civil rights, Spanish Loyalists, or even Henry Wallace could result in an informant-triggered investigation of the person. Harry Truman admitted, "some reports show that people were being fired on false evidence."

Between 1946 and 1948 Congress carried out 26 separate investigations of communism. The House Un-American Activities Committee was especially busy, including one on the "American Negro in the Communist Party" and the headline-grabbing investigation of the motion picture industry in 1947.

In the foreward to one of its reports on the "American Negro," it made it clear that all evidence supported the view that this was a race of very loyal citizens.

"The Communist Party in the U.S.A. in its continuing efforts to infiltrate and destroy the Constitutional Government of this country, has made the minority groups in the U.S. prime targets of attack. The control by majorities of minorities is a fundamental precept of marxism, and the individual communist agent and party member has been drilled and schooled in the techniques and tactics of achieving such control through organized and reliable minorities. To this end the communist conspiracy has concentrated on capturing smaller groups with the ultimate objective of seizure of the whole. One of the principal goals of the Communist Party in the U.S. is the infiltration and control of the Negro population in this country.

"The fact that the communist conspiracy has experienced so little success in attracting the American Negro to its cause reflects favorably on the loyalty and integrity of the vast majority of the 15 million Negro citizens. To attest to this fact we restate the words of Mr. J. Edgar Hoover, Director of the Federal Bureau of Investigation, which appeared in the congressional record:

"'We recently reviewed the origins of 5,395 of the leading members of the Communist Party. The results were most interesting. Only 411 were Negroes, but of the remaining 4,984, we found that 4,555, or 91½ percent, were either of foreign birth or born of foreign parents. The fact that only 411 Negroes were found in this select group is strong evidence that the American Negro is not hoodwinked by these false messiahs.'

"In furtherance of its traitorous designs, the Communist Party of the U.S. has exploited issues of genuine concern to the American Negro and to all Americans. But as this report will show, the communist has always been guided by the directives from the leadership of the international conspiracy, and has betrayed the Negro's cause whenever it was expedient to further the policies of turmoil, dissension and rebellion."

Information concerning the early efforts of the party to infiltrate and influence the American Negro population is reflected in the testimony of William Odell Norwell before the Special Committee on Un-American Activities on November 30, 1939. Norwell, an American Negro, had been a member and officer of the Communist Party U.S.A. from the summer of 1929 until the latter part of 1936. He testified that in 1929 he had gone to Russia as a representative of the party in America. While in Russia he had several conferences with the Negro department of the Communist International . . . who stated very definitely that the C.P. should organize the colored people of the South for the purpose of setting up a separate state and government in the South. Norwell recognized the communist purpose as twofold and described these as follows:

"In the course of publicizing, agitating for the immediate demands for the poor farmers, and so forth in the South, this movement would gain momentum. Therefore the resolution states in any contingency, while the workers of the North or industrial workers throughout the country were organizing to strike against the system of capitalism for their independence, and for the overthrow and the setting up of the dictatorship of the proletariat, this national minority will bring up the rear, so to speak. That is, the revolt will serve as a tremendous means of weakening the entire system and therefore furthering the possibility for the industrial workers of the North to achieve their objectives . . . such a program in its more elemental stages and form, can only lead to race riots and victimization of the colored people of the South, chaos, and eventually to a complete, sacrifice offer by the party itself."

Despite this and other very significant reports regarding black people's loyalty, the paranoia and wild thrashing that enmeshed many innocent people in guilt by association even extended to the members of the armed forces, and in particular to blacks in the military. The black veteran of World War II who had overcome the bigotry of training in the U.S. and had found a niche for himself via European combat duty of distinction, was in a dilemma after VJ Day. A return to civilian life in his old home town would often mean many steps down the socio-economic ladder from his hard-won service rank. Of course, some opted to go back to school under the G.I. Bill to train for new careers. But others who could not afford to do this, decided to make the military their life. Many of these found that they never attained their goals because of the red menace scare. Lt. Col. Roger Walden was representative of these. A paratrooper, he decided to stay in the Army after the war, married, received his commission in 1946 and served in the occupation of Japan. As soon as the Korean hostilities started, he was put into combat there and received a Silver Star for valor.

"Once back in the States, my Army career was one of slow, steady advancement. I was stationed at Ft. Campbell, Kentucky, when the time approached for me to make the rank of major. I had been made regimental adjutant, after being asked if I would accept the position. All seemed to be going well for about a month, when I was relieved of this job and placed in one below my qualifications. At Range Central I tried to make inquiries as to why I had been practically demoted, and was met at every turn by evasion or silence. I mentioned this to my commanding officer at Range Central and he quickly slid around the conversation. I noticed when he thought I wasn't looking, he would look at me and shake his head. To see my military career in which I had done a good job suddenly sidetracked was befuddling and infuriating. I tried to be patient and see what would come of all this. When the promotions for major came up, my name was not on the list. Twice I was passed over. That did it. I demanded a meeting with the division commander. He received me about a week later and listened to my story. He avoided any answers but said he would look into it. He did!

"Shortly after our meeting, I was told to report to a hearing at which I was to be interrogated by officers of the Army. At this 'Hearing' all of the missing pieces fell into place. Counter-intelligence had been responsible for the sudden change in my affairs. I was a security risk.

"The kind of questions they asked, and the methods and manners used in asking them, I resented very much. It was as if I was facing the Spanish Inquisition or, more befitting, the Gestapo. I couldn't believe what was happening. I was accused of being a communist and a traitor. Protest or denial was useless, as they bore in like sadistic animals relishing every minute of their cruelty and power.

"I was angry beyond imagination when they brought my wife into this sorry mess. This was the crux of the whole thing. I saw it as they hammered away at me. My brother-in-law, Captain Charles Hill, Jr., of the Air Force Reserves, had had the attempt made to force his resignation from the service on the grounds that his father, Reverand Charles Hill, was thought to be, or might be, or could be, a communist. He refused to resign and fought back. The Secretary of the Air Force sent him an apology saying a mistake had been made. However, he never was called to duty in Korea when there was a great need for experienced combat pilots. My wife Roberta, who was Charles's sister, had been mentioned in the vague non-particulars sent to Charles demanding his resignation.

"My inquisition noted that my car was seen at a certain address on West Grand Boulevard. (My in-laws lived there and my wife visited them a lot whenever I was away.) They said I attended meetings in the basement of Rev. Hills's home conducted by Paul Robeson, which was a lie. (I met Mr. Robeson exactly once in my life after a concert.)

"I had been allowed to go through World War II—I was engaged to Roberta at the time—allowed to fight in Korea and start moving up the ranks. . . . My career was short-circuited when I was reaching the level of coming in contact with security material. From here in I was to be kept in inconsequential jobs because I was tied into some kind of conspiracy against the government. I wish I could say I can laugh about it now, but I can't. What was done to me was done against the Bill of Rights, the Constitution, everything worthwhile for which this country is supposed to stand."

Accusations went against people much higher in the pecking order than majors in the Army. Truman's own Under Secretary of State Dean Acheson addressed the National Council of American Soviet Friendship and was from then on described by Mr. Hoover and the F.B.I. as a possible Soviet agent in the "enormous ring of Soviet espionage," whose purpose was atomic energy data. Hoover offered no evidence of illegal acts of Acheson, but wrote to Truman, "It has been made known to the Bureau through various sources in the past, that the political views of Under Secretary of State Dean Acheson, Assistant Secretary of War Howard C. Peterson and Secretary of Commerce Henry Wallace have long been pro-Russian in nature. And therefore it is not beyond the realm of conjecture that they would fit into the scheme as set out above."

These tactics were used even more flagrantly with people who did not have high office, and "not beyond the realm of conjecture" as substituted for hard evidence became the charge directed at anyone with a liberal or socialist past. Of course some few of these were actually card-carrying communists. But most were not.

Gordon Parks explained how intellectual curiosity and dissatisfaction with the status quo would have brought most black artists into some contact with leftist groups.

"Several times I found myself innocently seated in things that were disguised as something other than what they turned out to be—recruiting sessions for the Communist Party. The messages and doctrines handed down neither turned me toward socialism or away from it. I just sat there and listened. Nothing was ever said that I as a black man living in a racist country hadn't known all along. The reason I didn't join the party is simply because I'm not much of a joiner of anything. That trait perhaps more than anything kept me off Joe McCarthy's list. I had fought so hard and so long by myself, that I had grown comfortable with fighting alone. Communism wasn't the answer to Fascism. But neither was Jim Crow. The solution I realized was a democracy, but surely not the kind that tolerated—as it did in the autumn of 1946—the lynching of two black men and their wives in Walton County, Georgia."

Since the twenties, thirties and early forties were times when many young people were attracted to the left in a manner not threatening to the U.S. and its democratic principles, and since a great number of these youths later became part of the creative community of the entertainment industries, it wasn't long before show business figures were becoming targets of investigation. A very small percentage of these were blacks because there were relatively few black stars in all the performing arts except for jazz, and the committees only went after big names to make a strong propoganda impact.

But there were some blacks who were harrassed and there were some whites who suffered because of their allegiance to black causes that had some left-wing sponsorship. Often the involvement was totally innocent, albeit naive politically. For many of these, black and white, their liberalism, and their left of center explorations, were more emotional and humanistic than truly political. But for others, like the brilliant, Harlem rennaissance poet and playwright Langston Hughes, it was the natural extension of a genetic line of ex-slave abolitionists who were the pride of his family tree. Hughes was usually deeply involved with Soviet goals and was allied with bona fide communists.

Right after the Russian revolution there had been an abortive attempt to recruit American blacks. A decade later, black members of the Party in Harlem numbered less than two dozen. In an attempt to counteract this indifference and bring racial problems into sharper focus, the party formed the American Negro Labor Congress. Three years later at the Sixth World Congress of the Comintern, Joseph Stalin had identified black participation in the Party as a major issue, and developed the plan for self-determination for Afro-Americans in a separate, black controlled state as proof of the pro-black commitment of the Party effort in America. Five blacks were appointed to the Central Committee of the U.S. Party in November of 1930, the American Negro Labor Congress changed its name to the League of Struggle for Negro Rights, with self determination as one of its goals and Langston Hughes became its president.

The organization began to share his hostility toward most of the then current black leaders like Dubois, Marcus Garvey, A. Phillip Randolph, and the man Hughes had a love-hate relationship with all his life, Walter White. These two particularly clashed during the communist take-over of the Scottsboro Defense in 1931. Hughes's public favoring of the Communist Party's response to the case, vastly increased the organization's prestige in Harlem, while White led the NAACP counter-attack on the Bolsheviks by writing, "With Jesuitical zeal and cleverness, the American communist agitator . . . resorted to every possible means to impress upon the Negro that he had no stake in his own land, that a philosophy of complete despair was the only sane and intelligent attitude for him to take. All this was centered about the Scottsboro cases as the basis for emotional appeal."

Though grateful for Walter White's tremendous effort to help his race through his administration of the NAACP, Langston Hughes hated him for opposing the communists. But White would be true to his anti-communism all his life, as was A. Phillip Randolph. Randolph, head of the Brotherhood of Sleeping Car Porters, and the most powerful black labor leader in the U.S., had also twice been president of the National Negro Congress, but had resigned from the organization, accusing it of having lost its independence because it had accepted financial support from the American Communist Party.

At an April, 1940, meeting of this group, he had the courage to stand up and call for mass resignations from it by blacks. "It seems to be beyond the realm of debate that the Negro people cannot afford to add the handicap of being black to the handicap of being red."

At this same meeting, John Garfield, the Broadway and Hollywood star, gave an address in which he took the Communist Party stand against the U.S. entering World War II on the side of England and France. Attacking the intensive war drive underway in America, he urged that everyone present read Dalton Trumbo's *Johnny Got His Gun*, a pacifist novel appearing serially in both the *Daily* and *Evening Worker*, the U.S. Communist Party newspaper.

Mr. Carfield, a Jew and an intellectual, fully aware of the persecution beginning in Germany where other Jews were being murdered, also aware of Russia's decidedly non-pacifist alliance with Hitler in August of 1939, and her own invasion of Poland less than one month later, with the subsequent butchery of hundreds of thousands of Poles, both Christian and Jewish—Garfield managed to push all of this information out of his mind and still act as mouthpiece for the communist line. This speech among others was used as evidence against him when he was called before the HUAC in 1947. He was not, however, indicted on any charges then or at any time.

Langston Hughes was not the only member of Harlem's elegant community of artists to become infatuated with communism. Countee Cullen, the poet whose works caught the attention of wealthy whites like Nancy Cunard, and initiated the rush of these socialites to Harlem in search of the Cotton Club era, joined his friend Langston with the Party. This despite the fact that his father, Rev. F. A. Cullen of the Salem Methodist Episcopal Church, was Walter White's staunchest ally in his anti-communism.

New Masses, the Bolshevik magazine, became Langston Hughes's major outlet for his poetry, including the bitterly anti-capitalist parody "Advertisement for the Waldorf-Astoria" in 1931. And the September 1931 *New Masses* announced his even further involvement with the far left, describing his formation of the New York Suitcase Theatre in conjunction with the editor of the magazine, who was Whittaker Chambers, the author of short stories hailed in the Soviet Union as being the epitome of Bolshevik art in America. Chambers would a short time later go underground for the Party, then break with communism just before World War II, and finally become the critical witness against Alger Hiss in the espionage case that featured evidence hidden in a pumpkin in Chambers' garden.

For the 8th Convention of the Communist Party in the U.S., Hughes read a song lyric he wrote for a Scottsboro rally a couple of years before. He called it "One More "S" in the U.S.A., and it very overtly showed his revolutionary leanings.

> "Put one more S in the U.S.A.
> To make it Soviet
> One more S in the U.S.A.
> Oh, we'll live to see it yet.
> When the land belongs to the farmers,
> And the factories to the working men,—
> The U.S.A., when we take control,
> Will be the U.S.S.A. then."

And for the 10th Anniversary of the Communist *Daily Worker* newspaper, he wrote a passionate endorsement: "Every Negro receiving a regular salary in this country should subscribe to the *Daily Worker* and share it with his brothers who are unemployed." Even then in the mid-1930's, he was included in Elizabeth Dillings *Red Network*—a guide to American communists and their dupes.

A friend of Hughes's at that time in Chicago was Richard Wright, later the author of *Native Son*, but in 1936 not yet 30, and a communist who had served as the Executive Director of the John Reed Club of Chicago—a Soviet front organization. He had already authored one novel about black proletarian life in Chicago, *Land Today*. In the early 1940s when his *Native Son* novel was dramatized, Wright himself, in some productions, played the protagonist, "Bigger" Thomas. The novel was a spectacular success, the play, and later movie, only moderately so.

By 1937 Langston Hughes started a gradual drift away from the far left. At 34 he may have been tired of being poor, and the death of his father had possibly removed the single most important factor driving him toward radicalism. He wrote to a friend, "The only thing I can do is string along with the left until maybe someday all of us poor folks will get enough to eat, including rent, gas, light and water."

The greatest flashes of his talent like the "blues poems" of 1927, his touching novel *Not Without Laughter* and his dramatic play *Mulatto*, had been almost devoid of socialist thought. In contrast, late in 1937, all he presented to his agent Maxim Lieber was a book designed for near infants called *Sweet and Sour Animal Book*, which eight editors turned down. Radicalism was not a stimulant to his creative juices, and like many other American leftists, his confidence in the integrity of this pure Soviet revolution was finally eroded when the news exploded about the non-aggression pact that Russia had signed with Nazi Germany in mid-August 1939. It was particularly demoralizing and humiliating because just one week earlier Hughes had joined 400 signers of an open letter calling for close cooperation between the Soviet Union and the U.S. against Fascism, and denying "the fantastic falsehood that the U.S.S.R. and the totalitarian states are basically alike." An admirer of strong man Joseph Stalin, Langston had never questioned Russian internal or international policies. In fact in April, 1938, after Stalin began squashing dissent by means of prosecutions and executions, Hughes still signed a statement in support of what the *Daily Worker* called "the recent Moscow trials of Trotskyite, Bucharinite traitors."

His friend and editor at Moscow's *Izvestia*, Karl Radeky, still pro-Stalinist despite the purges, nevertheless was executed after confessing to treason in the "Trial of the Seventeen." When Russia invaded Poland, and two months later Finland, many of the American left like Langston lost their last vestiges of sympathy for the U.S.S.R.

When word of his disenchantment reached the communist press, they flailed out at him at a moment in his life when neither his art or his health were strong. On January 15, 1940, the *People's World* of San Francisco pulled no punches with

"Hughes has been bitten with the war bug. Not only is he pimping for ye imperialism, but now has renounced all the sentiments expressed in his 'Goodby Christ.' Instead of defending the poem, which rejected Christ because of all the crimes against blacks committed in *His* name, Hughes had timidly apologized for having written it. The time had come for the red faithful to turn their backs on this traitor.

"So goodbye Hughes," the columnist wrote, mocking the poet with his own flamboyant phrase from his days of radical exuberance in Moscow in 1932, "This is where you get off."

It was always easiest to fathom the politics of the artistic community, since they left a trail of their ideas in black and white for all to see, or they signed their names to petitions, or were used as bait to lure other participants to meetings. So in 1947 when the House Un-American Activities Committee was on a quest for publicity for its mission and for the government's anti-communism programs, Hollywood with its stars was a guarantee for headline attention. It was safe to expect that the film capital would have a standard proportion of radicals and even a few party members. So the committee plunged ahead into Tinseltown politics.

In some ways it was an odd arena to hunt for subversives because it had been very helpful in providing propaganda during the war and well into 1946. Newsreels, a highly sophisticated propaganda art, had reinforced the pro-American position. Henry Luce, owner of "The March of Time" newsreel series, called them "Fakery in allegiance to truth." By selective editing, a movie audience could receive an urgent message that was almost a Paul Revere-like call to arms. When President Truman or Cardinal Spellman made a speech, the anti-communist portions could be singled out for screening to the captive audience. Ironically, most of the movies that accompanied the newsreels were basically non-political. But the committee could always focus on dissecting the intention behind a specific scene or line, or the private life of the actor who delivered it, or the director who framed it—and this is the path they followed.

Hoping to stop the investigation, liberals like John Huston, Gregory Peck, Lucille Ball, Burt Lancaster, Frank Sinatra, Edward G. Robinson, Robert Young, Eddie Cantor, Kirk

Douglas, Ava Gardner, Katharine Hepburn, William Holden, Orson Welles and Groucho Marx formed a group called the Committee for the First Amendment. This had a reverse effect in merely bringing more of the attention and publicity that the House Committee wanted, and it rallied the conservatives in the industry to start speaking out. Adolph Menjou charged that Hollywood was a "world center of communism" and Robert Taylor urged that "reds be kicked out of the industry."

And of course there *were* some communists to uncover—no matter that it was a tiny percentage of those working in the industry. No one needs to purchase a good conscience more than an avowed leftist earning $200,000 a year. And no one is more confused by the contrast between the egalitarian phrases of his youth and the nouveau-riche life style he has adopted. It is difficult to give more than just lip service to these slogans when wearing cashmere and smoking Havana cigars, but from the mid-thirties to the mid-fifties about 300 film directors, actors, writers and behind-the-camera artists joined the American Communist Party. By 1950 all but 100 had resigned, either through an honest re-evaluation of their political position or pragmatically to save their careers.

There were also many others who although not de facto members of the party, were active in front organizations like the Hollywood Anti-Nazi League and the Hollywood Writers Mobilization, which first attracted excited New Dealers with its ultra-patriotic wartime discussions, and then flipped 360 degrees, post-war, when it parroted the Soviet line.

But the issues that really provoked the investigations might have been more economic than ideological. Labor union actions had been decimating the profits of the studios and moguls like Jack Warner saw that their stars were supporting these picket lines. Since 1945 there had been a struggle going on for control of the studio unions between the left wing Conference of Studio Unions and the mob-controlled International Alliance of Theatrical Stage Employees. Although mob shakedowns cost the studios plenty, it was a much lower figure than they would have to pay in potential wage increases if strikes had been allowed to occur more frequently. A decrease in left-wing power in the industry could only increase studio profits, so it is quite possible that studio heads urged the House Committee on at first, and then realized that the situation was getting out of hand and that too much negative publicity would also hurt their potential profits.

Ed Sullivan wrote in his column that Wall Street had 60 billion dollars invested in Hollywood at the time, and that the bankers had pressured the executives to emphatically reassure the committee that they would cooperate and clean their own house. Finally ten witnesses, most of them screenwriters, some of them communists, refused to answer questions about their political affiliations on grounds that such questions violated their First Amendment rights. The "Hollywood Ten" were eventually jailed for contempt of Congress, the moguls abandoned them to their fate, and promised Congress that not only would nothing critical of American democracy come out of their film laboratories, but that they would blackball any known Marxists from the industry. Studios fired 9000 C.S.U. painters, carpenters and others who were never allowed to return to film work, and Walt Disney did the same when his C.S.U. screen cartoonists dared to strike.

A bizarre twist of fate occurred while the "ten" were serving their prison sentences. Ring Lardner, Jr., one of the convicted men, while taking exercise in the yard of Danbury Prison, came face to face with another prisoner, J. Parnell Thomas, the Chairman of the House Committee, who had been convicted himself afterward of payroll padding and other financial crimes.

Unfortunately, the blacklisting also extended to many of those who merely supported the constitutional rights of the communists. The Committee for the First Amendment arranged radio broadcasts on ABC called "Hollywood Fights Back." Judy Garland said during one program, "It's always been your right to read or see anything you wanted to. But now it seems to be getting kind of complicated." Of 313 who signed C.F.A. advertisements in *Variety* on Oct. 28, 1947, twenty-one, including Katharine Hepburn, were black or gray listed.

Also during the course of the hearings unfriendly witnesses started pouring out testimony that named "names." Ex-communists scrambling to save their own careers, destroyed those of their friends—300 to be exact. Many of those "named" had done nothing worse than support constitutional rights and liberal causes, but they had to repent and get clearing from industry power brokers. Among these were José Ferrer, John Huston, Arthur Miller, Elia Kazan and Edward G. Robinson.

Kazan took out a full page ad in *The New York Times* apologizing for his backing of left wing organizations, and Edward G. Robinson published an article in the American Legion magazine "How the Reds Made a Sucker Out of Me," ghost-written by a House Committee approved writer.

Not to be outdone, the radio and TV industries were going through the same, agonizing, self-examination. A newsletter *Counter Attack* organized by ex-FBI agents, *Confidential Communications* detailing the political records of artists like Josephine Baker and Kim Hunter with the intention of barring their employment on radio and TV, and finally *Red Channels*, the ultimate report of communist influence in the media, all tried to emulate the tactics going on in Hollywood. Offshoot agencies of these publications would then, for a fee, offer to "rehabilitate" the artist and intercede with the networks for them to be employable again. Judy Holliday and Lena Horne had to utilize firms like "American Business Consultants" to get work, even though they were totally innocent of any actual wrongdoing, were exemplary citizens, and were an asset to the U.S. government by virtue of paying enormous amounts of income taxes.

Black actors who fell victim to American Business Consultants were William Marshall, star of TV's dramatic show "Harlem Detective" and later *Blackula* the black exploitation movie, and Canada Lee who had played Bigger Thomas in the Broadway production of *Native Son*. Lee, who was active in many anti-racist organizations listed as communist fronts by the Attorney General's office, was vilified during the Judith Coplon espionage trial. His F.B.I. file was thick, mostly with gossip and innuendo. After *Red Channels* listed him, his TV sponsor, the American Tobacco Company, dropped him, and this ban stood up across the industry. He was shattered in spirit and in fragile health. Steven Kanfer, a writer, described the actor's final years: "At last, destitute, he delivered an attack upon Paul Robeson. The film industry thereupon relented and granted him one final role, as the Reverend Stephen Kumalo in *Cry the Beloved Coun-*

try, filmed on location near Johannesburg, South Africa. . . . He returned to New York . . . affected by failing health, unable to work in his own country. Four TV sponsors offered roles, then withdrew. . . . He died penniless and alone."

A war erupted between the left-wing and moderate press as to exactly what his political stance was at his death.

According to the *Daily Worker* "those who joined with the torturers 3-1/2 years ago, now vulture-like seek to embrace their victim. Like one, the red-baiting obituary writers of the commercial press seize upon two sentences from the Negro actor while he was on the economic rack, "I am not a communist or a joiner of any kind" . . . they could not make Canada Lee into a Cold War stool pigeon. He fought for his dignity even when he did not understand the nature of that fight."

But Leonard Lyons, the columnist, disagreed: "The *Worker*'s trying to claim Canada Lee. The fact is that Lee worked with anti-communist groups for the past three years after he made *Cry the Beloved Country*. He told me, 'I'd rather be the lowest sharecropper in Georgia or Mississippi, than be in South Africa. America is the best place for the Negro, for no place else is there any real hope for decent living.'"

Another actor, Frank Silvera, like Lee not a "name," but familiar to stage, screen and TV audiences as a superb artist, had an equally tragic history because of the witch hunts. He was a light-skinned black, so much so that for the first half of his career he was never cast as a colored man. Classically trained, he played with Helen Hayes and Mary Martin in *The Skin of Our Teeth* and Joe Papp made him *King Lear* in Central Park. He had started with Boston's Federal Theatre from 1935 to 1939. By 1945 he was playing Anna's father in *Anna Lucasta* on Broadway, followed by Tennessee Williams' *Camino Real*.

He joined the Actor's Studio in 1950 and was father to Ben Gazzara and Tony Franciosa in the Broadway Production of *A Hatful of Rain*. When Elia Kazan made the movie *Viva Zapata* starring Marlon Brando, he cast Silvera as General Huerta, the first time in Hollywood history that a black actor played a non-black major role. Other film roles were in *Toys in the Attic* and *Mutiny on the Bounty* and for TV he played the white Lt. Tragg weekly on the "Perry Mason" series.

He was an intellect and innovator, and while doing these other jobs he dreamed of his own theater. When the opportunity came he called it the "Theater of Being Workshop" with the goal of "training actors toward the establishment of new criteria concerning the Negro image."

"A theater of being is one that goes beyond the stereotypes and clichés of acting to the experience. In the beginning there was not the work, but the experience. To provide a true image of the playwright's work, therefore, the actor must discover the experience that the words are meant to convey." James Baldwin's *Amen Corner* was the first play to come out of this workshop. Referring to new post-war opportunities for blacks, "I'm neither black nor white," declared the man who portrayed almost every nationality on screen except that of an American black. "There will be a far wider participation of Negroes all over the country who want to be actors. Just like baseball, they will see the walls are down, the green lights going. They'll go like hell."

But in 1950 he said, "The number of Negro actors who make a living out of the radio and TV can be counted on one's fingers. That is the real tragedy."

But the actual tragedy of his later career is best expressed in a letter from Arnold Perl to *The New York Times* mailbag right after Frank's death in July 1970.

"The time was 1950, the dawn of McCarthyism in the arts and elsewhere. Bill Robson, a CBS producer, commissioned a TV script that Walter Bernstein and I wanted to write. It was called 'Blind Spot,' and concerned the come-uppance of a white drifter who sold phony lottery tickets in Harlem. The story turned on the fact that the elevator operator in the drifter's hotel, although seemingly an outrageous Uncle Tom, was in fact a Negro undercover man. Hardly social drama, it was however a considerable advance for TV at that time.

"Robson liked the script and casting began. Silvera's name came up immediately. He was already an outstanding and distinguished actor. But he was asked to read for the part. This was of course one of the normal indecencies Negro performers faced, the equivalent of asking Burt Lancaster to read for a part, but Frank, as ever, faced the facts of life and came to read.

"He was brilliant. But Robson's brow furrowed during the reading. He thanked Frank and asked him to wait outside. 'He's too light for the part.' We groaned, 'You tell him' said Robson, 'you're a friend of his.' I said I'd tell Frank exactly what Robson had said, no more, no less.

"I told Frank at the open door of the outer office. He smiled, and without losing a beat, said 'Ask him if I'm light enough for the white lead.' Robson heard, blanched, and asked Frank to come in. 'You're right. You've got the part.' Frank smiled again, then letting no one off the hook, asked, 'Which part?' Every white person in the room (and we were all white except Frank), looked at the floor, the ceiling, anywhere—until Frank broke the tension by saying, 'Okay, when does rehearsal start?'

"The rest is anti-climax, or more accurately, total destruction. The script went into rehearsal with Frank in the black lead and high hopes. On the third day of rehearsal, the long arm of Mc-Carthyism reached into the studio and the show was cancelled. No explanation was offered. It was simply never done. Within less than a year, all of us connected with the show were pro-scribed, and indeed ideas like these in our play were consid-ered, leftist—and were verboten for the next decade. We were blacklisted, but for Frank Silvera it was nothing new—the word was named for him and for all black actors. He had been on that list from the day he was born, until the awful moment a few weeks ago when a lovely man was suddenly, stupidly gone."

Mr. Perl did not say that while repairing a garbage disposal unit in his kitchen in Pasadena, California, Silvera was acciden-tally electrocuted.

Josh White, the folk singer of Village Vanguard and Cafe Soci-ety fame, appeared before the Un-American Activities Commit-tee on September 1, 1950, at his own request. "For my sake and the sake of many other entertainers, who like myself, have been used and exploited by people who give allegiance to a foreign power."

He admitted that he, an artist who knew "mighty little about the ins and outs of movements and parties," had been duped into many communist front appearances. He justified his belief in Christianity and his hatred of Jim Crow with, "I was seven years old when I left my home in Greenville, South Carolina, to

Charlie Christian with Gene
Krupa. The last cog in the
perfect Goodman ensemble, he
was dead within two years. (Otto
Hess Collection. The N.Y.
Public Library Collection,
Performing Arts Research
Center)

Billy Eckstein. A great singer, he never
took the chance to become the first black
leading man. (The N.Y. Public Library
Collection, Performing Arts Research
Center)

Hammond brought together
Benny Carter and Charlie
Barnett. (The N.Y. Public
Library Collection, Performing
Arts Research Center)

Paul Robeson. The most versatile black talent to date. (The N.Y. Public Library Collection, Performing Arts Research Center. Columbia Pictures)

Sidney Poitier, the first major black movie star, won the Oscar for a starring role. (The N.Y. Public Library Collection, Performing Arts Research Center, Columbia Pictures)

Hattie McDaniel. The first black to win a supporting Oscar, for *Gone With the Wind*. (The N.Y. Public Library Collection, Performing Arts Research Center. Photo by "Janie")

Harry Belafonte presented with three gold records in one year by George R. Marek, RCA Victor Records Division V.P. and General Manager. (The New York Public Library Collection, Performing Arts Research Center. RCA Victor Records)

Radio stars Amos 'n' Andy in blackface. TV forced another cast. (The N.Y. Public Library Collection, Performing Arts Research Center. CBS Radio)

Redd Foxx. From Malcolm X to MGM in one short lifetime. (The N.Y. Public Library Collection, Performing Arts Research Center, MGM)

Stepin Fetchit. His own race hated what he was doing on film. (The N.Y. Public Library Collection, Performing Arts Research Center. 20th Century-Fox)

Lena Horne. MGM could excise her beautiful face and voice for Southern theaters. (The N.Y. Public Library Collection, Performing Arts Research Center)

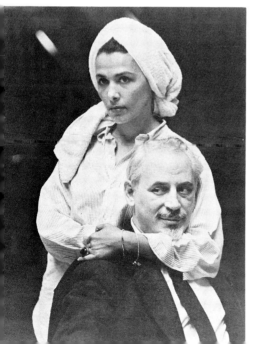

Lena with her white husband, conductor Lennie Hayton. (The N.Y. Public Library Collection, Performing Arts Research Center. Photo by Friedman-Abeles for Galaxy)

Duke Ellington and Cary Grant kidding around in the 1970s. The Mob would have forbidden this when Duke led the Cotton Club band 40 years before. (The Harvey Granat Collection. Photo by Mike Zwerling)

A very young Lionel Hampton with the genius Louis Armstrong, who was considered too black to play the Cotton Club. (The Lionel Hampton Collection)

An all-star session during World War II. Basie joins Hampton on vibes, while Artie Shaw, Tommy Dorsey, Ziggy Elman and Buddy Rich, among others, swing along. (The Lionel Hampton Collection)

Max Gordon and Thelonius Monk at the Village Vanguard. (The Lorraine Gordon Collection. Photo by Hozumi Nakadaira)

Lionel Richie, who was chosen to be the star performer at the 1984 Olympics in Los Angeles. (The N.Y. Public Library Collection, Performing Arts Research Center.

The artist and some of the photographs from *Gordon Parks: A Retrospective*. (The N.Y. Public Library. Photo by Michael Schenker)

Bill Cosby visits James Brown backstage at the Apollo. (Photo by Gordon "Doc" Anderson)

Nat "King" Cole, smooth and mellow at the Apollo. (Photo by Gordon "Doc" Anderson)

In 1987 Oprah Winfrey became the highest paid female performer ever. (Photo by permission of Harpo Productions)

The most versatile entertainer of modern times, Sammy Davis, Jr., is seen here just after World War II as part of the Will Mastin Trio. (The N.Y. Public Library Collection, Performing Arts Research Center)

During Sammy's first shot on national TV for Ed Sullivan, the cable failed and home viewers thought they were listening to a white performer doing impressions. (Photo by Joshua Greene)

Whoopi Goldberg with Isabel Stevenson of the American Wing at the time of her smash hit, one-woman show on Broadway. (Photo by James Chotas from the N.Y. Public Library Collection, Performing Arts Research Center)

lead a blind man while playing the tambourine. Before I was eight, I knew what it meant to be kicked and abused. Before I was nine I had seen two lynchings. I got to hate Jim Crow for what it did to me personally, and because Jim Crow is an insult to God's creatures and a violation of the Christian beliefs taught by my father."

He told of becoming a folksinger, recording at sixteen, and then having his hand paralyzed for five years in an accident, until his prayers were answered and the affliction disappeared, and he got a role in a play, *John Henry*, that starred Paul Robeson. Then he, like other black performers interested in getting back to work, took the option that was most effective toward that end. He denounced Paul Robeson. White performers named names, but since there were so few black star-quality leftists, people like Josh White merely disassociated from Robeson.

"I have a great admiration for Mr. Robeson as an actor and great singer, and if what I read in the papers is true, I feel sad over the help he's been giving to people who despise America."

Harry Belafonte had helped some so-called front organizations, but was cleared without either naming names, denouncing Robeson, or even appearing before the Committee. He was merely visited by a lady investigator of that group who questioned him about his motives for performing at a "Caravan for Wallace" benefit. She accepted his explanation that he made his living by entertaining and had sung for this group for the money they had paid.

She also questioned him about the night in February of 1953 when he smashed his hand through a car window in fury over the refusal of the Supreme Court to uphold the Rosenbergs' appeal. But she didn't make too much of this incident because she also was aware of physical threats against him by left wing blacks who thought he had made a deal with the government. According to Belafonte, "Sidney Poitier saved me one night in a bar in Harlem from a man with a knife who came at me—he was part of the left—because he thought how could I have possibly gotten on the Ed Sullivan show unless I finked."

The only other major black star to be given a very hard time during both the Hollywood and the television red menace investigations—excepting of course, Robeson—was Lena Horne. And most of her harassment was attributable to her lifelong ties to this same man who from her childhood on had been a friend to her family, and an inspiring symbol of pride to her own feelings of blackness. She certainly did not share his far left politics, but she liked and respected him, and, particularly in her younger years, felt she should participate in some of his activities because he was her mentor and example on how to live as a black.

Lena was never accused publically of leftist leanings or called upon to answer any formal charges by any government agency, but still in 1952 she was blacklisted as a communist sympathizer. She had joined the Hollywood Independent Citizens Committee of the Arts, Sciences and Professions which was later listed as a "front" organization, but her retort to this was, "I also belonged to all the same outfits that Mrs. Roosevelt did."

She of course joined Robeson in some of his causes, like the Council on African Affairs' appeal for funds for food to be sent to starving black South Africans. But she wasn't what some people started calling her, "the female Paul Robeson," and she involved herself in battles that he distanced himself from. Her studio and agency weren't thrilled with her participation in a benefit for the L.A. anti-KKK rally in 1946 that was organized by labor groups, Jewish groups and blacks to protest an upsurge of Klan activity against blacks and synagogues in the Los Angeles area.

She was drummed out of the Screen Actors' Guild, and commented years later, "This shook up the bosses at MGM, and they insisted I write the unions a letter clearing myself. The letter said, I'm black, I have these friends, I don't know anything about their politics! Nevertheless, MGM didn't put me back to work."

That same year she tried to get an apartment in Manhattan but was turned down. Whether it was because of the blacklist publicity or because the building didn't want a black who was married to a Jew (Lennie Hayton), both of whom were in show business, she could not tell. But it especially hurt that the luxury building, "The Eldorado" on Central Park West, was owned by C. M. "Daddy" Grace, a black religious leader who had bilked his black parishoners of millions.

Red Channels, the private agency that compiled lists of per-
sonae non grata and their past activities and sold the information to networks and advertisers, did an act on her at that moment, and she became unemployable on radio and TV. Only Tex
McCrary and Jinx Falkenburg invited her to appear on their
daytime talk show.

All these setbacks caused Miss Horne to lose her spirit and go
through a cold and distant phase. Only on-stage was she totally
free of criticism about color, marriage or associations, and yet
she started to withhold from audiences a sense of sharing with
them unless they responded to her as a human being. Ralph
Harris tried to explain it.

"Lena works on a crowd's insides until the crowd is giving
her as much as she gives the crowd. The crowd knows it. She is
not singing at them and they realize they've got to give something back or no dice. She's crystallizing something for them
that needs their help. They don't get whatever it is, until they
throw something back for Horne."

Because the red scare cancelled out her other work, she had
to go to Las Vegas to make a living and to fulfill herself as an
artist. But the gambling crowd gave nothing back. She hated the
place and couldn't wait to get away from it. Both the audience
and the mob bosses felt no allegiance to any color but dollar
green. It was imperative that she get off the blacklist and return
to films and TV.

She first met with the head of a large theatrical union. He
then arranged for her to have an appointment with one of the
clearance groups that had the power to erase the undeserved
bum rap. In her case it was the political columnist George Sokolsky, a solid conservative, but married to a Chinese woman
and personally supportive of blacks. Sokolsky, along with Tex
McCrary and Ed Sullivan, persuaded *Red Channels* to drop her
name from the list. Sullivan was a lifelong liberal, but he may
have had some ulterior motives in Lena's situation, because he
scooped the other TV variety shows by immediately signing her
for his show the moment she was cleared. Soon after, though,
both Steve Allen and Perry Como guest-starred her on their
programs, and from then on she was free to perform without
restraint. But Hollywood still made her very few offers.

It is unfortunate that the early 1950's were so difficult for Lena, because she had started the post-war period with one of her most satisfying engagements both from the standpoint of performance and what she accomplished for the integration movement in show business. This took place in 1948 at the Copacabana, her first New York gig since 1942. She was to appear in the main room where no black entertainer had ever been invited. On opening night, Billie Holiday came backstage and told her that blacks weren't being admitted. Billie had only gotten past the rope because one captain was a jazz buff and recognized her as one of his recording idols. When Bill "Bojangles" Robinson and a famous black actress were turned away the next night, the actress telephoned Lena and denounced her for working at a club where "your people are treated like that." She assured Lena that she was going to make a fuss to the black press about Miss Horne's insensitivity.

Lena called in two old friends for advice on the matter, reporters Ted Poston and Major Robinson. Poston, in 1956, wrote about the sequence of events for the New York *Post*.

"The reporters immediately set up a standard battle plan which even as recently as 1948 Negroes had to use to obtain their civil rights in New York City."

Enlisting the help of a white columnist for the *Post*, Victor Riesel, they called and made a reservation for a party of four in Poston's name. That night, on cue, Riesel arrived half an hour before showtime and said he was "with Mr. Poston's party." He was ushered in and when Jack Entratter, manager of the Copa (and later of the Sands in Las Vegas) saw this well-connected columnist, he immediately shifted the "Poston Table" to ringside and ordered a round of drinks "on the house."

When Poston arrived with his wife, the maître d' couldn't find any reservation in that name. Major Robinson soon appeared with a policeman, and Entratter, trying to avoid more bad P.R., rushed over to check out the problem and reinforced his employee's decision that no one could enter without a reservation. Riesel left his table, pointed out Poston as his host, reminding Entratter that there had in fact been a reservation, and so, reluctantly, they were all led to the ringside table.

Later, between shows, both Entratter and Lena joined them

and the manager explained the position of club owners about black patrons. As Poston remembered it:

"First of course was the oft-expressed fear that 'customers come here from everywhere. Suppose some southern patron comes in and saw Negroes here. Anything could happen.' He admitted, however, that he had never heard of anything untoward happening in downtown clubs which did admit Negroes, and nodded in half-agreement when he was told, 'Look, no matter how loud they holler down home, when crackers come to New York, they expect to see Negroes in places of public accommodation. The last thing a cracker would do is pick a fight in a community where he feels himself a minority.'"

"Entratter's second fear—and apparently that of his 1948 confreres—was that if one Negro was admitted to a club, the place would be flooded with Negroes later.

"'Why?' he was asked. "We've never been to the Copa before, nor had any desire to come here. If you hadn't kicked "Bojangles" and the actress around, we wouldn't be here now.'"

This incident turned out to be landmark, because from then on the Copa lifted restrictions on admitting blacks who had reservations, and due to its influence as the major New York nightclub showcase, other Manhattan cabarets followed suit.

But the most powerful post-war event to further the integration process and to influence the white majority's perception of blacks did not take place in politics or in show business, but in the all-American pastime of major league baseball. There are those who insist that all professional sports are essentially a form of show business, so maybe the entry of Jack Roosevelt Robinson as the first Negro ever in the big leagues was akin to a Carnegie Hall debut. But to blacks all over the country it was the symbolic giant-step beyond compare.

Branch Rickey, the white general manager of the Brooklyn Dodgers, had studied, analyzed, and almost psychoanalyzed all of the best young black athletes available before he came up with Jackie as the one he thought had not only the talent but also the intelligence, backbone, and self-control to take the brunt of both the abuse and idolation that this revolutionary role would bring to him. Rickey was a businessman first and foremost, and there is no question that he recognized the revenue to be derived from ticket sales to newly employed post-war blacks. But he also was a decent person and undoubtedly felt that the time had come for this type of integration.

He spoke to church and civic leaders of both races, trying to head off problems and marshal support for his explosive move. He wanted all of Brooklyn prepared. Jackie did his part at Montreal in the International League for one year while the majors were being readied for his 1947 debut. He won the league's most valuable player award with conduct impeccable by any standards. But there were no rednecks and no Dixie history of slavery up in Canada.

To avoid exposing Robinson to 1947 spring training problems in Florida, Rickey switched the spring warmups to Cuba, which made manager Leo Durocher and his hard-drinking, hard-swinging team of Hugh Caseys and Kirby Higbes very happy, since Havana was known for its rum, women, cigars and gambling. But many of these teammates of Jackie were southern, with their own prejudice problems, and they were stars in their own right who resented all the special attention and superlatives this black rookie was getting. It took every bit of Robinson's savvy as a player and a man to gain their respect and to prove to them that he was good, he was tough, and that they needed him in the lineup to win games.

He then had to prove to the fans and players in other cities that he had the stuff in him to weather the abuse and scorn, and still compete with them on the highest level. Rickey's scenario worked as he had dreamed it would. Despite all the pressure and distractions, Jackie Robinson was a hell of a baseball player and won Rookie of the Year, and later on all the other awards—Most Valuable Player and All Star—until he became the most dominant force in the game. And perhaps most important, he won the respect of everyone—fans, competitors, even bigots.

In terms of contribution to the progress of his race, Robinson was unquestionably the most significant athlete of his generation, and it was with great sadness that in 1949 political issues made him stand up as an antagonist to the greatest black athlete of the previous generation, Paul Robeson.

Chapter X

Paul Robeson

(All the Complexities of the Times in One Life 1898-1976)

No other American-born man of color ever possessed more raw power, talent, and intelligence to inspire his own race and to influence white attitudes toward that race than Paul Robeson. His life spanned the era from 1898 to 1976 and was intimately woven into all of the problems, defeats, progress and triumphs that have been investigated in all the previous chapters of this book. He had more potential even than DuBois, Booker T. Washington, Frederick Douglass or Martin Luther King, Jr., because he had the ability to do so many admirable things so well. His physical size, his athletic coordination, his handsome face, his powerful, controlled voice, his charismatic presence, his keen mind, all belonged to a superior being. By today's standards he would have created all the excitement of a pop star, movie idol, sports hero all rolled into one. And for his time, that's what he was. A superman. Perhaps because of this, or despite it, he was eventually undone by the world in which he had to live, and by forces within himself.

His life can really be divided into two sections. The first extending through VJ Day in 1945, is a series of triumphs. The second part, from 1946 to his death in 1976, has all the ingredients of a tragic opera.

His childhood was filled with the deprivation and trauma of most other American black offspring of escaped slave parentage. Born April 9, 1898, in Princeton, New Jersey, one of five children of the Reverend William Drew Robeson, he lost his mother Maria Louisa at the age of six in a nightmarish accident, when she burned to death after a coal from a kitchen stove ignited her dress. From then on, whatever stability he was exposed to came from the extended family of aunts, uncles and cousins who had just moved up from the cotton and tobacco fields of North Carolina.

Education was an unquestioned goal of the reverend's home, having struggled himself to get the finest classical, traditional type of learning after escaping the South via the underground railway, and persisting until he had been graduated from Lincoln University's Divinity School. Paul graduated from Somerville High as an honor student and a celebrated athlete. Word of the potential of this 6'4" giant with the steel-trap mind had spread along the northeastern black grapevine, and he received a scholarship to Rutgers University through the auspices of NAACP supporters, including Lena Horne's grandmother Cora.

Princeton in those days had the demeanor of an old southern town, and Paul was used to racial problems. When he moved on to Rutgers, the situation was not much better, since he was only the third black to ever attend the school. Still, producing good grades and performing amazing feats seemed to come ridiculously easy for him. As Carl Van Doren once wrote of Robeson, "As soon as he was ready, the times seem to have been ready for him." He won the major oratorical contests four years in a row. He achieved America's highest scholastic honor, the Phi Beta Kappa key, and for two years he became Rutger's first all-American football player. It makes one wonder, historically, how many of these football awardees could also display Phi Beta keys? And this fantastic athlete also caught for the baseball team, played center on the basketball varsity, and won letters in track.

But the Glee Club denied him membership, despite his resonant voice, and he was turned away from all social events and dances. Nevertheless, he graduated as valedictorian of his class in 1919. Law was the profession he thought could best utilize his debating talents, so he moved to Harlem and entered Columbia Law School. The tuition and board were a terrible burden, and the solution for an extra source of income was playing minor league professional football on weekends, particularly after 1921 when he married Eslanda Cardoza Goode, who planned a career as an analytical chemist.

In 1922, still at Columbia, and still seeking new ways to make money, he was attracted to the idea of the theatre. His debut was a very minor part, playing Simon in *Simon the Cyrenian* at the Harlem YWCA. But Eslanda had secretly invited two men from the then avante-garde Provincetown Theatre, who were so impressed with his stage presence that they offered him the title role in *The Emperor Jones*, a new play by a playwright just starting to acquire a reputation, named Eugene O'Neill. Paul turned down this role to continue with law, oblivious to the fact that fate would reprise this contact with the same theatre, the same play and playwright a few years later.

But first, another director, Augustin Duncan, brother of Isadora, was also taken with his performance as Simon, and convinced Paul to co-star with the famous Margaret Wycherly in *Taboo*. It was such a success that Mrs. Patrick Campbell optioned it for a London production, directing and starring in it herself, changing the name to *Voodoo*, and, most important, bringing Paul over to England to play opposite her.

It was a loosely constructed script that had dream sequences where Mrs. Campbell inserted spirituals like *Go Down Moses* for Paul to sing. The audience was so stunned by his singing voice that during the performance Robeson would often hear his director stage-whisper, "Another song, another," and he would add to his repetoire.

Finally, he decided to go back to New York and give the practice of law a whirl. Black lawyers in those days were rare, and the members of his prestigious law firm were not ready for a young professional who would not accept the role of an "Uncle Tom." After a few months of racial insult and abuse, he was firm in his decision to give up the law forever and concentrate on the entertainment arts, which gave him deep satisfaction, and surprisingly abundent earning potential, since he was one of a kind at that time. He also was sure that "only the singer, artist and writer are able to break the ban in America."

Now he sought out Eugene O'Neill. The author had Paul in mind ever since they had first met, and had written a second play for an integrated cast. Their plan was to open *All God's Chillun' Got Wings* with Paul in the lead role of Jim, not coincidentally, a black lawyer. But word leaked out that the final scene included an on-stage kiss between Jim and his white wife, and soon the reaction began. The Hearst papers started a campaign to rouse public opinion against the production, the mayor of New York indicated that he would harass it, and K.K.K. threats of violence arrived by mail daily.

O'Neill decided to fight another day, and instead of the new play, he revived *The Emperor Jones*, choosing Paul for the lead over Charles Gilpin, the top black actor of the day, who had introduced the part in the first production. The reviews were four star. According to one, Robeson was called back out, "by men and women who rose to their feet and applauded. When the ache in their arms stopped their hands, they used their voices, shouted meaningless words, gave hoarse throaty cries . . . the ovation was for Robeson, for his emotional strength, for his superb acting."

The Emperor Jones moved on to London and so did Paul. It was during this London run that the often reported incident of racial bigotry at the famous Savoy Hotel took place. Robeson had been able to gain admittance all over the city, received with great politeness at numerous restaurants and clubs. But when he tried to enter the Savoy Grill to meet friends this particular evening, he was turned away. A black publisher from Chicago had been denied rooms by 30 London hotels shortly before this, and Paul's friends took the issue to all the newspapers and ultimately to the British Parliament. He was never again insulted in England.

Returning to New York in the fall of 1924, another twist of fate directed him toward an extension of his career into concert engagements. He had had a brief fling with a musical in 1922, when Eubie Blake cast him for a short stint in the version of *Shuffle Along* that played at both the Plantation Club and the

Cotton Club. One night just after his return from London, Paul was asked to sing during a living room soiree at Walter White's apartment. Heywood Broun, a popular columnist, was a guest, and the next day he wrote a piece telling the city about this magnificent voice. Within three weeks, Jimmy Light, director of the Provincetown Theatre, had organized a concert for April 19 at the Greenwich Village Theatre with Larry Brown as accompanist. This duo of Robeson and Brown remained intact for the rest of Robeson's life both as musical partners and inseparable friends, travelling all over the globe together. Their first review read:

"All who listened last night in the first concert in this country made entirely of Negro music . . . may have been present at a turning point, one of those thin points in time in which a star is born and not yet visible—the first appearance of this folk wealth to be made without deference or apology. Paul Robeson's voice is difficult to describe. It is a voice in which deep bells ring." This was encouragement enough for Essie to quit her job as a lab technician to become their manager, and for the next four years the three of them toured the length and breadth of the U. S. for concerts that emphasized Negro spirituals like "No More Auction Block," "Goin' to Ride Up in de Chariot," "Every Time I Feel de Spirit," "Hear De Lam's a Crying'," "O' Give Me Your Han'," "Water Boy," and "Swing Low Sweet Chariot."

Robeson made it clear why he chose to saturate his audiences with this music. "These songs are to Negro culture what the works of the great poets are to English culture. They are the soul of the race made manifest. . . . But the suffering he has undergone has left an indelible mark on the Negro's soul, and at the present stage he suffers from an inferiority complex which finds its compensation in a desire to imitate the white man and his ways. But I am convinced that in this direction there is neither fulfillment nor peace for the Negro."

A few years later, the Viennese music critic Siegfried Geyer, knowing of Paul's minimal formal voice training, went to a concert fully expecting to hear a "Nine Days Musical Wonder." However, afterward he wrote: "When this man began to sing one of those Negro spirituals filled with the deepest melancholy—when slow and full came the first words "Wade in the

Water"—the hall suddenly grew hushed and still. We were listening to organ tones of purity seldom heard, and what followed—one spiritual after another—confirmed the phenomenon which the Negro singer represents—a voice which is no mere function of the larynx, but of which the motive of force is soul."

The musical *Show Boat* by Jerome Kern and Oscar Hammerstein II took him off the tour in 1928, and truly made him an international star. "Ol' Man River" was written specifically with him in mind. Through the years he used it, first only as a show-tune, and then by making minimal changes it became an activist song of resistance in the later years when all of his performing had taken on political overtones. *Show Boat* was a hit of immense proportions in New York and later in London and, although his part was not the lead, it was Robeson that people came to see.

Marie Seton describes the London opening night:

"Something happened in Drury Lane Theatre on the night *Show Boat* opened there in April, 1928. . . . Robeson sang 'Ol' Man River' and everyone else in *Show Boat* was forgotten by both audience and critics. His was the voice of a man speaking in the midst of a puppet-show. The audience did not realize that what moved them was the fusion point where real experience is transmitted into art.

"As the weeks passed and more and more people went to see *Show Boat*, the impact of Robeson was like a chain reaction. The first to "discover" him were the smart Mayfair set, who went in search of the latest sensations, and inaugurated new fashions. But soon the country people who came up to London for the 'season' were telling their friends to go to Drury Lane. Then the elderly, frowsty people, who go to matinees, began talking about Robeson's voice. Soon the 'intelligentsia' of Bloomsbury and Chelsea, who seldom deigned to go to musical comedies, were discussing him. At last, young people from Clapham and Tooting could be heard talking about him on the tops of busses and on the underground. . . . The expression on Robeson's face was not that of an actor."

"'I'm Scared of Livin' and Feared of Dyin'—'

"The pathos of Robeson's voice called up images of slaves and overseers with whips. How had a man with such a history risen?

"Sitting next to me was a middleaged lady with a dry yellowing face and the refined, dowdy clothes characteristic of certain English people who have repressed all strong feeling beneath a monotone of comformity. A child sat at her side. There was nothing beautiful or free in either the child or the aging woman, except the pleasure in their eyes as they listened to Paul Robeson. Their entranced expression seemed reflected in face after face up to the dim balcony. It proclaimed that Robeson, so classically African, with broad flaring nostrils, full lips and dark skin, expressed something they felt most deeply. They clapped wildly.

"A most startling quality appeared in Robeson as he accepted the applause. He stood as if it were his naked spirit which was receiving the response of the audience. He was visibly touched, and yet remote. He seemed to have no greed for applause, and he appeared to be a man stripped bare of mannerisms."

Paul and Essie by now felt very comfortable in London, which seemed to have an atmosphere more conducive to his artistic development than any city in America. And of course, because blacks were in such small minority in Britain, and no threat to the status quo, there was much less racism than at home. Living in London had stimulated profound changes in the Robesons, socially and politically. They were exposed to the most prominent and cultured members of English society, and more significantly, to many of the most outspoken radicals and political free thinkers of that era. It was in a conversation at a party, talking to George Bernard Shaw, that Paul realized he himself was totally ignorant of the socialist theories that Shaw brought up, and this led him to an immediate study of the subject. He began to give deeper thought to his role in the world and the aims of his life. And perhaps most important he was introduced to blacks from Africa, two of them later to become Heads of State of emerging African nations—Kwame Nkrumah and Jomo Kenyatta.

In his autobiography *Here I Stand* he tells us: "In 1927 I moved to England with my family. . . . London was the center of the British Empire and it was there that I discovered Africa. That discovery which has influenced my life ever since, made it clear that I would not live out my life as an adopted Englishman, and I came to consider that I was an African. And as I plunged with excited interest into my studies of Africa at the London School of Oriental languages, I came to see that African culture was indeed a treasure-store for the world. . . . I felt as one with my African friends and became filled with a glowing pride in these riches, new found to me."

In his enthusiasm for whatever place he was visiting, he would make similar statements in Wales, in Germany and in Russia. He seemed to adopt his host nation always. And at those deeply joyful moments in new surroundings, the problems of his native black Americans seemed to recede further into the past, and they seldom came up in conversations with friends.

The year 1930 brought another startling first for him, the role of *Othello* in a London production. Ira Aldridge had been the last black actor to play the Moor and that was in the deep past of 1860. Paul's interpretation was revolutionary, yet true to Shakespeare. He viewed the character as a colored man of noble ancestry, yet isolated in an alien and hostile white society. Sure that he has been betrayed, Othello kills not out of jealousy, but to instinctively defend his racial pride and integrity. This interpretation was nourished by Paul's explorations into African cultural roots.

The *Othello* production brought forth another racial brouhaha even in relatively tolerant London. The play calls for an obvious, strong, sexually satisfying aspect to the marriage of Othello and Desdemona. And on opening night when Robeson and Peggy Ashcroft clung to each other in a soul-shattering embrace, there was an audible gasp from the audience. For the next month Miss Ashcroft was hounded by the press as to how it felt to be kissed by a black. "It's quite like being kissed by any other actor," she insisted. Writing of this controversy, and speculating about a possible importation of the production to Broadway, Burns Mantle, the New York critic, said, "If Peggy Ashcroft comes to New York to receive and return Othello's kisses frankly and eagerly in character, a furor would result. But if Lillian Gish accepts the role, things could become quite terrible."

Late in 1930 Paul began a series of travels that took him away from England for long periods. The first move was to Berlin to work with Max Reinhardt, the most famous director in the world at that time. He left on the trip eagerly telling all who would listen that in Germany there was no color bar, and he would not be limited in scope. This sounded strange to British ears since they had been giving his talents the broadest possible forum in the most responsible manner. They had elevated him to stardom without posing one barrier. But Paul persisted in his praise: "Germany is the gateway now of all of Europe. Russia sends its artists and its directors." It was around this time that Eslanda gave the press a little insight into her star husband's priorities.

"He is lazy and uninterested in the presence of things which are of no fundamental importance to him. But he is roused to tremendous activity and excitement in the presence of things which are important to his development."

The year 1931 saw him star in still another O'Neill play in London, *The Hairy Ape.* His reputation grew, and the accolades became more heroic. Alexander Woollcott, the critic and raconteur, wrote of him: "By what he does, thinks and is, by his unassailable dignity and his serene, incorruptible simplicity, Paul Robeson strikes me as having been made out of the original stuff of the world. In this sense he is coeval with Adam and the redwood trees of California."

At the invitation of Sergei Eisenstein, the celebrated Russian film director, Robeson made his first trip to the Soviet Union in 1934, along with Essie and writer Marie Seton, his biographer. A movie *Black Majesty* was under discussion. They passed through Germany briefly, but long enough to be involved in an ugly incident provoked by Nazi storm troopers.

Marie was white, Essie was very light-skinned, and Paul noticed the SS men guarding the train station eyeing him ominously when their group changed trains. He understood enough German, particularly the racial epithets, to know that they suspected he had two white German campanions. Suddenly with a snarl, one officer and a few men started to surround Paul, separating him from the women, and in his mind becoming the image of a southern lynch mob. Fortunately, at that moment their train pulled in, and with his size he bulled his way through the circle and signaled the ladies to rush onto the train with him.

The incident was over, but he never forgot the fear he had felt, or the look in the Nazis' eyes.

Russia was another matter. He had studied the language for two years preparing for this trip which fostered within him not only a great love for the Soviet people, but a more serious interest in socialism itself, and its positive effect on underdeveloped peoples. Eisenstein's film about Haiti was never done, but there were other benefits. He met an African who called his attention to "something he had observed in the Soviet Union. On a visit to that country the man had travelled east and had seen the Yakuts. A people who had been classified as a 'backward race' by the Czars. He had been struck by the resemblance between the tribal life of the Yakuts and his own people of east Africa. What would happen to a people like the Yakuts now that they had been freed from colonial oppression, and were part of the construction of socialist Soviet? Well I went to see for myself . . . saw how the Yakuts and the Uzbeks and all the formerly oppressed nations were leaping ahead from tribalism to modern industrial economy, from illiteracy to the heights of knowledge, their young men and women mastering the sciences and arts. A thousand years? No—less than 20."

This last remark was in answer to colonialists who always predicted that it would take African cultures 1000 years to be capable of self-rule. But again, in hearing of Robeson's preoccupation with the future of primitive Africans, some American blacks were wondering why his thoughts were not for his own people at home, and if he had given up on them even though they were so much farther along the road to parity with whites. Did he consider the American racial scene less receptive to change than primitive tribes? Or was he just seduced by the exotic allure of whatever was on the other side of the mountain? Closer to the truth, probably, was that he saw a need for an overall devotion to the oppressed people of the entire world. But American blacks still felt he was treating them as second-class citizens. William L. Patterson, the black lawyer so involved in the fund-raising for the struggle of the Scottsboro Boys, met him in Moscow and begged him to return home to help in the fight for Negro causes.

Among his fellow black American artists this sense that he

was abandoning them had been building up for many years. Arnold Rampersad, the biographer of Langston Hughes, the literary star of Harlem, points out the signs of disenchantment:

"Meanwhile sorcery of another kind was taking place on behalf of Hughes who had conceived of *Emperor of Haiti* with the prepossessing Paul Robeson in mind, although Robeson showed no interest in returning from Britain where he was a lion. However, Godmother was working day and night to subdue the star, who was terrified of her."

And a while later: "Then Hughes received an urgent summons from Kaj Gynt, his collaborator on the musical *Cock of the World*. Paul Robeson, in the U.S. on a concert tour, was on the brink of a decision about appearing in the show. George Gershwin himself might do the music. Could Hughes return to New York at once? Although Carl Van Vechten advised caution, Hughes decided to cancel some engagements and dash to New York.

"Weary, Hughes reached the city on Thursday, March 24, just before the Easter weekend. But at the apartment building where Robeson's white manager lived, he was refused admission. The irony was almost too much for him. Paul Robeson's manager lived in a building where blacks were refused even as visitors. Then he discovered that Robeson had decamped and gone back to London, nor was the star much interested in their play."

Lena Horne, who met him just after he moved back from London, loved Paul and would abide no criticism of him. "Paul used to tell me that we would never win through anger or bitterness but only through pride and belief that our cause was just. . . . He used to tell me half-jokingly that I was too self-centered ever to be a very effective political militant. 'Lena's got too much temper,' he would tell people. Or, 'she likes nice things too much.' Both of which I fear are true. But in private, he did everything he could to reinforce my weakened, mostly dormant sense of racial identity. 'You are a Negro—and that is the whole basis of what you are and what you will become,' he said, 'when you live and learn some more, you will be Lena Horne, Negro.'"

If this conversation had taken place two years later, would it still have been "the whole basis of what you are"?

Later in 1937, while the Spanish Civil War raged, he cut short a second Moscow trip to fly to Albert Hall in London to sing and raise funds for the Loyalists. It was at this benefit that he first changed Oscar Hammerstein's lyrics of "Ol' Man River" to suit his new activist mood. That night they appeared in this form:

> There's an old man called the Mississippi,
> That's the ol' man I don't like to be,
> What does he care if the world's got trouble?
> What does he care if the world ain't free?
> Tote that barge, lift that bale,
> You show a little grit an' you lands in jail.
> I keeps laughin', instead of cryin',
> I must keep fightin' until I'm dyin',
> And ol' man river, he just keeps rollin' along.

A few months later he took his wife and his songs to the front lines and sang for the Loyalist troops in Madrid and Barcelona. At Tervel, the guns of both sides were stopped in a state of truce for a few hours to allow him to perform safely. Proximity to danger and battles seemed to alter the style of the public comments, making them more aggressive. Late in 1936 he told *The New York Times* that he would enroll his nine-year-old son in school in Moscow "instead of America so the boy need not contend with discrimination because of color until he is older and his father can be with him."

Robeson's very significant contributions to both the advancement to maturity of the movie industry and to the attempts at integrating black actors into the main stream of film roles between 1932 and 1939 has been covered in detail in the chapter on blacks in Hollywood. In a London interview he made it clear why he turned to other directions after seven disappointing years:

"I thought I could do something for the Negro race in the films—show the truth about them, and about other people too. I used to do my part and go away feeling satisfied, thought everything was okay. Well, it wasn't. Things were twisted and changed, distorted, they didn't mean the same.

"That made me think things out. It made me more conscious politically.

"One can't face the film companies. They represent about the biggest aggregate of finance capital in the world. That's why they make their films that way. So no more films for me."

He fared much better in his relationship with record companies and made dozens of albums under many labels through the years, starting with one for Victor in 1925. John Hammond had him record "Paul Robeson Spirituals" with great care for Columbia, and RCA did a wonderful album called "Paul Robeson, Songs of my People," that offered "Deep River," "Ezekiel Saw the Wheel," "Sometime I Feel Like a Motherless Child," and "Joshua Fit' the Battle of Jericho." Of course there were recordings of highlights from his films and excellent ones of the *Show Boat* songs. When he became known as a global traveler, he did tunes from other countries in other languages like "Schlof Mein Kind," "Fontana" and "The Song of the Volga Boatmen." But it was still and always the "Shortnin' Bread" and "Mighty Lak' a Rose" discs that sold the best.

There was a certainty in the Europe of 1939 that a new World War was imminent, and the Robesons felt a responsibility to their homeland after 11 years abroad. Paul and Larry Brown had just completed a harrowing tour of the continent and Scandinavia, with the very real threat of invasion by Hitler's forces at every stop. And so they shipped their belongings back to New York. The "welcome" home was at first rude, for when he arrived to keep an invitation to tea at a friend's suite in a well-known hotel, he was told to use the freight elevator.

But New York had its compensations, when he was signed to do the CBS broadcast of the premier of the 11-minute "Ballad For Americans" by Earl Robinson and John LaTouche. This performance resulted in the greatest audience response of calls to the CBS switchborad since Orson Welles's Martian scare program. The excitement was not only for Robeson's one of a kind voice, but for the daring realism of the lyric:

Man in white skin can never be free,
While his black brother is in slavery.
Out of the cheating, out of the shouting
Out of the windbags and patriotic spouting,
Out of uncertainty and doubting,   .

Out of carpet bags and the brass spitoon
It will come again—our marching songs will come again.
Simple as a hit tune, deep as our valley,
High as the mountains, strong as the people who made it.

His friend John Hammond insisted that Paul record this for
Columbia with Hammond producing, and the result sold 30,000
copies the first year. In a juxtapositon of parties, the Republicans
chose this liberal anthem as their theme song for the 1940 National Convention. Wendell Willkie more than likely influenced
this choice.

Stimulated by the success of the ballad, Robeson and Larry
Brown performed across the U.S. to the largest concert audiences ever—30,000 in Hollywood Bowl, 14,000 in Lewisohn
Stadium, 160,000 in Chicago's Grant Park and 22,000 at Wa-
tergate Park in Washington, D.C. There were no southern concerts because he still refused to perform before segregated audiences, and southern promoters refused to honor this clause in
his standard contract. In the critics' reviews of these concerts he
always received the highest praise. In fact, in his entire career as
a performer, it is difficult to find a negative analysis of his acting
or singing, whatever the fate of the vehicle in which he was
appearing.

During the Roosevelt era Robeson's reputation as an entertainer was now fused with an identification as a spokesman for
all those oppressed, struggling against any injustice—whether
anti-Semitism, colonialism or anti-labor legislation. He sang and
spoke at a rally of the citizens' committee to free Earl Browder,
head of the American Communist Party. Ironically, when Goli-
ath-like Russia invaded tiny, courageous Finland, he refused to
participate in fund-raising for this desperately needy underdog.

The vigorous concert schedule did not dilute his activism.
With W.E.B. Du Bois he was the co-chairman of the Council on
African Affairs to promote African liberation. He was very active
in the growth of unions, particularly the CIO, and was also
awarded honarary membership in the longshoremen's maritime
and auto workers' organizations.

Robeson's anti-Fascist fervor was no problem during World
War II when the "popular front against Fascism" was official

U.S. policy. And, of course, in 1942 Russia was our ally against a common enemy. He was also enjoying a new peak of popularity due to his brilliance in the 1943 New York production of *Othello* with Uta Hagen as Desdemona and Jose Ferrer as Iago. Hailed as the finest American Shakespearean production ever, it ran for 296 performances on Broadway and then went on a cross-country tour of major cities, omitting the south except for one-nighters at black colleges. That year Robeson won the Donaldson Award for best performance by an actor on Broadway. But even more impressive was receiving the gold medal award for best diction in the American theatre—a long move from the old theatrical black stereotype. This award, presented by the American Academy of Arts and Sciences, had only been won by nine people since its inception in 1924.

Once VJ Day passed and the cold war with Moscow had begun, the public's interpretation and toleration of Robeson's political stance changed dramatically. His pronouncements had also altered considerably. Verbal darts at "Fascism" began to fade into the background, and a more overt Leninist stand became evident in his public addresses. His very first post-war speech in accepting the annual Springarn medal from the NAACP in Chicago on October 17, 1945, jolted the Afro-American Pittsburgh *Courier*, which reported that he "shocked his several hundred listeners by voicing frank and pronounced preference for Soviet principles—economic, political, and social."

He followed this up by creating greater consternation before the Central Conference of American Rabbis, accusing the U.S. of having taken over the role of Hitler, and that it now "stands for counter-revolution all over the world." He urged the U.S. to share secrets of the atomic bomb with the Soviet Union, predicting it would be "the greatest guarantee against another war." This man who had such exquisite timing on stage was exhibiting the reverse politically.

In 1946, he devoted his energy to a flurry of activity on behalf of the Council on African Affairs which had strong alliances with the Soviet Union. He first joined Marian Anderson at a rally the council was organizing at Harlem's Abyssinian Baptist Church for South African Famine Relief. Then he spoke at a mass meeting for African freedom at Madison Square Garden sponsored by the council. In his speech he said, "Stop Russia, the brass voices cry in chorus, and the men behind the voices hope that people will be afraid and will turn against their wartime ally. Their fanatic cries mask the program of imperialist aggression which these men themselves are seeking to impose upon the world. The 'stop Russia' cry really means—stop the advance of the colonial peoples of Asia and Africa toward independence, stop the forces of the new democracy developing in Europe, stop organized workers of America from holding their ground against their profit-greedy employers. Stop the Negro people from voting and joining trade unions in the south. 'Stop Russia' means stop progress, maintain the status quo. It means let the privileged few continue to thrive and thrive at the expense of the masses."

Within a few days of each other he spoke first at a waterfront strike meeting in San Francisco of the Committee for Maritime Unity, participating as co-chairman of the National Committee to Win the Peace, and then at a meeting of the Civil Rights Congress, where he was elected vice president with William L. Patterson as executive secretary.

Almost immediately the first of his many subpoenas to appear before legislative investigatory committees arrived. This one was from the California Committee on Un-American activities, headed by State Senator Tenney, and they wanted Paul's testimony in his role as co-chairman of the National Committee To Win The Peace. During the session, Senator Tenney asked him: "You don't mean to tell this committee, I am sure . . . that merely because a man is a capitalist, and has some money . . . that he becomes a lyncher or would condone those things?"

Answer by Robeson: "No, I was giving a definition of Fascism, that it is not necessarily the beast in man, it is the necessity of certain groups to protect their interest, like a former witness said, against social change, that is all. They want the status quo or even much less than that. That was the essence of Fascism. When people in Europe were pressing forward to social change, the Fascists said no and beat them back. I feel that is part of what is going on maybe in our country today. . . .

Tenney: But are you a member of the Communist Party? I ask it of everybody, so don't feel embarrassed.

Robeson: No, I am not embarrassed. I have heard it so much. Every reporter has asked me that. I will certainly answer it, Mr. Tenney, only you might ask me if I am a member of the Republican or Democratic Party, as far as I know the Communist Party is a very legal one in the U.S. I sort of characterize myself as anti-Fascist and independent. If I wanted to join any party I could just as conceivably join the Communist Party, more so today than I could join the Republican or Democratic Party. But I am not a communist.

Tenney: "You are not? I suppose from your statement, would I be proper and correct in concluding that you would be more sympathetic with the Communist Party than the Republican or Democratic Partys?"

Robeson: "I would put it this way. I said I could join either one of them just as well. . . . I have no reason to be inferring Communism is evil or that someone should run around the corner when they hear it, as I heard here this morning, because today communists are in control or elected by people because of their sacrifice in much of the world. I feel Americans have got to understand it unless they want to drop off the planet. They have got to get along with a lot of communists."

Years later he continued to deny that he had ever been a card-carrying communist. "If the government officials had a shred of evidence to back up that charge, you can bet your last dollar that they would have tried their best to put me under jail. But they have no such evidence because that charge is a lie."

This committee labelled him a cooperative witness, but the vast amount of publicity in the media did not help his career. The number of offers to perform started shrinking drastically. In March of 1947, he sang "Joe Hill" by Earl Robinson and Alfred Hayes at the University of Utah in Salt Lake City, the place where Hill was executed in 1915. Robeson afterward announced: "You have just heard my final concert for at least two years and perhaps for many more. I'm retiring here and now from concert work. I shall sing now for my trade union and college friends. In other words only at gatherings where I can sing what I please."

On April 3, while honoring a previously made commitment, he was prevented from appearing in Peoria, Illinois, when

Shriners cancelled the contract for the use of the Shriners' Mosque, and the mayor would not allow the use of city hall as a substitute site.

The same sequence was attempted on May 9, when the Board of Education of Albany, New York, denied permission for his concert at Phillip Livingston Junior High School, but Supreme Court Justice Isadore Bookstein ordered that the school be made available and the concert was held after all. He continued his union work by giving four recitals in Panama for the United Public Workers of America, CIO, who were trying to unionize Panamanian workers. And he spoke at the National Maritime Union Convention, the last to which he was invited, since leadership under Joseph Curran turned to an anti-Communist line of action.

In December of 1947 he became an integral part of the Henry Wallace for President of the U.S. Committee from which the Progressive Party emerged. In March he told the Honolulu *Star Bulletin* that he planned to continue his work on behalf of Wallace because "if anybody continues the New Deal traditions of Franklin Roosevelt, it is Wallace." He scoffed at the idea that Wallace was a communist and said he believed Wallace was a "progressive capitalist." "Continuing with this whole talk about communism is absurd. Either we get along with the communists, jump in the ocean, or blow up the whole world. Saying you can't get along with communists is like saying you can't get along with the birds."

Speaking to the International Fur and Leather Workers Convention in May, 1948, he asked:

"How can we stand and allow our government to suggest that we can think more of the profits of a few people of Standard Oil of this very state, than the lives of one of the great peoples of the world, a people who gave us the very basis of our ethics and our religion? Am I to say, or to allow to say, a Forrestal [Secretary of Defense], who went to Princeton about the same time as I went to Rutgers. I know a lot of these fellows on the Board of Standard Oil—they say, 'Roby, why do you take the side you do?' They care nothing for the rights of the ordinary laboring man. Let them starve, they say, just so we get the profits. But I say to them, never, for example shall my son go to a foreign land to take up a gun to shoot a people that are close to him, in the interest of any kind of oil."

He spoke out nakedly against capitalism once more at the Progressive Party Convention in July, 1948:

"What Mockery! Our high standard of living for a minority in the richest country of the earth! Absentee ownership still rules supreme, one percent of the population owns as much wealth as 1/3 of the ill-housed, ill-fed whom Roosevelt so feelingly described. The spectacle of the Pells, Grundys, the Sullivans and Dulleses in full view on the Republican side and the DuPonts, House of Morgan, Dillon and Forrestal on the Democratic side, shows the contempt of big business barons for the great majority of the American people."

Early in 1949 he rewrote history: "If today we Americans move freely on earth, we owe this to the heroic defenders of Stalingrad." At the same time, he said he had visited the South where his father lived and worked as a slave 100 years ago, but found everything the same for the Negro—nothing changed. "Such is the policy of a country where Wall Street rules," he said.

But the actual moment when the fortunes of his life, his career and his reputation took an irreversably negative turn, came during his acceptance speech of the top political award at the Russian-sponsored Paris Peace Conference on April 20, 1949, when he said it is "unthinkable that American Negroes could go to war on behalf of those who have oppressed us for generations, against the Soviet Union which in one generation has raised our people to full human dignity." With that he went past the point of no return.

These attacks less than four years after the exhausting and costly effort to defeat Germany and Japan severely offended the average decent American citizen. But worse, from everyone's standpoint, his words unleashed the repressed hatred of the lunatic fringe, a dangerous minority that now felt justified in spewing venom not only on Robeson, but on all its traditional enemies—blacks, Jews, immigrants, and anyone with liberal, ethical or humanitarian leanings. The mood throughout the spring became increasingly ugly wherever Robeson went, and the inevitable explosion happened in Peekskill, New York, on

August 27, 1949, although it could just as well have occurred somewhere else.

Robeson and Pete Seeger were scheduled to give a concert for the benefit of the Harlem Civil Rights Congress, but organized groups of whites, armed with tire irons, baseball bats and rocks, sealed the roads after only 200 of the audience had arrived. The concert organizers and Robeson were diverted by their own security before they reached the trouble spot, and the event was cancelled. All law enforcement personnel left the site, and Howard Fast, the white novelist, and 42 other men and boys battled the mob to help the early arrivals, including women and children, escape.

A week later, in the same location, the concert took place surrounded by an atmosphere of riot police, and coverage by an international press corps. Despite the available protection, a nightmarish attack followed as the crowd left the grounds afterward. One hundred forty people were seriously injured, while many of the police turned their backs or just stood by. Local law officers did not want to molest local rednecks for the sake of "outsiders." But the cameras were clicking, and Americans all across the country were sickened by the photos of the mob gone mad.

And though the forces of reason defended Paul's right to his political positions, and the right of free assemblage for his rallies, he had moved so far beyond the mainstream that he was separating himself more and more from these defenders. And to many moderate black leaders he was becoming more of a hindrance than an asset to the cause of black racial equality.

Walter White, in his role of executive secretary of the NAACP, had already attacked Robeson's Paris speech in detail during a press conference ten days after it was made. And a full month before the Peekskill debacle, a number of prominent blacks had not defended his peace congress remarks while testifying before special hearings of the House Un-American Activities Committee. Manning Johnson in a flamboyant statement accused Robeson of dreaming of becoming a "Black Stalin."

But it was Jackie Robinson who delivered very carefully thought-out testimony that best expressed the position of moderate blacks in defense of their race, while at the same time acknowledging the debt that all blacks owed the Robeson of the twenties, thirties, and early forties. Before his Washington, D.C., appearance, Jackie was pressured from all sides. Some warned him about "becoming a traitor to the Negro," or becoming "a tool of the witch hunters." And he was very aware of the strong efforts Paul had made in 1943 to get baseball commissioner Kennesaw Mountain Landis to open the major leagues to blacks, efforts that must have helped Branch Rickey to finally sign Jackie three years later. These were his own thoughts as he wrestled with so many conflicting emotions before leaving for Washington.

"I knew that many Negroes welcomed Robeson's remarks, not because of disloyalty, or of any tender feelings toward the Soviet Union, but because they feared that white America would never grant the Negro a portion of equality simply out of a sense of justice and decency. These Negroes believed that the only way to get Americans to do right was to frighten them, to hold a big stick over their heads. The Soviet Union appeared to be that big stick.

"Yet as I turned these things over in my mind, I could not convince myself that the average American white man was so devoid of a sense of justice that he would do right only out of fear. In fact I feared that the threat implied in Robeson's remark might warp whatever sense of justice American white men possessed.

"Against the facts, Robeson's Paris remarks seemed silly to me. Even in the days of legalized peonage, when my mother was battling for a minimum standard of decency on that plantation in Georgia, Negroes had stormed the hills of San Juan with Teddy Roosevelt, for whom I was named. In the First World War Negroes had gone to the Marne, to Château-Thierry, to Belleau Wood, where they had proudly born the burden of second-class citizens playing second-class soldiers, even as they pledged allegiance to the same noble causes other Americans professed in fighting this war . . . and in the Second World War, even in the face of insults and attacks on soldiers in their homeland and work-horse duties in the farthest corners of the globe, the Negro had fought some, though not always with his heart in it. . . .

"But what about Robeson? With what was I to take issue specifically? Had Robeson betrayed me? The Negro? The nation? The cause of freedom? How much justification was there in the things that Robeson had said in Paris and elsewhere? . . . And I remembered how as children we had thrilled to Robeson's success, had hummed the tunes made famous by his booming bass voice. . . . What Negro by 1949 had not heard Robeson tick off the background to his bitterness, 'Man, in Princeton, New Jersey, where I grew up, they would push Negroes off the sidewalk. It was like darkest Alabama.' We had heard him recall the episodes that he could not or would not forget. The resentment of having to sit out a football game against a southern college which refused to play against a Negro. The anger of being invited to sing in city after city where his sponsors did not have the courage to make it possible for him and other Negroes to stay at a local hotel without eating their meals in their rooms or riding freight elevators?

"It was a sordid story in which the life of every Negro is a tear-tinged little chapter, and I knew that even Negroes who considered Robeson politically naive and tactless would sympathize with him.

"Yet there was the question of responsibility to the bigger issue of personal freedom, to the future of humanity involved in an ideological struggle that would be the world's most consuming issue for years. How best could a Negro right the glaring wrongs of his native land? Certainly to give the impression that no Negro would go to war against Russia, that all Negroes were waiting eagerly to betray the U.S., was not only a lie, but a gambit designed to push millions of frustrated white Americans into replacing terror with terror. Even more tragic, to imply that a bright future for the Negro was possible only through violent revolution, most surely would convince millions of whites that the only way to retain the noble part of America's past would be through blind reaction. And how tragic this would be, not just for Negroes, but for all Americans and all those who had begun to look to America for wise leadership."

Having sorted out his thoughts in this manner, Jackie met with Branch Rickey and Lester Granger, the Executive Director of the National Urban League, and together they composed a statement that they felt represented the blacks' place in America with pride, and a clear conscience toward both Negro and white America. Because the text is bold and wise, it warrants inclusion here almost in its entirety. This is what Jackie Robinson said to the House Committee on Un-American Activities on July 18, 1949:

"I don't pretend to be any expert on communism or any other kind of politicalism . . . but you can put me down as an expert on being a colored American with 30 years of experience at it. . . .

"The white public should start toward real understanding, by appreciating that every single Negro who is worth his salt is going to resent any kind of slurs and discrimination because of his race. And he's going to use every bit of intelligence he has to stop it. This has got absolutely nothing to do with what communism may or may not be trying to do. And white people must realize that the more a Negro hates communism because it opposes democracy, the more he is going to hate any other influence that kills off democracy in this country. And that goes for racial discrimination in the Army, and segregation on trains and buses, and job discrimination because of religious beliefs, or color, or place of birth. . . . Negroes were stirred up long before there was a Communist Party, and they'll stay stirred up long after the party has disappeared—unless Jim Crow has disappeared as well!

"I've been asked to express my views on Paul Robeson's statement in Paris to the effect that American Negroes would refuse to fight in any war against Russia because we love Russia so much. I haven't any comment to make except that the statement sounds very silly to me. But he has a right to his personal views and if he wants to sound silly when he expresses them in public, that's his business. He's still a famous athlete and a great singer and actor. . . . But I know that I've got too much invested for my wife and child and myself in the future of this country, and I and other Americans of many races and faiths have too much invested in their country's welfare, for any of us to throw it away because of a siren song sung in bass. I'm a religious man, therefore I cherish America where I am free to worship as I please, a privilege which some countries do not give, and I expect that 999 out of almost any 1000 colored Americans you meet will tell you the same thing. But that doesn't mean that we're going to stop fighting race discrimination in this country before we've got it licked. It means that we're going to fight it all the harder because our stake in the future is so big. We can win our fight without the communists, and we don't want their help."

Paul tried to ignore the severity and the implications of these stands by prestigious black Americans. He appeared for the defense at the ongoing trial of 11 leaders of the American Communist Party, but was prevented by his advisers from saying anything other than that he knew the defendants. He toured extensively on singing and speaking engagements sponsored by the Council on African Affairs, each of which was picketed by the American Legion and the Veterans of Foreign Wars. His spirits were raised in October when Russia named one of its highest peaks Mt. Robeson in his honor.

But 1950 brought with it a series of drastically effective reprisals against him. Demands were made to Rutgers University that Robeson's name be removed from alumni rolls and athletic records and honorary degrees be rescinded. In March, NBC cancelled his scheduled appearance on Eleanor Roosevelt's TV program, ostensibly with her approval. Charles B. Denny, an executive vice president, told the press, "no good purpose would be served in having him speak on issues of Negro politics." On June 28 Robeson made a major speech against U.S. participation in the Korean hostilities, and that same day, agents of the State Department demanded that he hand over his passport to them, "because the Department considers that Paul Robeson's travel abroad would be contrary at this time to the best interests of the U.S." They knew that he had completed arrangements for a trip to Europe to attend meetings, fulfill some speaking engagements in a number of countries, and to sing concerts in Italy and England, along with recording sessions.

Every American who wanted a passport in those years was obliged to sign an oath swearing he was not a communist, but Robeson refused, saying it was nobody's business. At a meeting at the State Department on August 28th he also refused Secretary of State Dean Acheson's offer to give back the passport so that he could make a living fulfilling his entertainment contracts for the concerts and recordings, if he would sign a statement swearing that he would not make any political speeches while out of the country. The day after his refusal of this compromise, Madison Square Garden refused to rent the arena to the Council of African Affairs for a rally, and a few weeks later the mayor of Boston banned the exhibition of Robeson's portrait anywhere in the city.

During 1951, the pressure on him continued. Walter White wrote a bitter attack on him in *Ebony* magazine entitled "The strange case of Paul Robeson." Legal actions to regain his passport were meeting with failure. Son, Paul Jr., was denied a passport to attend a youth festival in Berlin, and *Crisis*, the NAACP magazine featured an article "Paul Robeson, the Lost Shepherd." In December, Paul himself heaped coals on the fire by heading a delegation petitioning the UN to charge the U.S. with genocide, on the grounds that "15 million black Americans are mostly subjected to conditions making for premature death, poverty and disease."

Early in 1952 he attempted to cross the border into Canada to speak at a Mine, Mill and Smelter Workers meeting in Vancouver, B.C. He was advised that if he went across, he would be subject to five years imprisonment and a $10,000 fine. Instead he spoke and sang to the meeting by a telephone hook-up. His income had dwindled from $150,000 a year to $6,000, since concerts and recording dates were not forthcoming.

Late that year, Russia awarded him the 1952 Stalin Peace Prize, which brought with it a check for $25,000. Whether this honor was bestowed by the Soviets to help his finances or to milk the Robeson situation for further propaganda can never be ascertained. But his acceptance of it removed any last possibility that he and his family could salvage a tolerant atmosphere for his future in the United States.

The I.R.S. presented him with a bill for their tax share of the $25,000 income. He resisted, stating that if the Nobel Prize money was tax free, why not the Stalin prize? The government's answer was that the sum obviously was paid to him for "services rendered."

He was denied a public auditorium in San Francisco and in Oakland later that year, and his sponsor, the Negro Labor Council, requested that the Berkeley Board of Education lend them the magnificent new Berkeley Board Theater. The Berkeley Board called a special open meeting at which 1200 Berkeley citizens voted by a show of hands 4 to 1 in favor of granting Robeson use of the hall. During the debate before the voting a minister pleaded:

"To my mind the real threat to democracy lies not in the idea which Robeson may have, but in the use of the fear of communism as a justification for the undermining of all the constitutional safeguards of individual rights. It was just precisely this supposed danger from communism first, and other minorities later, which Nazis used to silence all opposition while they hacked away at the very foundation of government in Germany."

Many of those who voted to allow use of the theater wondered whether there would have been this flexibility of thought and action in Robeson's beloved Soviet Union when faced with dissident criticism.

The years of trauma continued and finally, in 1958, at age 60, he got back his passport when the Supreme Court, in a related case—not his own—ruled that Congress had not authorized the State Department to have the power to withhold passports because of beliefs or associations. Paul had the joy of announcing the passport victory before a sell-out concert at Carnegie Hall, his first appearance there in ten years. He also told this audience of plans to go immediately to London, Prague, Berlin and Moscow, but made it clear he was not "deserting the country of my birth." Throughout that summer he performed in those four countries, to acclaim, but in August when his autobiography *Here I Stand* was reviewed, along with a biography of him by Marie Seton, the personal criticism was again deep and painful. In addition, not one leading American publisher would handle his autobiography, and he had to publish it in the U.S. himself under a hastily organized company, Othello Associates."

For purposes of objectivity, neither the American nor Russian reviews of both of these books are examined here, but it is interesting to see what was said in the British press, since that would have been his most sympathetic western audience in 1958. The review by Peregrine Worsthorne in the *Daily Telegraph* in London on August 22, 1958, went as follows:

"Paul Robeson is blessed with a superb voice, better perhaps than any other singer alive. He can express man's deepest feelings—compassion, anger, suffering and joy.

"Yet unlike most actors who rest content to express their vision of truth without attempting to realize it in this world, Mr. Robeson has sought to do both—to share as well as sing about the human condition. In other words, he has combined two conflicting functions, artist and politician.

"As a result, his personal testament, *Here I Stand*, and Marie Seton's biography are both studies in frustration, and frustration of a man who in the mundane level of political action has only succeeded in arousing interest and contumely. It is easy to see why the artist who never sings a false note and whose voice can give depth and meaning to the simplest melody, cannot as a politician ever strike a true one, nor can he probe beneath the surface of the obvious.

"His passionate and wholly understandable concern over Negro rights in America, gives him a black and white view of the world which grossly oversimplifies the true picture. Because his father was a slave over 100 years ago, he refuses to see today, that the true threat of slavery comes from the Soviet Union, rather than from the U.S.

"Because in Moscow a Negro can eat next to a white man in a public restaurant whereas in New York he sometimes cannot, he believes Russia is freer than the U.S. Again, because Negroes are poor, and working classes in general are poor, he believes racial discrimination to be a rich man's conspiracy, whereas the tragic truth is that it is the poor whites rather than the rich ones, who today feel most passionately about segregation.

"His political understanding in short is as narrow as his musical range is broad . . . in themselves, his politics are frivolous. He has nothing serious to contribute to the problems of Negro rights or political freedom. His views are only interesting insofar as they have interrupted and influenced a great musician. . . . *Show Boat, Emperor Jones, Othello, All God's Chillun', Sanders of the River*, are magic names. The other side of the coin—visits to the Soviet Union leading to withdrawal of his passport by the State Department—tell us only what we know already—that folly begets folly!"

And this is what appeared in the literary supplement of the *London Times* on September 5, 1958:

"Although it's only within the past ten years that Paul Robeson's political leanings have caused his career as a singer to be affected and interrupted, the fact remains that he has always felt strongly about the Negro problem in the U.S. And since the early 1930's when events in Germany began to impinge on his consciousness, he has been greatly concerned with oppression everywhere. When he played *Othello*, it was in order to prove something about and on behalf of the Negro. When he sang spirituals and folk songs it was to and for 'ordinary people.' A little later than many of the intellectuals, artists and writers, he allied himself with the communist cause, without, it seems, ever actually joining the party. And now, years after the dissillusionment of most of his contemporaries about communism, he hangs on with a kind of stubborn simplicity to the now discredited catch words and slogans of 20 years ago. Impossible to doubt his sincerity and his humanity as he lifts those huge arms wide like an Old Testament prophet in order to emphasize the hymn of brotherhood and love he sings.

"But he so obviously means one thing, while the words he sings mean another. Brotherhood turns uneasily into solidarity. People become masses. The false international voice breaks in and overwhelms even the strong resonant and heartfelt sound of Robeson. . . . In an autobiographical section he tells how years ago he came to love the English country and the English people, and decided to make his home in England:

"'And so I found in London a congenial, stimulating, intellectual atmosphere in which I felt at home. To an American Negro, the marked respect for law and order which is common among all classes throughout the British Isles was especially pleasing. They simply would not put up with Faubus over there. In those happy days, had someone suggested that my home should be back home in Jim Crow America, I would have thought he was out of his mind. Go back—well, what in heavens name for?'

"But later the urge to speak for, and in a sense to lead the American Negro, proved too strong for him. He returned to his own country where he was treated as a national hero during the war years and as virtually a traitor in the following decade. It is easy to find fault with the argument of his book. Its great virtue lies in its candid statements of the facts. *Here* are sentences from his speeches, *there* are those same sentences after they had passed through the distorting mirror of the American press. *Here* is what he was asked by the Un-American Activities Committee, *there* is what he replied. We can judge for ourselves. Sir Arthur Bryant, who can hardly be accused of sharing Robeson's politics, says in a foreword to Miss Seton's biography, 'It is not only his burning convictions, the depth and range of his sympathy and superb technique that move us, but the feeling that behind the voice is a man of rare human calibre. He acts on our sympathies as Dr. Johnson and Walter Scott do, because we feel that we are in the presence not only of an artist, but of a man of high nobility and honour.'

"This is sincere and well spoken, but some of us will continue to admire Paul Robeson most on those occasions when he can say simply in the words of Pablo Neruda that he's fond of quoting, 'I came here to sing, and for you to sing with me.'"

Paul ended the year 1958 in London as the first black person ever to stand at a lectern in St. Paul's Cathedral singing to 4000 persons inside and 5000 more standing outside. But on his return to Moscow something critical and vital happened to his body or mind just after a Kremlin New Year's ball where he was welcomed by Premier Nikita Khrushchev. He fell mysteriously ill, was rushed to a Moscow hospital, confined there for a short time, and then flown to a London private clinic for further treatment. During the next four years he would be in and out of hospitals. The clandestine approach regarding news of his condition and the absence of any frank and definite statements from the various doctors who treated him have led to charges of "cover up" and deception regarding the illness or illnesses. Russian sources spoke of chronic fatigue and circulatory problems. But old friends and associates in London theorized that after having sacrificed so much personally and professionally to maintain his Leninist integrity, he was shocked to the core on being faced with concrete evidence of the Stalinist purges on his arrival in Moscow in January of 1959.

Herbert Marshall, a very close friend and associate from as early a period in London as the Unity Theater productions in the twenties and thirties, is sure that Paul had a mental break-down in Moscow. Writing from his post as Director and Professor Emeritus of the Center for Soviet and East European Studies at Southern Illinois University in Carbondale, Illinois, he speaks first of Russia's failure to ever produce even one of the much-heralded series of Robeson films.

"The role Paul should have played with Eisenstein directing was Toussaint L'Ouverture. True! I was involved in it. But the film was banned by Stalin and the C.P.S.U.

"Paul's second proposed Soviet film which I was going to make with him in the Leningrad Film Studios, based on the life of Ira Aldridge, was supported by Khrushchev but was also banned by his successor, and then Paul had his mental break-down in Moscow, not in England or the U.S.

"The first treatments were in Moscow and these failed. Paul came back to England and was put in a mental hospital by Essie. My only bitter regret is that Paul didn't recover under any treatment anywhere. . . . Now, of course the party line is to say that it wasn't mental, but physical. They don't want him to have had a mental breakdown in Moscow for reasons which I have explained. . . . In other words, when Paul, in Moscow learned the full truth of the Stalin terror and what it had done to his dearest comrades there, especially his Jewish friends like Mikhoels and Pfeiffer, he had his breakdown in 1959."

Personal letters from Eslanda to friends give lengthy descriptions of symptoms that both of them were feeling, but whereas she is very specific and professional about her own diagnosis, she is more rambling and vague about her husband's condition. These letters can only elicit the greatest compassion and sadness in their depiction of a previously vigorous couple now ravaged by not one but multiple diseases, which unquestionably owed some of their etiology to the terrible emotional and physical stress to which they had long been subjected. Eslanda writes from Moscow's Kremlin Hospital on January 29, 1959, to her Indian friend Rajni:

"Of course all this is very hard for Paul to take. He has only had the one illness in his life and is very restless and unhappy, and not at all reconciled yet. When he thinks of standing up to sing or even speak, he realizes that at any moment he may get dizzy, and it is only this which makes him resigned. Even here in the hospital now, he sometimes gets very dizzy and has to hurry to bed. This infuriates him, and only when I tell him that it has happened to many and better men than he is, and is not unusual at his age with his background—only then does he simmer down.

"After consultation, the doctors here have cancelled the *Othello* at Stratford for this spring and said under no circumstances could he undertake such a role for the time bring. This was to have been the icing on the cake of his career, so you can imagine what a blow that was. The contract has already been cancelled, although it has not yet been publically announced.

"Also, all concerts here and all concerts in England have been cancelled, and he will have to consider an altogether new career, something leisurely, like an occasional radio broadcast and some recording under quiet, easy conditions. He will make no plans until about six months from now, because we have already had two warnings and two are enough."

She wrote to Marie Seton on March 12, 1959, again from Kremlin Hospital in Moscow, explaining that she was having gynecological problems and had had a biopsy which found "precancerous cells at the mouth of the uterus." She and Paul were in adjoining rooms at the hospital where he was being treated for "terrible chest colds due to chronic exhaustion over a prolonged period." The doctors were building him up and had now changed their mind and would let him do *Othello* in the near future, but an Indian trip of concerts had definitely been cancelled. She was getting a series of gamma ray treatments at the Cancer Institute, and a transfusion each week.

"Both Paul and I have changed our plans for living. We mean to do less each year and live to work and fight for some time yet. We know we cannot do this if we try to do everything as we have up to the present."

But these estimates were overly pessimistic. English doctors gave him more range of activity, and although there were frequent setbacks for both of them medically through the years, and the pace of life slowed, Paul was still amazingly productive both artistically and politically. That same year, in April, he *did* open his *Othello* at Stratford-on-Avon, and in August he addressed the International Youth Festival, criticizing U.S. foreign and domestic policies. In 1960, he even made a final concert tour of all of Australia and New Zealand. The years 1961 and 1962 were spent mostly in hospitals in Russia and East Germany.

When the major political civil rights victories started to be won in the U.S., he was excited, and speaking of the 1963 march on Washington, he told a reporter, "The turning point has come for the American Negro people."

Reports started to circulate that Paul had become terribly disillusioned with communism and was being involuntarily detained in East Berlin. His son denied this, but nevertheless he *was* spirited out of an East German clinic, and on December 22 arrived in New York to retire in the U.S.

In the early 1970's, with the political climate in America having adjusted to the continuing Cold War, and with Robeson himself obviously no longer such a "threat," certain deserved honors that had been withheld were finally bestowed. The President of Rutgers University criticized the National Football Foundation for having passed over a two-time All-American for its Hall of Fame. *Ebony* magazine proclaimed him one of the "ten most important black men in American History." The National Urban League gave him the Whitney M. Young Memorial Award and Carnegie Hall held a "Salute to Paul Robeson" on his 75th birthday. Each of these sources of honors had at one point been his public detractor.

The award that was tinged with the greatest irony was finally having his "star" implanted on Hollywood Boulevard's "Walk of Fame" on the same day the industry also honored super-rightist John Wayne with an Academy Award. Sidney Poitier, speaking at the Robeson ceremony, said, "There would need to be a ceremony like this every day for the rest of our lives for us to ever begin to be aware of the impact he had on the role of blacks in the film industry."

Paul Robeson died on January 27, 1976. For the last five years of his life he had been practically a recluse living in his sister's house in Philadelphia. His estate, which had diminished to about $150,000, remained a symbol of the division of loyalties that had raged throughout his lifetime. Most of the assets of the old Leninist were in U.S. Treasury Bonds at his death.

But all the obituaries as usual were written too early, too close to his times and to all the furor to accurately evaluate his role in both the history of the entertainment arts and the political history of the pre- and post-World War II period.

Now over a decade later, it is incontrovertible that he was one of the purest, most versatile talents to ever grace a stage, a screen or a recording studio. The man could literally do nothing wrong in quality, timing and taste, when he was performing.

Politically, the true tragedy of the Robeson story is also timing. If he had been born 20 years before or 20 years after, there would have been a different ending. He met the U.S. government head on at a time when there was a post-war blend of patriotism and sense of righteous justification in having been the premier instrument in the settlement of the world's major problems. And here, in its first moments of world leadership, Russia was providing a challenge by rapidly heating up a potential war.

Martin Luther King, Jr., made statement after statement deploring U.S. involvement in the Vietnam War, and was not put upon. His position was not all that different in content from Robeson's 1949 Paris Peace Prize Acceptance speech, but because of the disparity in the type of man, the tone, and the timing, it didn't provide the same sequelae. King was working to bring about change *within* the system, and didn't espouse treason, as Robeson indirectly did, to accomplish those goals. And in the passage of over a decade between their remarks, all the other factors had altered.

It is also impossible to believe that the reaction to Robeson by the federal executive and legislative branches would have been this unfortunate and extreme if he had appeared a decade before or after.

For any valid agency of the U.S. government to ignore the constitutional protections provided by the First and Fifth Amendment is unforgivable. And it is also amazing that Congress and the State Department failed to make a full-blown martyr out of Paul Robeson with their imprudent overkill tactics, unleashing a firepower far beyond what his so-called "crimes" deserved. The reason that this martyrdom did not result can be attributed to the methods that he himself employed on his side, using far too broad a stroke in both his vilification of the U.S. and his santification of the Soviet Union—so simplistically broad that even the liberal sectors of the American public did not find his position supportable by the kind of soul-searching, objective, intellectual integrity that this moment in time, particularly, required.

One can empathize totally with the tortured human being, Paul Robeson, and passionately attempt to protect him from all the basically undeserved abuses he received in his lifetime. One can also thrill to the experience of seeing his athletic skills, hearing the color and tone of his singing, watching his power on a theatrical stage or at a meeting, and still be puzzled and disappointed by the simplistic aberrations of his politics. Did he never realize that he was bestowing adoration on a country that had enslaved far more millions than all the southern states together ever did? Why did he have to attach naive praise of Russia to sometimes valid criticism of the U.S.?

The ultimate failure of Robeson in his intense desire to help all people of color hinges on the identical factors that made for the success of Martin Luther King, Jr. All of King's energy and thought was channeled into the causes of his own race. Robeson lost sight of his own father's advice to "be black first and always" and watered it down with the element of red. He even lost sight of his own fine advice to Lena Horne that "being a Negro is the whole basis of what you are and what you will become." Karl Marx should never have been confused with Frederick Douglass or even John Brown in his mind. And because of this confusion, his influence on the civil rights movement was disruptive and counter-productive.

Despite all his early accomplishments, in the final analysis, he did not protect the black image as did his fellow athlete Jackie Robinson, and his fellow performers Lena Horne, Sammy Davis, Jr., and Bill Cosby, all of whom were content to influence by weight of their talent and not to proselytize. Instead he sullied and distorted this image in his later years by his obsessive attachment to an antagonistic political credo that in his hands had never been constructive or convincing.

Epilogue

(Where It All Is Today)

So what has really happened to white-black chemistry since 1932? Perhaps the key word is perception. The perception of both races toward the other is changing.

Certainly in the entertainment world it all comes down to the way white audiences perceived blacks then and now. In 1932 whites viewed blacks as fumbling, dimwitted servants and so the public was fed a diet of Stepin Fetchit images again and again. Audiences of today have a conception of black performers no different from the one they have of whites. If they exhibit special talent, they perceive them as innovative, intelligent and as role models to emulate. Latch on to Michael Jackson's fashion plate glitz, copy Eddie Murphy's cool, Bill Cosby's cerebral overview and Diana Ross's glamor.

"Hey, that Wynton Marsalis is some classy dude! He blows it hot and longhair in a three-piece suit, rep tie and rimmed specs. Looks like a Cal Tech prof—but I like it, and I'm gonna try it!" That's what's going on in America today in the late eighties. If you don't believe it, examine what has happened in the meteoric rise of 34-year old Oprah Winfrey. "The Oprah Winfrey Show" should be the biggest grossing series in the history of first-run syndications according to industry officials. Her contract calls for her to get 25 percent of the show's revenue, which is estimated at $125 million for the 1987-88 season. In 1986, she was also nominated for an Academy Award for the supporting role of Sophia in the film *The Color Purple*.

What is most significant is that white middle America tunes in with pleasure to hear this friendly, chubby black lady ask intelligent questions about very sensitive subjects. This same audience sees a news clip of Elizabeth Taylor embracing Michael Jackson at a fundraiser and doesn't blink, whereas it would have been enraged decades ago.

Perhaps the most sharply etched measure of just how far America has come was seen in the closing ceremonies of the 1984 Olympics in Los Angeles, an extravaganza that was being beamed to not only every living room set in the U.S., but all over the world. Producer David Wolper, with every star available, chose Lionel Ritchie, a black, to be the singer, dancer, cheer leader to close the festivities in a long, glorious crescendo of color, sound and energy that had Ritchie front and center throughout, in red, white and blue.

At another commemorative gala in 1986, with all the luminaries of Broadway gathered at the Majestic Theater to pay homage to composer Harold Arlen, the three stars chosen to perform the cavalcade of hits in memorium, were Lena Horne, Harold Nicholas and Tony Bennett. This is the same Lena whose parents couldn't sit in the white-only audience of the Cotton Club to watch her dance in the chorus, and whose black obstetrician was barred from entering a northern Ohio hospital to deliver her first baby in 1937.

This is the same Harold Nicholas who starred in hotel shows in the early days of Las Vegas but would have been beaten up if he had dared to step into the casino itself.

Fifty years ago, a black citizen standing on the street looking up at the massive Public Library at Fifth Avenue and 42nd Street in New York would more than likely be approached by a policeman and told to quickly return "back uptown where you belong."

During March of 1987, a gigantic banner with the name Gordon Parks was suspended from this massive façade. Gordon Parks is black, is a photographer, a writer, a film director of movies like *The Learning Tree* and *Shaft*, and for an entire month the largest library in the U.S. was dedicated to the exposition of his unique art. But in 1944 the editor of *Harper's Bazaar* saw his portfolio of pictures one-half hour before Parks's interview with him, admired them very much, and then buzzed his secretary to show Gordon in. He became pale and confused when he got his first look at the young photographer, and started shuffling the prints nervously.

"Fine work," he said. . . . "I must be frank with you. This is a Hearst organization. We can't hire Negroes. I'm embarrassed and terribly sorry, but that's the way it is."

The world is still far from perfect. There are still pockets of bigotry where white supremacists try to set the clock back. In January, 1987, Charles A. Blackburn, a white man in Forsyth County, Georgia, invited a black women's club to courses in his home and set off an Old South reaction of death threats, Klan warnings, and racial tension that hadn't been seen in 20 years. But the difference was that this time the authorities immediately upheld the law of the land, and the vast majority of whites viewing the scenes on television news programs rooted not for the segragationists but for the civil rightists.

The very intelligent Nat "King" Cole always felt the answer was shared exposure. "One of the biggest problems is that we have white and colored in the same world and they don't know each other yet. By listening to the same singer and enjoying him together—by having a good time together—people forget about prejudice, if just for a few minutes."

As long ago as 1950, Billy Eckstine, making a tour of the South with his own band for the first time since his days as Earl Hines's vocalist, was in a state of elation and relief over the difference in attitude in just one decade. A white policeman in Jackson, Mississippi, asked him, "How are they treating you?"

"It's a lot better than it ever was before," said Billy.

"Good," the cop smiled, "we're trying to become civilized."

In Roanoke, Virginia, the manager of the swank Ponce De-Leon Hotel invited him to stay as a guest, and in Charleston, South Carolina, a perfect stranger, a businessman, insisted he play golf with him at a restricted course. Ten years before on the Hines's tour, the band stayed at ghetto rooming houses and played for "colored only" audiences.

Sammy Davis, Jr., views racial perceptions from another angle. "The difference between love and hate is understanding. That understanding is obstructed by the images which are imbedded in people's minds. Obviously it's not the dark skin that's unattractive to white people or they wouldn't spend 100 dollars a day in Florida trying to get it—right?"

When Sammy was asked if he was satisfied with the strides in his lifetime of opportunities for blacks in show business, he answered: "I'm more than satisfied. I'm not satisfied to the point where I'll be a Pollyanna, but the strides have been tremendous. We now have executives, we now have black people behind the cameras, we have black producers, black directors, black writers not exclusively doing black shows—that to me is even more significant because they are not visual out there. I would have liked it to have come a little quicker so that some of the talent, some of the deserving ones wouldn't have been ignored and would have gotten recognition." On December 6, 1987, President Reagan presented one of the Kennedy Center honors to Sammy Davis, Jr., and Harold and Fayard Nicholas led the onstage festivities paying respect to Sammy.

And an awareness of the difference in Bill Cosby's position 20 years ago and now, allows for gauging the degree of progress. Bill said in the mid-1960's while making "I Spy," "writers and producers seem to think you need a special reason for a role to be played by a Negro—that he has to pounce on someone or to be pounced upon. Because of this, Hollywood has helped to promote a negative image of the black man. When a Negro comes on the screen, the audience immediately tenses up. They know they are about to witness some violence, whether physical, verbal, or emotional. If someone were to make a film about a Negro who didn't have any great conflict because of his color, who loved and was loved by a black girl and raised a black family, the audience would come back to see it again looking for some hidden meaning."

But in 1986 Cosby made his series about that black who was loved by a black girl and raised that family—and viewers just came back to see it again and again because it was enjoyable and entertaining.

There are many people still singing the blues, but in objectively assessing the rapid improvement in racial relations in the U.S. and more specifically in the performing arts in the last 50 years, we might borrow Bill Robinson's marvelous phrase that

Lionel Hampton always used, and agree that things are "copasetic."

But, oh God, it hasn't been easy.

Bibliography

1. *Franklin D. Roosevelt, His Life and Times*, edited by Otis L. Graham, Jr., and Meghan Robinson Wander. G.K. Hall, 1985.
2. *Fiorello, His Honor the Little Flower*, by Gloria Kamen. Athenium, 1981.
3. *John Hammond on Record*, by John Henry Hammond, Jr., and Irving Townsend. Ridge Press, Summit Books, 1977.
4. *Live at the Village Vanguard*, by Max Gordon with introduction by Nat Hentoff. A De Capo Paperback, St. Martin's Press, 1980.
5. *The NAACP, Its Fight for Justice*, by Minnie Finch. Scarecrow Press, 1981.
6. *Letters from the Jim Crow Army*, introduction by L.D. Reddick. Periodical "Twice a Year," New York, 1947.
7. *The Invisible Soldier*, compiled by Mary Motley. Wayne State Press, 1975.
8. *The U.S. Army in WW II: The Employment of Negro Troops*, by Ulyssis Lee. Office of the Chief of Military History, U.S. Army.
9. *The Nazi Olympics*, by Richard D. Mandell. MacMillan, 1971.
10. *A Study of the Negro in the Military Service*, by Jean Byers. Written for the Dept. of Defense, 1947.
11. *The Great Red Menace*, by Peter L. Steinberg. Greenwood Press, 1985.
12. *Wait 'Till Next Year*, by Carl Rowan and Jackie Robinson. Random House, 1960.
13. *The Dark Ages, Life in the U.S. 1945 - 1960*, by Marty Jezer. South End Press, 1982.
14. *Lena*, by Lena Horne and Richard Schikel. First Limelight Edition, June 1986.
15. *The Hornes*, by Gail Lumet Buckley. Alfred A. Knopf, 1986.
16. *Bill Lees Jazz Letter 1986-1987*, P.O. 240, Ojai, CA 93023
17. *Hard Times*, by Studs Terkel. Washington Sq. Press, Pantheon Books, 1970.

18. *Josephine,* by Josephine Baker and Jo Bouillon. Harper & Row, 1977.

19. *Yes I Can, the Story of Sammy Davis, Jr.,* by Sammy Davis, Jr., and Jane and Burt Boyar. Farrar Straus & Giroux, 1961.

20. *City of Nets,* by Otto Friedrich. Harper & Row, 1986.

21. *The Raw Pearl,* by Pearl Bailey. Harcourt Brace & World, 1968.

22. *Belafonte—An Unauthorized Biography,* by Arnold Shaw. Chilton Co. Book Division, 1960.

23. *Lena—A Personal and Professional Biography of Lena Horne,* by James Haskins with Kathleen Benson. Stein & Day, 1984.

24. *Paul Robeson, Citizen of the World,* by Shirley Graham. Negro University Press, 1971.

25. *"The Great Fear," The Anticommunist Purge Under Truman and Eisenhower,* by David Caute. Simon and Schuster, 1978.

26. *Arma Bontemps Langston Hughes' Letters 1925-1967,* edited by Charles H. Nichols. Dodd Mead & Co., 1980.

27. *Naming Names,* by Victor Navasky. Penguin Viking Press, 1981.

28. *Robeson Speaks—Writings, Speeches, Interviews 1918-1974,* edited and introduction by Phillip S. Foner. Brunner Mazel, 1978.

29. *The Life of Langston Hughes,* Volume 1, 1902-1941. Arnold Rampersad. Oxford University Press, 1986.

30. *To Smile in Autumn,* by Gordon Parks. Norton, 1979.

31. *Of Minnie the Moocher and Me,* Cab Calloway and Bryant Rollins. Crowell, 1976.

32. *Blacks in Hollywood—The Black Performer in Motion Pictures,* by Gary Null. Citadel, 1975.

33. *Paul Robeson, A Tribute,* by J.D. Douglas for Lambeth Council Construction Services, 1987.

34. *Slow Fade to Black,* by Thomas Cripps. Oxford University Press, 1977.

35. *From Sambo to Superspade, The Black Experience in Motion Pictures,* by Daniel J. Leahr. Houghton Mifflin, 1975.

36. *The Golden Webb, a History of Broadcasting in the U.S., 1933-1953,* Vol. I & II, by Eric Barnour. Oxford Press, 1968.

37. *Tune in Yesterday, The World Encyclopedia of Old Time Radio,* by John Dunning. Prentice Hall, 1976.

38. *Show Time at the Apollo,* by Ted Fox. Holt Rhinehart Winston, 1983.

39. *Paul Robeson, The Great Forerunner,* by the editors of *Freedomways.* Dodd Mead & Co., 1985.

40. *The American Negro in the Communist Party,* by the Committee

on Un-American Activities. U.S. House of Representatives, December 22, 1954.

41. *The Whole World in His Hands, A Pictorial Biography of Paul Robeson*, by Susan Robeson. Citadel Press, 1981.

42. *Paul Robeson*, by Marie Seton. D. Dobson, 1958.

43. *A Man Called White*, Autobiography by Walter White. Indiana University Press, 1948; Arno Press, 1969.

44. *Little Flower, The Life & Times of Fiorello La Guardia*, by Lawrence Elliot. William Morrow, 1983.

45. *The Paul Robeson Family Papers and Letters*. From the Marie Seton collection at the Marx Memorial Library, London, England.

Index

Acheson, Dean, 194, 236
Adams, Joe, 149
Addams, Jane, 70
Adomis, Joe, 116, 117
Albritton, David, 180
Aldredge, Ira, 220, 242
Alexander, Will, 176
Alexander, Willard, 38, 45
Alhambra Grille, 30
Alhambra Theater, 24, 25, 33
Allan, Lewis (Abel Meeropol), 60
Allen, Fred, 144, 147, 160
Allen, Henry "Red", 24
Allen, Steve, 209
Allen, Woody, 62, 64
Altshuler, Dick, 34
Ameringer, Oscar, 6
Ammons, Albert, 20, 50, 51
Ammons, Gene, 173
Amos 'N' Andy, 143, 145, 149, 158, 159, 160, 161, 162, 163, 164
Anderson, Eddie (Rochester), VIII, 92, 100, 102, 103, 144, 145
Anderson, Ernest, 104
Anderson, Mariam, 74, 178, 227
Arlen, Harold, 32, 100, 248,
Armstrong, Louis, 4, 8, 25, 29, 41, 95, 103, 131, 137, 138, 154
Ashcroft, Peggy, 220
Astaire, Fred, 89

Bacon, Peggy, 50
Bailey, A. Peter, 163
Bailey, Mildred, 20, 37, 38
Bailey, Pearl, 64, 83, 119, 120, 138

Bates, Ruby, 11, 13
Bautzer, Greg, 116
Bean, Orson, 62
Beavers, Louise, 89, 96, 97, 146
Beebe, Lucius, 50
Beenwkes, Lambert B., 149
Beery, Wallace, 8
Balafonte, Harry, VII, 62, 64, 106, 107, 108, 109, 110, 129, 130, 131, 155, 207
Belafonte, Julie, 130, 131
Belafonte, Marguerite, 130
Benchley, Robert, 54
Bennett, Joan, 97
Bennett, Tony, 111, 248
Benny, Jack, 99, 134, 144, 145, 147, 160
Benson, George, 20, 45, 46
Berg, Gertrude, 162
Bergen, Edgar, 89, 144
Bernstein, Artie, 28, 30, 32, 33
Bernstein, Leonard, 62
Bernstein, Walter, 205
Berrigan, Bunny, 37
Berry, Chu, 16, 33, 34, 138
Best, Willy, 145
Bethune, Mary McLeod, 176
Billingsley, Sherman, 18, 80, 81
Bioff, Willie, 111, 112, 113
Bishop, Joey, 132
Black, Ivan, 60
Blackburn, Charles A., 249
Blake, Eubie, 216
Blakey, Art, 62
Bledsoe, Jules, 145

Baldwin, James, 205
Baker, Josephine, 78, 79, 80, 81, 82, 84, 123, 124, 203
Ball, Lucille, 200
Baltimore Afro American, 27
Banks, Louis, 9
Barefield, Eddie, 142
Barnett, Charlie, 20
Barry, Phillip, 8
Basie, Count, 20, 27, 38, 42, 44, 45, 102, 103, 131, 151, 171, 185
Bates, Daisey, 170
Bogart, Humphrey, 47, 105, 107
Bonnano, Joe, 117
Bookstein, State Supreme Court Justice Isadore, 230
Brando, Marlon, 204
Brown, Heywood, 217
Browder, Earl, 226
Brown, Ada, 139
Brown, James, 107
Brown, John, 147, 246
Brown, Larry, 217, 225, 226
Browne, George, 111, 112, 113
Bruce, Lenny, 62, 157
Buchalter, Louis Lepke, 111
Buck, Pearl, 8
Bunch, John, 40
Bunche, Ralph, 157
Burke, William E., 104
Burwell, Evelyn Pope, 90
Buttons, Red, 111

Cafe Society (Downtown and Uptown), 45, 47, 49, 50, 51, 52, 53, 54, 55, 56, 59, 60, 61, 102, 129, 206
Cagney, James, 54
Caldwell, Eskine, 8
Calloway, Cab., VIII, IX, 4, 100, 103, 137, 138, 139, 140, 141
Campbell, Mrs. Patrick, 215
Canova, Judy, 145
Cantor, Eddie, 98, 151, 152, 200
Capone, Al, 2, 3, 111
Carmichael, Hoagy, 146
Carnegie, Mrs. Andrew, Jr., 211
Carter, Benny, 8, 12, 20, 28, 30, 138
Carter, President Jimmy, 65
Carter, Ray, 182

Casey, Hugh, 212
Catlett, Big Sid, 26
Chambers, Whittaker, 198
Cheatham, Doc, 138
Chicago Defender, 27, 126
Childress, Alvin, 161
Chittison, Herman, 146
Cholly Knickerbocker, 50
Christian, Charlie, 20, 41, 42, 43
Churchill, Winston, 186, 187
Clark, Kenny, 185
Clay, Shirley, 33
Club Saratoga, 24
Cochran, Gifford, 92
Coffin, Henry Sloane, 21, 22
Cohen, Octavus Roy, 90, 143
Colbert, Claudette, 96
Cole, Cozy, 138
Cole, Nat "King", 108, 109, 110, 122, 151, 153, 154, 155, 156, 157, 249
Collins, Joan, 108
Columbo, Russ, 27, 31
Collier, James, Lincoln, 6
Comden, Betty, 62
Como, Perry, 209
Condon, Eddie, 28
Connely, Bob, 143
Cooley, Spade, 151
Coplon, Judith, 203
Corey, "Professor" Irwin, 62
Correll, Charles, 143, 159, 160, 161
Corwin, Norman, 150
Cosby, Bill, VIII, 111, 152, 156, 158, 246, 247, 250
Costello, Frank, 117
Cowan, Louis G., 147, 148
Crosby, Bing, 99, 110, 155
Coughlin, Father, 173
Covan's, 27, 44
Cowell, Henry, 8
Cowley, Malcolm, 14
Cox, Wally, 62, 64
Crawford, Joan, 84, 97
Crow, Bill, 39, 40
Crowther, Bosley, 104
Cugat, Xavier, 39, 117, 122
Cullen, Countee, 197
Cullen, Rev. F.A., 197
Culp, Robert, 152
Cunard, Nancy, 197

Curtis, Tony, 108

Dameron, Tad, 109
Dandridge, Dorothy, 106, 108, 146
Dandridge, Ruby, 145, 146
Dandridge, Vivian, 146
Daniels, Billy, 145, 146, 153
Darrow, Clarence, 71
Darro, Frankie, 96
Davis, Col. Benjamin O., 166
Davis, Bette, 104
Davis, Miles, 62, 65, 185
Davis, Sammy Jr., VIII, 98, 106, 107,
    109, 111, 115, 121, 124, 125, 126,
    127, 129, 131, 132, 133, 134, 135,
    136, 143, 150, 151, 152, 155, 246,
    249, 250
Davis, Sam Sr., 125, 126, 131, 150
Debs, Eugene V., 16
Dee, Ruby, 146
Dehn, Adolph, 50
Delta Rhythm Boys, 119
Dempsey, Jack, 9, 38
Denny, Charles, B., 236
Disney, Walt, 8
Dewey, John, 70
Dies, Rep. Martin, 187, 188
Dillings, Elizabeth, 198
Donald, Eddie, 181
Dos Passos, John, 14
Douglas, Frederick, 213, 246
Douglas, Kirk, 200, 201
Douglas, Paul, 145
Dubois, W.E.B., 69, 70, 73, 82, 196,
    213, 226
Duncan, Augustin, 215
Duncan, Isidora, 215
Dunham, Katherine, 130, 131
Dunston, Rudolph, 49
DuPont, Lamont, 35
Durante, Jimmy, 5, 117
Durocher, Leo, 212
Dylan, Bob, 20, 46

Earhart, Amelia, 8
Eckstine, Billy, 108, 109, 110, 111,
    119, 122, 134, 151, 154, 173, 185,
    249
Edwards, Frances, 103
Edwards, James, 106

Edwards, Ralph, 145
Eisenhower, President "Ike", 41, 114,
    178, 179
Eisenstein, Sergei, 221, 222, 242
Eldridge, Roy, 26
El Glaowi, 80
Ellington, Duke, VIII, 2, 3, 4, 8, 12,
    37, 42, 45, 100, 101, 102, 103, 137,
    138, 151
Ellis, Herb, 99
Entratter, Jack, 210, 211
Epstein, "Bookie" Joe, 116
Ericson, Frank, 17
Evans, Horace, 181

Factor, Max, 102
Faddis, John, 67
Falkenburg, Jinx, 209
"Farina", 88
Farmer, Art, 6
Farmer, James, 85
Fast, Howard, 149, 232
Feather, Leonard, 51, 157
Ferguson, Sen. Homer, 189
Ferrer, Jose, 203, 227
Ferrer, Mel, 108
Fetchit, Stepin, VIII, 89, 247
Fibber McGee and Molly, 160
Field, Frederick Vanderbilt, 189
Fischer, Bill, 143
Fitzgerald, Ella, 78, 172
Fontaine, Joan, 108
Ford, James M., 7
Forrestal, Sec. of Defense James,
    230
Foster, William Z., 7
Foxx, Redd, 156, 157, 158
Franciosa, Tony, 204
Francis, Kay, 97
Frank, Waldo, 14, 15
Franklin, Aretha, 46
Franklin, Raul, 143
Freed, Arthur, 83, 101
Frishberg, Dave, 143
Froeba, Frank, 32

Gabin, Jean, 55
Gable, Clark, 109
Gale, Moe, 4
Gallard, Eugene, 168

Garber, Jan, 172
Gardner, Ava, 201
Gardner, Ed, 149, 150
Garfield, John, 197
Garland, Judy, 89, 202
Garvey, Marcus, 196
Gazzara, Ben, 204
Gehrig, Lou, 65
Geyer, Siegfried, 217
Genovese, Vito, 117
Gershwin, George, 8
Gibbs, Georgia, 50
Gillespie, Dizzy, 62, 109, 138, 157,
    173, 185
Gilpin, Charles, 216
Gish, Lillian, 220
Glaser, Joe, 41
Gleason, Jimmy, 145
Goldberg, Whoopie, IX
Golden Gate Quartet, 20, 50
Golson, Benny, 6
Goodman, Alice Hammond
    Duckworth, 30
Goodman, Benny, 20, 27, 30, 31, 32,
    33, 34, 37, 38, 39, 40, 41, 42, 43,
    51, 99
Goodman, Harry, 39
Gordon, Lorraine, 61, 66
Gordon, Dexter, 109
Gordon, Max, 18, 47, 48, 61, 62, 63,
    64, 65, 66, 67, 132
Gosden, Freeman, 143, 159, 160, 161
Gossett, Louis Jr., 97
Goulet, Robert, 111
Grace, C.M. "Daddy", 208
Gramaphone Magazine, 27, 30
Granger, Lester B., 174, 234
Granz, Norman, 99
Greaves, William, 94
Green, Adolph, 62
Green, Jack, 172
Green, Silas, 34
Greenbaum, Gus, 118
Greene, Freddy, 20, 45
Griffith, D.W., 73
Grimke, Francis J., 20
Grofe, Ferde, 8
Gropper, William, 50
Gruening, Ernest, 26
Gynt, Kaj, 223

Hagen, Uta, 227
Hall, Edward, 51
Hall, Juanita, 146
Hammerstein, Oscar II, 218, 224
Hammond, Esmee, 40
Hammond, John Henry Jr., 12, 14,
    15, 16, 18, 19, 20, 21, 22, 23, 24,
    25, 26, 27, 28, 29, 30,31, 32, 33,
    34, 35, 36, 37, 38, 39, 40, 41, 42,
    43, 44, 45, 46, 50, 51, 55, 61, 85,
    132, 171, 172, 225, 226
Hammond, Mrs. John Henry Jr.,
    (first wife), 51, 171, 172
Hammond, John Henry Sr., 21, 22,
    23, 26, 27, 28, 35
Hammond, Mrs. John Henry Sr., 21,
    22, 23, 26, 27, 46
Hammond, Ogden H., 21, 35
Hampton, Gladys, 41, 42, 43, 44, 151
Hampton, Lionel, 20, 34, 41, 42, 43,
    44, 78, 99, 141, 142, 151, 251
Handy, W.C., 108
Harris, Ralph, 209
Hastie, William H., 166, 176
Hawkins, Coleman, 20, 30, 31
Hawkins, Erskine, 4, 138
Hayes, Alfred, 229
Hayes, Helen, 8, 204
Hayton, Lennie, 121, 122, 208
Helm, Harvey, 143
Henderson, Bobby, 29
Henderson, Fletcher, 8, 30, 36, 39,
    137, 169, 185
Henderson, Horace, 169, 170
Henderson, Luther, 146
Hernandez, Juano, 146
Heywood, Eddie, 50, 62
Hentoff, Nat, 65
Hepburn, Katherine, 201, 202
Higbe, Kirby, 212
Higginbotham, J.c., 19, 24
Hill, Captain Charles Jr., 193, 194
Hill, Rev. Charles, 193
Hill, T. Arnold, 165
Hill, Joe, 229
Hill, Virginia, 116, 117, 118
Hines, Earl "Fatha" 32, 45, 109, 249
Hinton, Milt, 138, 142
Hitler, Adolph, VII, 50, 59, 167, 174,
    176, 180, 197, 225, 227

Hodges, Johnny, 37
Hoff, Sid, 50
Hoffman, Joseph, 23
Holden, William, 107, 201
Holiday, Billie, VIII, 6, 8, 20, 29, 30, 33, 38, 39, 42, 50, 55, 56, 58, 60, 210
Holliday, Judy, 62,, 64, 203
Hoover, J. Edgar, 116, 187, 188, 189, 191, 194
Hope, Bob, 99
Hopkins, Harry, 176, 177
Horne, Cora, 82, 114
Horne, Lena, VIII, X, 5, 50, 52, 53, 54, 56, 57, 82, 83, 84, 92, 95, 97, 98, 99, 100, 101, 102, 103, 104, 119, 120, 121, 122, 126, 149, 150, 153, 169, 170, 203, 208, 209, 210, 211, 214, 223, 246, 248
Hotckhiss School, 25
Howe, Quincy, 14
Hughes, Langston, 15, 130, 195, 196, 197, 198, 199, 200, 223
Humes, Helen, 20, 26, 50, 61
Humphrey, Sen. Hubert, 190
Hunter, Alberta, 53, 61
Hunter, Kim, 203
Hurok, Sol, 42
Hurst, Fannie, 96
Huston, John, 200, 203
Hyman, Earl, 146

Ickes, Harold, 176
Illo, Shirley, 143
Impelliteri, Mayor, 80
Ingram, Rex, 92, 100, 103, 145
Ink Spots, 172
Ives, Burl, 62

Jackson, James, 153
Jackson, Mahalia, 146, 147
Jackson, Michael, 247, 248
Jacoby, Herbert, 64
Jacquet, Illinois, 130, 138
James, Ida, 50
Jessel, George, 117
Johnson, Cornelius, 180
Johnson, George P., 95
Johnson, Jack, 3, 130
Johnson, John, 126, 127, 128, 129

Johnson, Manning, 232
Johnson, Marion Montero, IX
Johnson, Noble, 95
Johnson, Pete, 20, 50, 51
Jolson, Al, 2, 88, 138
Jones, Jo, 44
Jones, Jonah, 138
Jones, Tad, 63, 62
Josephson, Barney, 18, 45, 47, 48, 49, 50, 51, 52, 53, 54, 55, 56, 57, 58, 59, 60, 61, 66, 67, 91, 102, 132
Josephson, Leon, 50, 59, 60
Jourdan, Louis, 151, 172

Kanfer, Steven, 203
Kapp, Dave, 45
Karl, Artie, 32
Katz, William, 105
Kaufman, George, 8
Kaye, Danny, 134, 146
Kazan, Elia, 203, 204
Kelly, Gene, 54, 62, 98
Kennedy, Flo, 163
Kenyatta, Jomo, 219
Kern, Jerome, 218
Kern, Jodge John, 112
Khrushchev, Nikita, 241, 242
Kilgallen, Dorothy, 110
King, Martin Luther Jr., 84, 85, 213, 245, 246
Kirk, Rahsaan Roland, 65
Kirsten, Lincoln, 171
Kitt, Eartha, 64
Klein, Manny, 32
Knepper, Jimmy, 65
Knight, Thomas Jr., 12, 13
Knox, Judge John C., 81
Koeningswater, Baroness Nica De, 66
Korda, Zoltan, 105
Kriendler, Jack 18
Krimsky, John, 92
Krupa, Gene 20, 27, 31, 39, 42
Kyser, Kay, 142

Lafayette Theater, 24
LaGuardia, Fiorello, 17, 54, 55, 63, 174, 177
LaGuardia, Marie, 177
Lancaster, Burt, 200, 205

Lanchester, Elsa, 33
Land, Edwin, 81
Landis, Kennesaw Mountain, 233
Langford, Frances, 134
Lansky, Meyer, 116, 117, 118
Lardner, Ring Jr., 202
Larkins, Ellis, 50, 61, 62
La Touche, John, 225
Lauder, Sir Harry, 23
Laughton, Charles, 33, 150
Lee, Canada, 105, 149, 203, 204
Lee, Johnny, 143
Lees, Gene, 40, 99
Leibowitz, Samuel S., 13
Leonard, Ada, 172
Leonard, Jack E., 111
Leroy, Mervyn, 97
Lewis, Jerry, 133
Lewis, John L., 14
Lewis, Meade Lux, 20, 50, 51
Lewis, Mel, 40, 63
Lewis, Ted, 134
Lieber, Maxim, 199
Light, Jimmy, 217
Lindbergh, Charles, 8
Long Avon, 51
Louis, Joe, 169, 170, 181
Louis, Louis I., 59
L'Overture, Toussaint, 242
Lowe, James B., 89
Lowe, Mondell, 172
Lubin, Sigmund, 87
Luce, Clare Booth 50
Luce, Henry, 200
Luciano, "Lucky", 117, 118
Lunceford, Jimmy, 4, 5, 137, 185
Lyons, Leonard, 204

McCarron, Sen. Pat, 116
MacArthur, Gen. Douglas, 7
McCarthy, Charlie, 89, 144
McCarthy, Sen. Joseph, 187, 188,
　　195, 206
McChesney, John, 25
McCoy, Clyde, 17
McCrary, Tex, 209
McDaniel, Hattie, 89, 92, 97, 145,
　　146
McDonough, Dick, 32
McGee, Howard, 173
McKinney, Mima Mae, 90, 91, 100

McQueen Butterfly, VIII, 58, 62,
　　103, 146
Madden, Owney, 3, 4, 5
Malcolm "X", 157, 158
Mandell, Richard D., 179
Mansch, Max, 59
Mansur, Graham Jr., 37
Mantle, Burns, 220
Marcello, Carlos, 117
March, Fredric, 8
Marcus, Stanley, 43, 44
Marsalis, Wynton, IX, 67, 242
Marshall, Gen. George, 166
Marshall, Herbert, 242, 242
Marshall, William, 203
Martin, Dean, 132
Martin, Mary, 204
Martin, Tony, 151
Marx, Groucho, 201
Marx, Karl, 246
Mastin, Will, 125, 131, 150
Mathis, Johnny, 62
Maxey, Leroy, 140
Maxwell, Elsa, 50
May, Elaine, 62
Mayer, Louis B., 84, 103
Meara, Anne, 62
Meeropol, Abel (Lewis Allen), 60
Melies, George, 87
Melodymaker Magazine, 27, 30
Menjou, Adolph, 201
Mercer, Johnny, 29, 150, 153
Metcalf, Lt. Ralph, 172
Michaeux, Oscar, 93, 94
Miller, Arthur, 203
Miller, Flournoy, 143, 161
Miller, Glenn, 98, 184
Miller, Lauren, 15
Mills Brothers, 122, 137
Mills, Irving, 12, 36, 37
Minelli, Vincente, 100
Mingus, Charlie, 65, 66
Mitchum, Robert, 105
Monk, Thelonius, 62, 66, 185
Montgomery, Little Brother, 16
Montgomery, Robert, 112
Moon, Henry, 15
Moore, Monette, 29
Moore, Tim, 161
Moreland, Manton, 96
Morgan, Richard, 34, 42

Morris, William, 37
Mortimer, Lee, 110
Moser, Bill, 143
Moskowitz, Herman, 70
Moss, Bob, 143
Mostel, Zero, 54, 59, 60
Moten, Benny, 27, 44
Mulligan, Gerry, 185
Mundy, Jimmy, 39
Murphy, Eddie, VIII, 247
Murray, Kel, 39
Muse, Clarence, 89, 94

Navarro, Fats, 109
Neruda, Pablo, 241
Newman, Joe, 40
Newman, Paul, 107
Newton, Frankie 16, 28, 34
Nicholas Brothers (Harold and
    Fayard), VIII, 1, 4, 5, 83, 91, 92,
    97, 98, 99, 107, 119, 145, 248, 250
Nichols, Mike, IX, 62
Nitti, Frank, 111, 112, 113
Nixon, Rep. Richard, 189
Nkrumah, Kwame, 219
Noble, Peter, 105
Norman, Maidie, 143
Morris, Frank, 173
North, Lt. Col. Oliver, 59
Norvo Red, 20, 33, 38
Norwell, William Odell, 191, 192

Oakie, Jack, 57, 58
Oakie, Mrs. Jack, 58
Oliver, King, 45
Olivier, Laurence, 150
Oneill, Eugene, 92, 215, 216, 221
Ovington, Mary White, 69, 70
Owens, Jesse, 180, 181

Page, Oran "Hot Lips", 44
Page, Walter, 44
Papp, Joe, 204
Parker, Charlie "Bird', 109, 173, 185
Parker, Maj. Gen. Edwin F., 182
Parks, Gordon, 128, 129, 195, 248,
    249
Patterson, Assistant Sec. of War, 165
Patterson, William C., 12, 149, 222,
    228
Patton, Gen. George, 181

Payne, Benny, 128, 139, 140
Payne, Felix Jr., 141, 142
Payne, Felix Sr., 141, 142
Peace, Elroy, 134
Peck, Gregory, 200
Perl, Arnold, 205, 206
Peter, Paul and Mary, 62
Peters, Brock, 106
Peterson, Sec. of War Howard C.,
    194
Pick and Pat, 145
Phillips, Wendell, 24
Pittsburgh Courier, 27, 126, 227
Pod and Jerry's Log Cabin, 30
Poindexter, Admiral, 59
Poitier, Sidney, VIII, 97, 106, 107,
    108, 139, 207, 244
Poston, Ted, 15, 210, 211
Powell, Adam Clayton, Jr., 56, 57,
    82, 130, 174
Powell, Bud, 172
Powell, Dick, 152
Premice, Josephine, 62
Presley, Elvis, 115, 137
Price, Victoria, 11, 13
Pryor, Richard, VIII

Quinlon, Ronnie, 153

Radeky, Karl, 199
Raft, George, 47, 115, 117
Rampersad, Arnold, 223
Randolph, A. Phillip, 165, 196, 197
Raye, Martha, 12
Reagan, President Ronald, 250
Redmond, Don, 33, 138
Refrigier, Anton, 50
Reinhardt, Max, 220, 221
Reuther, Walter, 190
Rickey, Branch, 76, 77, 211, 212, 233,
    234
Rico, Roger, 80
Riesel, Victor, 210
Ritchio, Lionel, 248
Roach, Hal, 88
Roach, Max, 185
Robeson, Maria Louisa, 214
Robeson, Eslamda, 92, 215, 217, 219,
    221, 237, 242, 243
Robeson, Paul Jr., 237, 244

Robeson, Paul, VIII, 15, 51, 57, 82,
91, 92, 93, 149, 150, 153, 189, 194,
203, 207, 208, 212, 213, 214, 215,
216, 217, 218, 219, 220, 221, 222,
223, 224, 225, 226, 227, 228, 229,
230, 231, 232, 233, 234, 235, 236,
237, 238, 239, 240, 241, 242, 243,
244, 245, 246
Robeson, Rev. William Drew, 214
Robinson, Bill ("Bojangles"), VIII,
89, 100, 124, 139, 170, 210, 250
Robinson, Earl, 225, 229
Robinson, Edward G., 93, 150, 200,
203
Robinson, Jackie (Jack Roosevelt), 75,
76, 77, 157, 211, 212, 232, 233,
234, 235, 236
Robinson, Major, 210
Robinson, Smokey, 107
Robson, Bill, 205, 206
Rockefeller, John D., 7
Rollins, Bryant, 139
Rollins, Jack, 64
Romero, Caesar, 47
Rooney, Mickey, 89, 131, 132, 134
Roosevelt, Eleanor, 57, 74, 174, 176,
177, 178, 190, 208, 236
Roosevelt, Franklin D. Jr., 57
Roosevelt, Franklin Delano, VII, 7,
74, 165, 167, 174, 175, 176, 177,
178, 226, 230, 231
Roosevelt, Teddy, 233
Rose, Billy, 38, 72, 78
Rosen, Morris, 118
Ross, Annie, 62
Ross, Diana, IX, 247
Ruark, Robert, 134
Rudd, Wayland, 15
Rushing, Jimmy, 44
Russel, Luis, 24
Russell, Charles Edward, 70
Russell, "Nipsy", 111
Russell, Pee Wee, 28
Rysking, Morrie, 8

Sachs, Walter, 70
Sahl, Mort, 62
Sam 'n' Henry, 160
Sampson, Edgar, 39
Sanders, George, 117
Saunders, Red, 16

Savoy Ballroom, 4, 25
Schenk, Joseph, 112, 113
Schenk, Mick, 112
Schwartz, Yonkel, 4
Scott, Hazel, 50, 53, 56, 57, 58, 59,
119
Scott, Sir Walter, 241
Scottsboro Boys, 12, 13, 14, 97, 196,
198, 222
Sedway, "Little Moe", 116, 118
Seeger, Pete, 62, 232
Selvin, Bob, 31
Seton, Marie, 218, 221, 238, 239,
241, 243
Shakespeare, William, 220
Shaw, George Bernard, 219
Shilady, John R., 71, 72
Simpkins, Arthur Lee, 119
Siegel, Benjamin "Bugsy", 115, 116,
117, 118, 119, 120, 121, 122
Silvera, Frank, 204, 205, 206
Singleton, Zutty, 28
Sinatra, Frank, 60, 110, 115, 132, 133,
134, 154, 155, 156, 200
Sissle, Noble, 78, 162
Skelton, Red, 143
Slauder, Arthur, 143
Sloan, Alfred P. Jr., 35
Sloane, Emily Vanderbilt, 21
Sloane, William Douglas, 21
Small, Ed, 19
Smiley, Allen, 118
Smith, Bessie, VIII, 8, 20, 24, 28,
33, 34, 36
Smith, Gerald, L.K., 173
Smith, Pinetop, 17
Smith, Rufus,
Smith, "Wonderful", 143, 144
Sokolsky, George, 209
South, Eddie, 55
Spellman, Cardinal, 200
Spencer, Kenneth, 104, 105
Spielberg, Steven, IX
Springsteen, Bruce, 20, 46
Stacey, Jess, 39
Stadler, Joseph "Doc", 117
Stalin, Joseph, 119, 237, 242
Stark, Herman, 5
Sterling, Sir Louis, 30
Stevens, Inger, 108
Stevens, Morty, 127

Stewart, Jimmy, 19, 97
Stewart, Ollie, 183
Stiller, Jerry, 62
Stimson, Sec. of War Henry, 166
Stokes, J.G. Phillips, 70
Stowe, Harriet Beecher, 88
Strayhorn, Billy, 101, 102
Streicker, Julius, 181
Sturges, Preston, 104
Sullivan, Ed, 151, 202, 207, 209
Sullivan, Maxine, 62
Sylvester, Bob, 116
Symphony Sid, 109

Tatum, Art, 16, 32, 50
Taub, Allan, 14, 15
Taylor, Billy Sr., 34
Taylor, Elizabeth, 248
Taylor, Robert, 105, 201
Teagarden, Charlie, 32
Teagarden, Jack, 32, 34
Temple, Shirley, 89
Tenney, State Senator, 228, 229
Terry, Clark, 62
Terry, Peggy, 10
Tharpe, Sister Rosetta, 62
The Beatles, 13
The Blue Angel, 47, 61, 64
The Cookery, 47, 60
The Copocabana, 216, 211
The Cotton Club, X, 1, 3, 4, 5, 32,
    49, 97, 103, 137, 138, 140, 197, 217,
    248
The Kingston Trio, 62
The Reviewers, 62
The Plantation Club, 216
The Stork Club, 18, 78, 80, 81, 84
The 21 Club, 18
The Village Vanguard, 47, 61, 62, 63,
    64, 65, 129, 206
Theremin, Leon, 8
Thomas, Danny, 151
Thomas, J. Parnell, 202
Thomas, Norman, 7
Thompson, Kay, 62
Trafficante, Santo, 117
Truman, President Harry, 187, 188,
    189, 190, 194, 200
Trumbo, Dalton, 197
Tubbs, Vincent, 128

Tucker, Orrin, 172
Turner, Big Joe, 50
Turner, Mary, 72, 73
Tuvim, Judith (Holliday), 62

Vallee, Rudy, 138
Vanderbilt, Cornelius, 21
Vanderbilt, Gloria, 21
Van Doren, Carl, 214
Van Eps, George, 39
Van Santvord, George, 25
Van Vechten, Carl, 223
Vaughn, Gen. Harry, 189
Vaughn, Sarah, 50, 109, 173
Vaughn, Stevie Ray, 20, 46
Venuti, Joe, 30
Vidor, King, 89, 90
Villard, Oswald Garrison, 70, 73
Von Schirac, Baldur, 180

Walden, Roberta, 194
Walden, Lt. Col. Roger, 192, 193,
    194
Walker, Frank, 28
Walker, Jimmy, 2, 17
Wallace, Henry, 190, 194, 207, 230
Waller, Fats, 6, 8, 20, 25, 29, 36,
    100, 139
Walling, William English, 69, 70
Walton, Lester A., 162
Ward, Ada, X
Ward, Helen, 39, 42
Warner, Jack, 201
Washington, Booker T., 69, 70, 147,
    213
Washington, Buck (of Buck and
    Bubbles), 34, 103
Washington, Dinah, 122
Washington, Fredi, 96, 97
Walters, Alexander, 70
Waters, Ethel, VIII, 58, 93, 100, 102,
    103
Wayne, John, 244
Weaver, Dr. Robert, 176
Webb, Chick, 16
Webb, Clifton, 29
Webb, Del, 116
Webster, Ben, 138
Welles, Orson, 201, 225
Wells, Dickie, 16, 26
White, Josh, 51, 62, 206, 207

White, Lindsey, 78
White, Paul, 134
White, Walter, 11, 20, 72, 73, 74, 78,
  80, 82, 83, 84, 85, 162, 163, 165,
  174, 196, 197, 217, 232, 237
Widmark, Richard, 101
Wien, George, 65
Wilkie, Wendell, 74, 226
Wilkins, Roy, 20, 73, 85, 174
Williams Brothers, 62
Williams, Clarence, 17
Williams, Cootie, 172
Williams, David, 181
Williams, Hannah, 38
Williams, Mary Lou, 42
Williams, Spencer, 161
Williams, Tennessee, 204
Wilson, Edmund, 14
Wilson, Garland, 19, 27, 28

Wilson, Teddy, 20, 32, 33, 37, 39,
  40, 42, 43, 44, 50, 53, 61, 99, 146
Winchell, Walter, 60, 78, 80, 81, 138,
  153
Winfrey, Oprah, VIII, 247
Wise, Rabbi Stephen, 73
Wolfe, Louis, 23, 24
Wolper, David, 245
Wonder, Stevie, IX
Woods, Charles, 163
Woolcott, Alexander, 221
Wooley, Mary E., 70
Worsthorne, Peregrine, 238, 239
Wright, Richard, 198
Wycherly, Margaret, 215

Young, Lester, 20, 44
Young, Robert, 150, 200
Young, Whitney M., 244